Chicago yesterdays; a sheaf of reminiscences

Caroline Kirkland

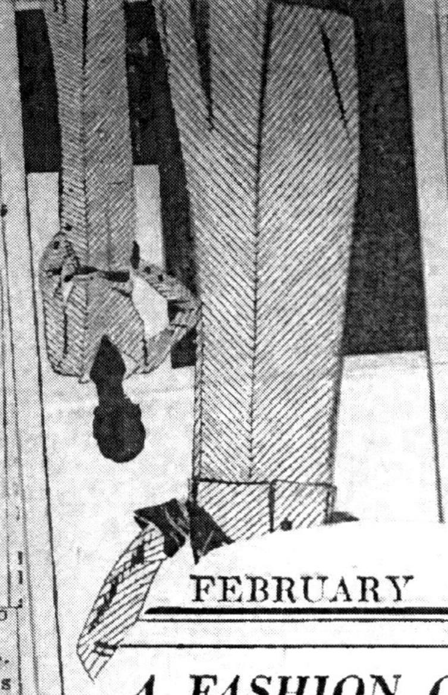

came when Mrs. Chalmers' grandson, Norman Williams, unvelled St. Gaudens' statue of Lincoln.

Of particular value is the photograph in the Chalmers home of Mr. Pinkerton with Lincoln and Gen. John A. McClernand, taken just before the bloody battle of Antietam, in 1862. Hanging by its side is Robert Lincoln's favorite picture of his father.

As for the Country Home for Convalescent Children near Wheaton, now under the direction of the University of Chicago, Mrs. Chalmers founded it 1 years ago, and has ever since given irelessly of her energy to build a model institution for the care of handicapped children. Today the bronze tablets on the walls of the hospitals, workrooms, and the library bear tribute ... and the gifts of other old ...cago families.

...ontinues her ...nd year in the many

FEBRUARY 5. 1932.

A FASHION OF '70S-'80S

a bit of meat and a few potatoes or beans to mix with it into the national dish—the "sancochade"—he doesn't pay much attention to politics.

The weather is ordinarily much to his liking also, never coming within ten degrees of freezing nor more than 30 degrees above that mark.

Roto Depicts 75 Years of Easter Finery

Milady of Yesteryear Knew Nothing of One Piece Frocks or Stepins

By James O'Donnell Bennett.

BEHOLD, O woman now in your thirties—woman of the one piece gown, the step-ins, and the diaphanous hosiery—behold the bales of fabric which your mother, grandmother, and great-grandmother carried on their backs and hung from their hips in the 19th century.

On the color page of this morning's THE TRIBUNE rotogravure section of THE TRIBUNE you have those ladies as they glided across the American scene from 1826 to 1899. Three-quarters of a century of fashions make the page gay with

MISS KIRKLAND, MADAME X OF TRIBUNE, DIES

Was Writer on Society

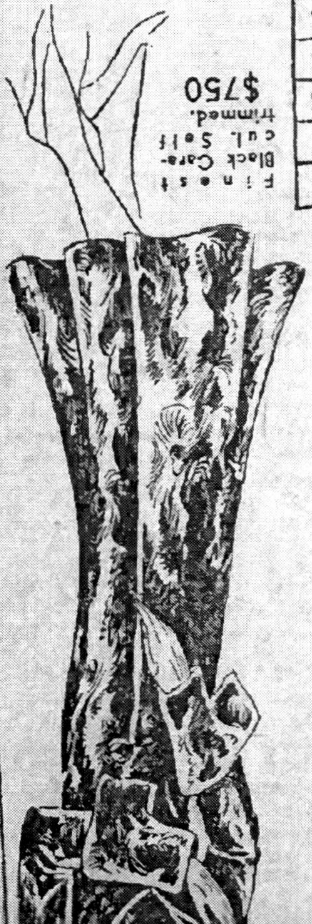

CHICAGO YESTERDAYS

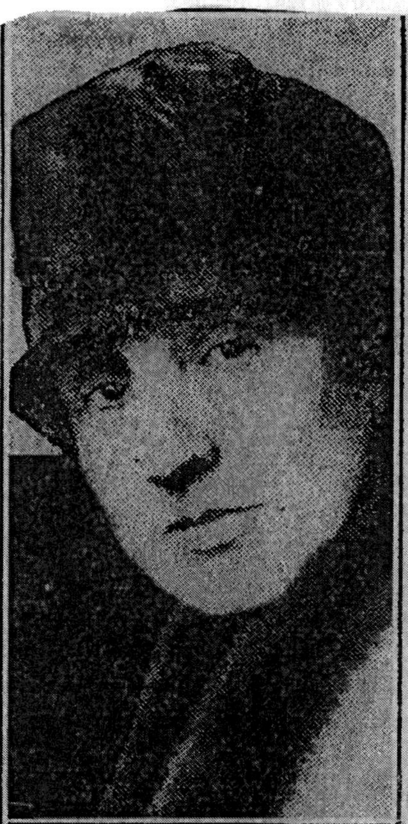

[Copyright: Eugene Hutchinson.]

TRIBUNE WRITER DIES. Miss Caroline Kirkland, known as Mme. X,

and a log wing ... Exchange:

"Mark, observing us, took off his hat and executing a bow with a French grace that would have made a Beau Brummell envious extended his hand to father, remarking:

"'Youse is certainment une strangers. I keeps zat Sauganash hotels, he's bang up good place for youse stops. Mine madam ze is une bully good cook, my pets ze pe gooses fed- ... etz su, I sleeps zu, une dollair ... folks ze day. Ze boys and goil ... out by gar."

... senior Gale for some reason ... ed Green Tree tavern, across ... y. His son remembered:

... the dining room were tables ... ngth of the room, covered with ... checked oil cloth loaded with ... d wild ducks, fricasse of prairie ... ens, wild pigeon pot pie, tea, ..., creamless, but sweetened with ... ulated maple sugar procured from ... red brethren. These furnished a ... uet that rendered us oblivious to ... ped dishes, flies buzzing, tangled ... the butter, creeping beetles, and ... ic of the mosquito band.

Pewter Spoons, Castors.

"We paid no attention to pewter ... stors containing such condiments ... mustard in an uncovered pot, and ... ack pepper coarsely crushed by the ... ood housewife, or to cruets with broken stoppers filled with vinegar and pepper sauce. Our appetites put to flight fastidiousness, and even though the case knives and forks had never been scoured we took for granted that they had been washed after every meal."

The Green Tree tavern served for breakfast the following delicacies: Fried perch just out of the river, venison steak, griddle cakes, white honey, and maple sugar.

A splash of color in the drab prairie colony were those occasions when the sporting blood dressed up in bright toggery and rode to the few hounds in town. There were balls in the big unfinished room over Wolf Point tavern. Sleighing parties would stop at the tavern for a slice or two of cake.

Empty Whisky Into Lemonade.

On July 4, 1836, a social event took place at Canalport honoring the beginning of the Illinois and Michigan canal. There is a story told that the social committee chopped lemons and threw them in the nearby spring to make lemonade for the temperate onlookers. Then some one spoiled the lemonade by emptying a barrel of

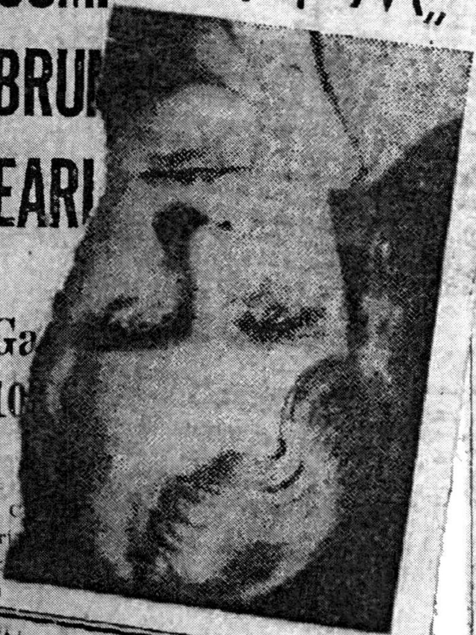

back of first piece

From the portrait by G. P. A. Healy — By courtesy of the Chicago Historical Society

WILLIAM BUTLER OGDEN

CHICAGO'S FIRST MAYOR

CHICAGO YESTERDAYS

A SHEAF OF REMINISCENCES

GARNERED BY
CAROLINE KIRKLAND

Chicago
DAUGHADAY AND COMPANY
1919

PUBLISHED DECEMBER · 1919

FOREWORD

The historian sifts and sifts through his sieve, and from the residue — that which is too thick and solid to go through his meshes — he constructs his story. In this book we lovers of Chicago have done differently. Only that which would slip through the sieve is here offered the reader. Truth lies in the dust that the scholar rejects as well as in the solid nuggets he gathers. From this dust we hope to reconstruct for your delectation at least a vision, a mirage of the simple, hard-working, every-day existence of the men and women of yesterday whose dutiful, industrious lives bequeathed to us of to-day one of the wonders of this age.

Fourth city on the globe in point of size as the census goes, Chicago is second to none in importance as the great market of the western and eastern hemispheres. Reapers made in Chicago reap the grains of Siberia and the Argentine. Products of Packingtown support life at the North and South Poles, and in the loneliest, remotest of the Polynesian isles. Steel from our great mills forms the skeletons of ships on the seven seas, and the rails of transcontinental railways in distant countries.

The strenuous industrial and commercial present is reflected in the city's social life. The families of the men at the head of the vast enterprises, which are the sources of the city's power, are the directing force in Chicago's society. They organize and run entertainments, charitable institutions, clubs, and reform movements of all kinds. So absorbed are our men and women of to-day, however, in their many activities that they give small heed to the city's very honorable and interesting past. They are more inclined to hang it up in a dark closet like an outworn cloak, instead of wearing it like a bright diadem as do older, more mellow cities. This lack of heed to our predecessors is a sign of our youth. It is only as we grow older that our thoughts turn backward.

It is but the lifetime of an octogenarian since Chicago got its city charter in 1837. At that time it had no water system, no drainage, no street pavements, no railways entered or left it. It was the crudest of frontier towns. But its inhabitants even then had a peculiar pride of place. Writing on March 22, 1833, Mrs. R. G. Hamilton, an early resident, said:—

"For in all my lifetime I never saw a place where nature had done so much. Our society is very good and large for a place so new. We have the military here, who are very agreeable, rather gay and extravagant for my turn of mind . . . . " and so on and so forth.

In the letters of Mr. and Mrs. Augustus Burley, in Mr. Joseph T. Ryerson's invaluable memoir, in Mrs. Leander McCormick's charming and artless account of the furnishing of her first house here, we get the homely, sweet flavor of those early days. Mrs. William Blair and Mrs. Arthur B. Meeker deal delightfully with later decades and bridge the time to the period of that genial and friendly west-side settlement — mainly from Kentucky — of which Mr. Carter H. Harrison gives so vivid a description.

Mrs. Joseph Frederick Ward, Mme. Charles Bigot, and Miss Mary Drummond make the sixties and seventies live again for us. Mrs. Frederick T. West and Mrs. Frederick Greeley, daughters of eminent pioneers, give us vivid glimpses of the aspect of a north-side residence district, a place of pleasant homes, set in large gardens on quiet streets. They also call up visions of Chicago's greatest disaster — the catastrophe that set her in the same category with Pompeii, London, and Lisbon, the Chicago Fire of 1871. Mrs. B. F. Ayer brings before us old Hyde Park.

Mr. Edward Blair's entertaining narrative, describing the founding of the Chicago Club, shows our society growing sophisticated, and links the past to the present. There is no stronger contrast in the book, however, than Mrs. Robert G. McGann's lively picture of early Lake Forest as it stands against the elegance, fashion, and up-to-dateness of that community to-day.

Mr. Hobart C. Chatfield-Taylor's chapter on "The Yesterday of the Horse" taps wells of personal memories of people who — well, who don't consider themselves entirely ancient.

To conclude this collection of yesterdays with a chapter from Mrs. William J. Calhoun, on the World's Fair, is to put the cap-stone on a fair edifice built of material no historian would use. Yet who shall say that Chicago of other days — yesterdays — does not live and breathe and move in these pages as no mere searcher after dry-as-dust facts could make her? It is men and women, and the children they rear, who make a city, not the streets that are laid out, the houses that are built, nor the laws that are passed. And, if after reading the words herein set down, thoughts may occasionally come to you of those who once lived here in Chicago as ardently as you, with ideals of civic and domestic life as high as yours — if not higher — then this book has not been achieved in vain, though it be composed only of historian's dust.

CONTENTS

CHICAGO YESTERDAYS

CHICAGO YESTERDAYS

I

THE TWENTIES AND THIRTIES

By Caroline Kirkland

Where Madison Street crosses State Street is said to be the most traffic-congested spot in the world to-day. On foot and awheel thousands of people of every race on this round and rapidly shrinking globe of ours pass and repass. The roar of this constant movement is punctuated by the shrill whistle of the traffic policeman. The warning clang of the street-cars is almost lost in the general din that rises skyward in waves of reverberation to vanish in the upper ether.

A hundred years ago this same spot was an unnoticed part of a flat, marshy, windswept expanse that stretched from the sedge-bordered banks of a sluggish little river south to a distant, knoll-dotted prairie, and west to one of the two forks that fed the little river. Instead of to-day's high buildings, a few widely scattered, one- or two-roomed wooden houses dotted the green waste of water-logged land. Instead of to-day's deafening uproar, the breeze whispered among the reeds. The quail's clear call represented the policeman's warning whistle. State Street, now flanked by magnificent shops and towering office buildings, was then a shallow, fern-bordered slough, emptying its muddy surface drainage, by a slow ooze, into the sluggish river, called by the Indians the "Che-ca-gou," or Garlic-weed creek.

This anemic stream staggered, now eastward, now westward. Spring freshets carried its waters over a low water divide into the Desplaines River, and thence, by the Illinois and Mississippi rivers, into the Gulf of Mexico. The rest of the year it drifted nonchalantly lakeward. At its mouth a sand-bar opposed its career, whereupon it turned docilely southward to meet the lake about where Madison Street now touches the shore.

The chief sign of man's handiwork in the landscape was Fort Dearborn, consisting of a regulation blockhouse, characteristic of our frontiers of those days. This, with a few low buildings, such as barracks, officers' quarters and storehouses, all built of rough-hewn logs, was enclosed by a stockade. The fort was the second on this site, having been built in 1816 on the ruins of its predecessor, which had been looted and burnt by the Indians who perpetrated what is now known as the Chicago Massacre, on August 15, 1812.

Across the river and a little to the east of the fort, John Kinzie's house stood, — about where the new boulevard abutment and Kirk's soap factory now meet, — in a fence-enclosed space, with three tall poplars in front and a giant cottonwood tree shading it from the rear. This house was the center of many social activities for several years.

In the forest of low scrub-oaks and other deciduous trees which covered what is now the "North Side," deer crashed through the underbrush. On the river's brink the unmolested crane stood for hours at a stretch in a one-legged contemplation of life and time. Innumerable water-fowl, wild swan, wild geese, and wild ducks, semi-annually settled in vast clouds of bird-dom on the soggy, sedge-grown reaches adjacent to the river.

Where now the West Side lies in a huge, more or less rectangular conglomeration of streets, parks, and buildings, in 1819 was a wide, flower-grown prairie where as late as 1837 deer were hunted with hounds, and where wolf packs roamed, filling the night with their melancholy and disturbing hullabaloo. They even prowled about the habitations of man and were our first scavengers. The children of that era after nightfall cowered in their beds, hiding their heads under the blankets when the fierce and mournful howls came too near the scattered hamlet. The pack loved best to congregate near Charlie Cleaver's soap factory, on the North Branch, to devour the scraps thrown out from there. Their quarrels disturbed every one within a radius of half a mile.

Ashbel Steele, an early resident, had a fine team and sleigh, and two dogs with which he used to hunt wolves in the winter time over what is now the West Side. He took with him his wife and two little girls, well wrapped up in buffalo robes, and in his letters, now in the archives of the Chicago Historical Society, he describes the thrill of the swift flight of his long-tailed team over the smooth, flat surface of the snowbound prairie. The dogs roused the wolves and ran them down, the Steele family following the chase in their low sleigh.

The same writer describes an afternoon walk between Clybourne's house and Huntoon's sawmill, both on the northwest side of the city, when he came upon the bodies of two dead Indians. One corpse was wrapped up and laid in the branches of a tree. The other was placed in a fenced-in inclosure, facing eastward, in a sitting posture, his back against a tree, his pipes by his side, his gun across the lifeless knees. Mr. Steele didn't know that this strange apparition was the body of an Indian chief, Big Thunder, who had requested to be so placed after death, saying:—

"Out of the East shall come great danger to my people. When it comes I will arise and lead my braves to victory." There is no record of the time when this strange spectacle disappeared from that part of the country.

On this same stroll Mr. Steele describes what he calls "Indian ladders," which were used to climb to the tops of trees for racoons and wild honey. As much as two hundred pounds of honey was taken at a time from one tree.

Browsing among the records and yellow, musty, old letters at the Chicago Historical Society is a far from unpleasant occupation. Notes there gathered mention I. K. Botsford's tinshop as being the first building on Lake Street, the principal thoroughfare in Chicago. Near-by was Charles Follansbee's "family grocery store," and Tuthill King's clothing store.

One Thomas Church, who landed here June 2, 1834, with his wife and two little girls, has left some letters describing his impressions and experiences. He says that he found less than half a dozen dwelling-houses on South Water Street; also several stores and the huts of Indian traders. There was then not even a foot-path where Lake Street now runs east and west. He was urged by the residents at Wolf Point to buy land and settle there, as they contended that the boggy condition of the territory south of the river would forever prevent its being usable. During the periods of inundation frequently the garrison at the fort could only be reached by boat or on horseback. When he wanted to get title to land near South Water Street, either it was marked as preëmpted, or there was a worn-out and stalled wagon stuck in the mire which it would have cost five or six dollars to dig out and haul away, an expense the value of the site did not warrant. Finally he built a store and house in "a pathless region" on what is now Lake Street west of Dearborn. Here he sold groceries, hardware, tools, crockery, and paints, and dealt with the Indians, who paid him, not in cash, but in furs, deerskins, and game, while the squaws brought in wild berries and maple sugar in birch-bark baskets.

After the death of his wife in 1839 he married again; this time a widow, Mrs. Benjamin Jones, and built for her and his daughters a new home on Lake Street just west of where the LeMoyne block now stands. He had a garden full of flowers, fruits and vegetables, and the west of his lot he planted thick with sunflowers and hollyhocks to neutralize "the odiousness of Johnston's soap factory." A heavy growth of shrubbery concealed his house from the street, and a "snow-white picket fence, whose massive posts were surmounted by massive balls," earned for his place the sobriquet "the snowball garden."

Mr. Church mentions the old burial ground on the lake front south of the present Madison Street, and says that easterly storms frequently washed away the earth, exposing and battering to pieces the coffins, and strewing the shore with ghastly remains.

Everyone was not buried there, however. In 1832 the

first cholera epidemic visited Chicago, brought here by troops from Detroit. Lack of any appliances for combating the disease resulted in many deaths both in the fort and outside of it. The corpses of the luckless victims were hastily tossed into a big general grave or trough, dug where now Wabash Avenue touches River Street. As the burial squad, on one occasion, was hurrying through its grewsome task, one corpse sat up and remonstrated, which sent the squad helter skelter back to the fort.

I think it was of a later cholera visitation — Chicago had many — that that delightful wit and *raconteur*, Dr. Charles Dyer, — now long dead, — used to love to tell of his own part. A ship-load of cholera-stricken people arrived in port. He was delegated to take off such as he thought could be saved. Looking over the miserable victims he selected fifteen, leaving another fifteen to certain death, as he supposed.

Man proposes; God disposes! Dr. Dyer's fifteen all died of the disease; those he left on the ship got well! What can medical science do with such obstinate, unappreciative mortals?

Life in the third decade in Chicago, was simple, rugged, and fairly wholesome. The fort, with its little group of army officers and their families, was the center of sociability. A debating society, which met there, was the acme of gaiety. Scarcely second to this, however, were the impromptu dances which took place in the old Sauganash Hotel when the innkeeper, that gay and genial Frenchman and pioneer, Mark Beaubien, would take down his fiddle and set all feet twinkling in the square-dances of that period. This once popular old hostelry stood on the southeast corner of Market and Lake streets. On this same site Abraham Lincoln received the Republican nomination for president on May 18, 1860, in that famous old convention hall, the Wigwam.

As the many men and women of that neighborhood transact their daily business, could magic turn to-day's sights and sounds into those that filled the eye and the ear on that spot on a certain day eighty-four years ago, these same dutiful clerks, stenographers, accountants, and other workers would forsake desks and typewriters and rush to doors and windows that command that part of Lake Street.

On August 18, 1835, eight hundred Indian braves celebrated the signing of the treaty which gave all their claims to land in and around Chicago to the "pale faces" by organizing a great war-dance. Starting on the north side of the river about where the northeast corner of Rush and Kinzie streets now is, this band of warriors proceeded along the river's brink westward to the north branch. They were naked except for loin cloths; their faces were streaked with paint — vermilion and red predominating — with accenting splashes of black. The coarse, long, black hair of each brave was gathered up in a scalp-lock on the top of the head, and adorned with hawks' and eagles' feathers. Leaping, crouching, creeping, bounding, they advanced to the hideous din of their own band. The savage rhythm to which their wild capers corresponded was given by measured beating on hollow vessels and striking war-clubs together, accompanied by discordant yells, made more horrible by the rapid clapping of the mouth with the palm of the hand, — that blood-curdling Indian war-whoop which is fast fading even from our traditions, but which, a century ago, was the signal for terror and foreboding.

Crossing the north branch the howling, leaping savages turned southward until they came to what was then known as Wolf Point, a collection of rude cabins clustered at the junction where the north and south branches met to form the main river. They crossed the south branch at about where Lake Street now runs, and advanced to the space in front of the Sauganash Hotel. The windows of the hotel parlors on the second floor looking westward were crowded with spectators, among whom was the young lawyer, John Dean Caton, and his pretty bride, Laura Sherrill, of Utica. When the Indians saw white women watching them, their frenzy increased. Writing of the scene afterwards, Judge Caton thus vividly describes it:—

"The morning was very warm and the perspiration was pouring from them. Their countenances had assumed an expression of all the worst passions . . . fierce anger, terrible hate, dire revenge, remorseless cruelty — all were expressed in their terrible features. . . . Their tomahawks and clubs were thrown and brandished in every direction . . . and with every step and every gesture they uttered the most frightful yells. . . . The dance consisted of leaps and spasmodic steps, now forward and now back or sidewise, the whole body distorted into every imaginable position; most generally stooping forward with the head and face thrown up, the back arched down, first one foot thrown far forward and withdrawn and the other similarly thrust out, frequently squatting quite to the ground, and all with a movement almost as quick as lightning.

"When the head of the column reached the hotel, while they looked up at the windows at the 'Chemokoman squaws' . . . it seemed as if we had a picture of hell itself before us and a carnival of the damned spirits there confined."

Passing on eastward, they disbanded under the Fort Dearborn stockade with parting yells, to end their last day in Chicago in a final glorious debauch.

The thirties of the last century in Chicago were as lively as the twenties were quiet. Speculators, gamblers, adventurers of all kinds flocked to the frontier settlement, along with the solid and substantial citizens who came to found families and fortunes in this outpost of civilization. Many arrived by the big, canvas-covered wagons called "prairie-schooners" and camped in a semicircle on the confines of the village. Frequently more than a hundred campfires dotted the night landscape. Land was the great speculation then; lots in 1833, for instance, selling for $3,000 that had cost their owners $80 the year before. All this, however, is a matter of written history and therefore not within our province. But of interest alike to housekeeper and householder is the cost of living in that era. Viewed in the light of today's expense account, it looks like the golden age to you and me. Beef was six cents a pound; butter the same. Flour was three dollars a barrel; grouse a dollar a dozen; quail thirty-seven cents a dozen; venison a dollar and a half the carcase. Fruits were more costly, as they had all to be brought from the East over land and lake — a long and laborious journey. The water supply was primitive, to say the least. A man collected water from the margin of the lake in a hogshead and peddled it from door to door.

Social customs were informal and animated by that spirit of boundless hospitality which is to this day the unwritten law in Chicago — to the amazement of our eastern visitors. In 1837 the daughter of one of our earliest settlers, a French-Canadian, La Framboise, was married to a Chicago postal clerk, name not recorded. (Later she became the wife of Médard Beaubien.) The bridegroom had fifty invitations struck off on the village printing-press. On hints he had another fifty printed and distributed; then a hundred more. Still the demand for invitations grew, so he announced that tickets were not necessary and that every one might come.

In 1831 the first bridge over the river and its branches was thrown across the south branch between where now it is crossed by Lake and Randolph streets. It cost $286.20 and for some unexplained reason the Pottawotamies paid $200 of this sum. Near the present Kinzie Street bridge a foot-bridge was built in 1832. In 1834 at Dearborn Street a "jackknife" bridge was constructed. This was three hundred feet long, with a sort of gallows frame at each end, and was drawn up and let down by cables worked by hand-power.

The first steamboat entered the river on May 4, 1834. It was the S. S. *Michigan,* Captain Blake, and owned by Oliver Newberry of Detroit, brother of Walter L. Newberry of Chicago, whose fortune founded the library bearing his name.

The first grain elevators were on the north side of the river, which made south-side business men so envious that they tried to do away with the bridges and cut off the North Side from any communication with their part of town, except by the tedious hand-worked ferry which ran back and forth where Rush Street bridge now is. Some years later, to improve communication between the north and south sides, William B. Ogden and Walter L. Newberry, both of whom owned much north-side property, gave the present block bounded by State, Superior, Cass streets and Chicago Avenue, where stands the Cathedral of the Holy Name and other church-owned buildings, to the Roman Catholic Church so as to get the Catholic vote for the proposed Clark Street bridge. This vote is supposed to have carried the measure, greatly to the ultimate advantage of both the north and south sides of the city.

In 1832, Chicago taxes totalled almost $400, which was considered a matter for great rejoicing. In 1833 the settlement became a regular village, with old John Kinzie's son, Major John H. Kinzie (his title came from Governor Cass of Michigan), as first president of the board of trustees. On this board were T. V. Owen, Mark Beaubien, and John Miller.

Chicago early acquired the fire habit which culminated in the famous orgy of October 9, 1871. Her first great fire was in 1838, when seventeen wooden buildings on Lake and Dearborn streets were swept away, including the original Tremont House on the northwest corner of these two streets. In 1835 a fire company had been formed at a general meeting of citizens called for this purpose in Ike Cook's saloon, on South Water Street. A month later the village board created a fire department. If this is mentioned here it is because the fire brigade was a part of fashionable, social life in those days. Among those composing this first fire company were John K. Wilson (father of the subsequent proprietor of the *Chicago Journal*), P. F. W. Peck, E. C. Brackett, John Holbrook, Silas B. Cobb, Arthur B. Meeker,

James K. Botsford, Grant Goodrich, William H. Taylor, George W. Snow, Jeremiah Price, B. W. Raymond, Ira Couch, H. O. Stone, T. B. Carter, James Wadsworth, Tuthill King, P. C. Sheldon, Samuel N. Davis, and J. M. Adsit. The company bought a hand engine for $894.38, and it was the correct thing for everyone to go to a fire in those days; the men to take a hand in passing buckets while the women passed cups of hot coffee. As the buildings were practically all of wood and were hastily and not too carefully constructed, there were many of these pleasant social occasions. In the Burley letters in a later chapter you get an interesting account of the firemen's ball, which was the chief social event of that season.

In 1837 Chicago became a full-fledged city, with William Butler Ogden as its first mayor.

Among the eminent citizens who came to Chicago in this and the previous decade and left descendants, direct or collateral, were William B. Ogden, John Wentworth, Justin Butterfield, Philo Otis, H. O. Stone, P. F. W. Peck, George W. Dole, George W. Snow, Charles Follansbee, Walter L. Newberry, E. K. Rogers, Silas B. Cobb, Augustus and Arthur Burley, Isaac N. Arnold, Henry Hubbard, Daniel Brainerd, Norman B. Judd, Thomas Bentley, J. Y. Scammon, Mark Skinner, Grant Goodrich, Alexander Wolcott, Arthur B. Meeker, William Bross, Henry W. Blodgett, Stephen Gale, and Isaac N. Harmon. Chicago's most notable pioneer, however, was Gurdon Saltonstall Hubbard, who came for the Astor fur-trading company in 1821, and was practically a resident of this city from then on until his death in 1886.

One name among those of the pioneers prominent in local

annals about that time here listed recalls a romance which connects Chicago with one of the most celebrated English writers of the past thirty years, Rudyard Kipling, and, as this chapter purports to be merely a not too coherent assembling of personalities and incidents, I venture to bring it in here.

Ellen Marion Kinzie, eldest child of John Kinzie, who married Dr. Alexander Wolcott, had a niece-in-law, Caroline Wolcott, gay, pretty and much admired, who came to visit her Chicago connections, the John H. Kinzies, in the late thirties. She was only sixteen years old at the time. Therefore, when young Joseph N. Balestier, a brilliant and enterprising citizen who had come to Chicago from the South, met and fell violently in love with her and she with him, her Chicago hosts strongly opposed the marriage. One story goes that the ardent young couple were on the eve of elopement when they were intercepted and induced to ask once more for the consent of Miss Wolcott's temporary guardians. This was finally secured. The marriage took place and the Balestiers ultimately settled in Brattleboro, Vermont. A grandson, Wolcott Balestier, became Rudyard Kipling's Fidus Achates, and a collaborateur in one or more of his books. After the death of the former, the now famous English author married the sister, Miss Caroline Balestier, and in this roundabout way established a relationship with Chicago. In his children's veins runs the blood of some of Chicago's early settlers, that fine crop of citizens who gave this city its best characteristics.

Kipling's one visit to Chicago, some time in the last decade of the last century, left such a bad taste in his mouth that, of all his bitter comments as to his trip across this continent, his diatribe on Chicago was the most stinging. But then he had not yet married a descendant of one of our f. f. C.'s.

From this point on, lights are turned on some of Chicago's yesterdays by the various contributors to this volume, who, for the love of Chicago, have kindly searched family archives and their own memories for material that may, we hope, for a moment hold the attention of impatient to-day.

Perhaps the narratives here set forth will leave a permanent impress on the minds of their readers, so that never again can they feel detached from the intangible, but inescapable clutch of the past, even of so vibrantly young and lusty a city as Chicago.

After all, what is it that makes any city interesting and gives it its charm and flavor? Is it its present? Decidedly not. It is the centuries of turmoil and achievement which lie behind London, Paris, Florence, Rome, and Athens that draw us and thousands, even millions, of other tourists to these cities. So it behooves us Chicagoans to cherish our city's past and to write its history in street names, parks, and monuments, as well as in books and memoirs.

II

A PIONEER COUPLE

Letters of Mr. and Mrs. Augustus H. Burley

Two of Chicago's early and eminent citizens were Arthur Burley and Augustus H. Burley, brothers, who in 1837, the year Chicago became a city, came from Exeter, N. H., by rail, Sound steamer, river boat, canal boat, lake ship, and horse and wagon to the uncouth, unkempt frontier settlement that sprawled along both banks of a shallow stream. The new town had been in turn a halting place for wandering Indians, a fur-traders' camp, a military outpost of civilization, and now was fast becoming a business center for a rapidly developing agricultural district.

The two Burleys were preceded by their half-brother, Stephen Gale, and followed later by their younger brother, Charles. From the beginning Augustus, and later his wife, Harriet, kept up a continuous correspondence with their eastern relatives — a correspondence which gradually unfolded a graphic picture of the conditions of life in this part of the world.

From this carefully treasured bundle of letters their son, Mr. Clarence Burley, has allowed me to cull what I need, to give as vivid an idea as such fragments can of the crude conditions and interesting development of domestic and social life in Chicago from 1837 to 1852.

Augustus H. Burley writes to Miss Harriet M. Gale in New England:—

"*Chicago, September* 7, 1837

". . . . The times are exceedingly dull in this city of Chicago; there is no business, no balls, no parties, some shooting, some riding, and plenty of *loafers*, and to-day, after the rain, a plenty of mud which completes the picture, excepting watermelons, which we have here in any quantities (alias slathers of them) and of the most delicious flavor. . . .

"We[1] have started a Circulating Library, and have a room, 'most finished to keep it in, and another room for a sleeping room, which form an addition on the back part of the store.

"Chicago is a pretty good place for men that are in business for making money, but it is a miserable place for loafers, — for there is no 'Valient,' no 'Hampton Beach,' no theater, no museum, or any other place except our store, which is generally allowed to be the best loafing-place in the city. . . .

"*Chicago, November* 20, 1837

". . . The prairie takes fire every dry day that we have, and in the evening burns beautifully and lights up the whole sky. The weather is very warm for the season, with more than the usual quantity of rain. The Indians predict an open winter."

Of the rugged conditions of life in the thirties in Chicago

[1] His older brother, Arthur Burley, was associated with him in this and other business enterprises.

these extracts give proof: —

"I am glad to hear that Edward S. is coming West, for it is one of the best countries for young men that can be found; it completely cures them of all greenness, also of weak stomachs and fastidiousness. I can eat 'most anything, and pull a long hair out of my mouth with perfect nonchalance.

"You can tell Uncle Gray that it was told me on the way that I should learn to drink rum, brandy, etc. before I had staid here long, but I have not drunk anything of the kind but once, and then I was actually sick. It is true that the water here is first-rate bad, and the only way we get along is by drinking a great deal of coffee and tea — two coffees to one tea. The weather, till within two or three weeks, has been very mild. In that time there has not been snow enough to stop the burning of the prairies.

"*Chicago, June* 20, 1838

". . . . Our weather this spring has been pretty much the same as usual, rather cold, but changeable of late. We have had some warm weather, and a great deal of thunder and lightning. The trees and the earth are now clothed in their beautiful garment of green; the prairies are enlivened by thousands of beautiful flowers and the birds, insects, and the snakes (O, delightful idea!) are as lively as you can imagine, and I will renew my promise to get you some flower seeds if I can. . . .

"I suppose that you will laugh when I tell you that I have got the itch, and I believe that I have never been fairly rid of it since I caught it of Harrison. It does not trouble me, only by its breaking out. It does not itch any. It is called, through courtesy, the 'Prairie' itch, but it is the old-fashioned variety. It is as common here as it is to have warts on the hands or any other little troubles.

"*Chicago, August* 14, 1838

". . . To me and to the rest of us the distance between here and Exeter seems only a step, but to you I know that it seems a long way. If the waters of Lake Michigan continue to rise for a year or two more Chicago and all the surrounding country will be covered with one vast sheet of water, finding an outlet through the Mississippi, and the inhabitants of this place must find a home elsewhere,—and I for one will find said home farther east.

"Chicago is very healthy for the season; we have had some very warm weather indeed, but now we have a cold snap which will probably last a day or two longer, and will conduce very much to the health of the city. Water-melons begin to come in in large quantities and of excellent flavor. Doesn't your mouth water?"

To his half-sister, Harriet M. Gale, he writes:—

"*Chicago, December* 28, 1838

". . . We have moved from our store in South Water Street to a new one on the corner of Lake and La Salle streets. Lake Street being our principal business street, the stand is much better for our business than the old one. The store is large and airy. We have it hung around, in the back part of the library room, with portraits of Indian chiefs, of which more anon.

"The store is well finished and, when we first came into it with our new stock, looked very well. Now some of the shelves are getting to be rather bare, which, by the way, is not to be regretted, only as it spoils the uniformity of our arrangements.

"The Indian portraits I spoke of are from a work published at Philadelphia under the patronage of the Government, entitled *Indian Biography,* being portraits of distinguished Indian chiefs and warriors, with their biographies connected. It is published by subscription; (the Government subscribed $100,000 towards it).

"Stephen is agent in Chicago, and subscribed his pay as agent for it, amounting to more than the subscription, which for the whole is $120, being six dollars a number and twenty numbers, the first nine numbers being published and received. Stephen has had his framed in black walnut, which I think is very appropriate. They hang around us in gloomy majesty, and form an excellent ornament to our store, exciting a great deal of interest and curiosity among visitors in general, and more especially among some Indians of the Winnebago tribe who were brought in to see them. They appeared very much pleased with them,— expressing it in frequent grunts, and recognizing several of the likenesses.

"As to Chicago, it is pretty much the same old place— full of bustle, activity, and the flower of American young men. The business this fall has been very much increased by the southern rivers being so low as they are, and their navigation being closed. This has forced a great deal of southern trade to Chicago. This trade has been so great that it has nearly emptied Chicago of everything. Salt being in great demand at the South, Chicago has been drained of nearly all except a lot in the hands of one man who wants it for his own use, and the remainder is selling at six dollars per bushel. All other articles in the grocery line have risen nearly one hundred per cent. . . .

"My letter has now had a resting spell for about one week, during which time I have been too busy to write, and now commence again. The old year is past and gone, and the new year has come, and with it we must renew the cares and troubles of those which are past. My Christmas and New Year's day passed the same as usual,—in the store all the time. Stephen attended a ball at Joliet New Year's night. The ball was very large, there being about sixty couples, everything being in the best style.

"There was also a ball in town, but it was small and did not go off with great *éclat*. The New York fashion of calling upon the ladies and taking a glass of wine, or of something else, on New Year's day, is in vogue here, but, as my time was so much taken up, I made no calls. . . .

"*Chicago, January* 11, 1839

". . . On Tuesday evening there was a ball which I attended and danced until two o'clock among the *élite* of Chicago. Last night there was a party which I did not attend. For a few days the weather has been very mild, and the mud is up to one's knees nearly. The ladies ride out in one-horse carriages without any seat or top, and a tail-board like a potato cart. The river is breaking up and it is very much feared that it will not be closed again.—Here comes Arthur with a green blind over his eye.—During this bad going, business is very dull; we have nothing to do but stand at the door and see people get into the mud."

The flight of time somewhat developed Mr. Burley's gregariousness and letters to his mother in the winter and summer of 1841 show Chicago's early social tendencies:—

"*Chicago, January* 10, 1841

". . . The New Year commenced here with the New York custom of calling on all acquaintances. I mingled with the rest, making, myself, thirty-three calls, most of which will last until the first of New Year again. Stephen made thirty calls, a wonder for him."

By 1843 Mr. Burley had married and a daughter had been born to the young couple. A letter of Mrs. Burley's describing a journey from New York to Chicago is especially recommended to the modern traveler who is accustomed to stepping on the Twentieth Century train at two o'clock in the afternoon, and arriving at his destination in eighteen or nineteen hours:—

"*Chicago, September* 5, 1843

". . . We left New York Saturday eve for Albany. About an hour before, I received a letter from Gus with directions for me to buy some things, as he had concluded to keep house. But I did not, as we had no time. We arrived in Albany early the next morning. I went to see my cousin Charlotte and spent the forenoon with her. She was well and very glad to see me. I believe she is to be married soon. At one o'clock we took the cars for Buffalo. Baby was very good all the way. We had a large car but no saloon. There were but seven or eight on board. I made a bed for baby on one of the seats and she slept there all night as well as though she had been at home. Monday eve we reached Buffalo so I had all day Tuesday to rest, and Wednesday noon we went on board *The Western* and started for home. Tell Harriet we stopped at Detroit after I was abed and asleep, but Charles went on shore and saw the folks. They were all well. You know I have a habit of retiring very early. Thursday, Friday, and Saturday it was delightful on the lakes. It was as calm as could be. If Harriet remembers, we could have no music on board *The Western* when we went home because one of the band was sick. He died in a few weeks and his father died just before we reached Mackinaw, and was buried while we were there. They both died from bleedings at the lungs caused by playing on wind instruments. There is another son in the band and, as the father was dying, he motioned for the son not to play any more.

"Mrs. Howe was at Mackinaw waiting for *The Western* to bring her child to Chicago. It is quite sick. The boat was so crowded that she could not come. I was thankful she did not, afterwards, for I do not know what would have become of her poor child. Just before we left Mackinaw it began to blow a little and kept increasing, and that night we had as severe a storm as has been known on the lakes. The boat pitched so that the man at the helm had to be chained fast to keep from going overboard. Some horses on the lower deck got nearly drowned from having the waves wash over them all the time. We saw a light and thought it was the landing place at Manitou and cast anchor, but the cable soon parted and we lost the anchor, and, as we drifted on, we found that the light proceeded from a scow. Sometimes we would go on a minute and then we would go back, and only went three miles in five hours. About daylight we anchored off the Manitou and were safe, but could not go near the shore, for there were one or two vessels aground already. In the midst of all this storm, there was a child born on the boat to a deck passenger. I believe the woman was made quite comfortable. There we had to stay three long, long days, and were nearly out of provisions and had to live on two meals a day. Finally we found that the forward deck passengers were almost starving. They were all brought up and had one good meal. Then there was but enough for two meals more and nothing to be got from the island, and all the other boats in the same condition, so Wednesday morning we put out in quite a blow, but it went down towards night. Thursday noon I saw the pier at Chicago and standing on it was my dear husband. We had six hundred people on board. There was a good deal of anxiety felt here about the boat.

"I did not mean to fill my letter with my journey home, but Stephen will tell all about Chicago and its inhabitants. We have concluded to stay at Mrs. Heights' this winter, and have a girl for a dollar a week who will do our washing and work for Mrs. Heights in the morning to pay for her board, and I have her in the afternoon to take care of the baby. Do you think it a good arrangement?"

The following is especially interesting to our real-estate experts. Mr. Burley writes to his father, James Burley, of Exeter, N. H.:—

"*Chicago, December* 15, 1845

". . . There is a three-story brick store a short distance above our present situation, on the second twenty feet from the N. E. corner of Lake and Clark streets, which can be purchased for six thousand dollars, and we have thought it not improbable that Mr. Robinson would like to make an investment here which would pay him good interest.

"The store is three stories high with attic and 80 feet in depth — the lot is 100 feet deep, with a passage way at the back end (for the use of it and the next 20 feet) across the corner lot, to remain forever open; the store has been built seven years and is good, tho' in need of some repairs, to plastering, etc., and wants also the addition of iron shutters; the roof is tinned and painted.

"Clark Street is the street on which the bridge crosses the river, and the corners of Lake and Clark streets are considered the most desirable in town.

"We should be willing and glad to take a five-year lease, paying $500 rent besides insurance and taxes. This, as stores now rent, would be low.

"I should prefer hiring the money and making the purchase for ourselves, as we then should get the benefit of the rise in its value, which we consider unquestionable, but we suppose it impracticable to borrow the amount on long time, tho' the security would be good and the interest at six or seven per cent easy for us to pay, and be a low rent.

"Chicago's prospects never were so good, nor has it ever done so much business in the same time, as this fall. The receipts of wheat have been immense, varying from 20,000 to 25,000 bushels per day for weeks together, and some days reaching 28,000 bushels. The cash price now is 95 cents and $1.00. One house has made actually $30,000 in wheat operations, and have now on hand 100,000 bushels at an average cost say of 73c or 75c.

"The speculating mania is getting fast hold again of the people, there is no disguising it, and another season will see '36 reënacted in Chicago. Our business necessities will keep us clear, but it is hard to avoid wheat, copper, stock, land, or some of the other operations in which 'most all take a chance. . . .

"You may think my expectations extravagant and my picture highly colored, but it is not, and, could you see the immense strides of increase our city actually takes, and the business it does, in a moment you would feel that any reasonable investment would repay many fold.

"With due deference, I remain,

"Your affectionate son,

"Augustus H. Burley."

To the few Chicagoans whose memories go back to the fifties of the last century the names, Mrs. Humphrey and Mrs. Payson, will recall two charming sisters of French extraction, their father, Eugene Canda, having been born in France. They played a conspicuous part in local society. Their names, as well as those of other early Chicagoans, progenitors of to-day's prominent families, appear in this exceedingly sprightly letter from Mrs. Burley: —

"*Chicago, November* 15, 1846

". . . I suppose ere this you have heard that Mr. Payson is married!!! as he has been married over a month. They were engaged only two weeks, and his sister only knew of it two or three days before. Dr. Stuart's family and Mr. Bishop's family were all that were invited to the wedding. Some of Mr. Payson's friends are very angry with him because he deceived them so. He said that he was only going to Buffalo with his sister. Wilder said he was sorry, as he wanted to send a package by him to Boston; this was the night before he left. They were married in the morning before breakfast and left at nine o'clock. They expected to stay in Boston till June, so I expect that you will hear of nothing but 'the beautiful Mrs. Payson who is flourishing in Boston.' Wilder and Payson have been acquainted from boys and Nat felt a little hurt. He and some others went down to see the boat off. They merely nodded to Mr. Payson and said 'good morning Miss Canda,' and walked off. They made believe that they did not know he was married, and he looked *so sheepish.*

"I understood that George Meeker said to her, 'I congratulate you, Mrs. Payson.' She put her hand over her mouth in her *usual fascinating style,* and said, 'Dear me, I cannot answer to that name!'

"Mrs. Charles Larrabee was here. One day she said that when Mr. Payson visited her, he came one eve and said that he had just been to call on Mrs. Humphrey and she was a very pleasant woman, but, said he, 'I should not think that Dave would like to have that sister of hers staying there, she is so inferior to his wife.' Poor Matty, she cried all day after they were gone. She declares that neither of them want the other, but Mrs. Humphrey forced them both into it. But enough! I guess you are tired of Payson.

"Mr. Ogden [1] inquired very particularly of Gus about you, Mary. I really think you must have made an impression on him. Poor Carry! I dread to speak of Mr. Forrest. Jane has jilted him; she is engaged to someone at the East. He felt dreadfully about it and went to Mary Ann Maxwell for sympathy, and she seemed to sympathize so well with him that he has about concluded that perhaps she will do

[1] William B. Ogden, Chicago's first mayor.

just as well as Jane. They go to our church sometimes, and then walk up by our house and around the block home so as to make the walk as long as possible. I am afraid that your chance is small, and I hear that you are getting fat. So am I, just think of that! Judging from my own feelings I suppose you must be delighted. Would you not like to know if I have an 'x' under my name? Well, guess if you can; I shall not tell you. I have gained twelve pounds in six weeks. My weight now is 116 pounds, *just to think it!* I shall catch up to you soon. I never felt better in my life than I have the last week. Gus has got a barrel of cider and I drink it two or three times a day. I think it does me a great deal of good. I forgot to say that Miss Cotton is an uncle and they are very much disappointed, as she wished to be an aunt. Such a looking baby you never saw in all your life; it looks like a little monkey.

"Gus brought me lots of pretty things from New York. A cherry-colored scarf; a gingham dress with a silk stripe in it — very pretty; a Thibet cloth cloak, a dark mulberry color; a bonnet, trimmed so heavy, which he only paid ten shillings for because it was old-fashioned. It weighs more than the worth of that. It is perfectly plain and just what I wanted. I went down to Mrs. Daniel's to get my bonnet trimmed and she asked me if I would not bring down my silk quilt and show it to her. Mrs. King had told her of it, and she said that she would save me some pieces. I took it down and she gave me a peck of most beautiful velvets, all colors; they have almost set me wild they are so pretty. I had to piece two blocks before I could do anything else. I will describe them to you. One is purple satin center, next row white uncut velvet; next blue velvet and the last row orange-colored silk. The other block is cherry satin center, next white velvet, next green velvet, and last pink satin. Don't you think they must be pretty?

"Would you believe it? I am almost to the end of my plain sewing. I have my cloak to make and then I shall go at my quilt, and that is all I expect to do this winter. I mean to go out and enjoy myself, study French, etc. I have a great many plans laid out for the winter. I have just got an extract book to try and improve myself in writing and I shall practice on my guitar all I can. The piano is sold.

"News! News! News!!! I have just come from down town. Mrs. Walter has twins! Two boys — did you ever hear the like of that? She was here the other day and said she was going to have twins so as to let me have one. She has been married just eight months and two days. Joel is almost beside himself; he thinks he is so much smarter than other folks. . . ."

A ball in January, 1847, was the great event of that social season. Mrs. Burley gives this picture of it: —

"The Firemen's Ball was the 22nd of January and was the grandest affair that Chicago has ever known. Gus was one of the managers. There were thirty-five. He was on the committee for invitations. They sent out 1,050, just think of that! Both the dining- and the dancing-hall were used for dancing. They were trimmed with bunting in festoons all over the ceiling. The firemen's caps, trumpets and buckets were hung all around, with innumerable lamps. The new engine, No. 3, was trimmed with flowers and ribbons and set in the lower hall. There was a bell hung in each hall and at the end of each set they gave a stroke on it instead of a tap on the fiddle. Both bands of music were very good, as they have been practicing all winter for the occasion. They had supper-tables set in three rooms all the time, so as not to stop the dancing. Parties of about two dozen could sit at one table, which made it very pleasant as we could pick our company. . . ."

In that decade Chicago was just rising from the marshy banks of the river. Her streets were at times impassable sloughs only to be traversed, as Mrs. William Blair points out in another chapter, by men in hip-high boots and by women in two-wheeled carts, into and out of which they had to be lifted by strong arms.

The men of the community were all hard workers then as now, frequently staying in their offices and shops until after ten o'clock in the evening The women were as industrious as their men-folk. Servants were few and far between, and none too competent. The women of that epoch cooked and washed and scrubbed and cleaned house, with sewing, tending children, and church work as recreation. Several times in her home letters, Mrs. Burley refers to a patchwork silk quilt on which she was working. Returning from a visit in 1848 to her husband's family in Exeter, in writing to her mother-in-law she completes the tale of the quilt, which was evidently a work of art of much renown:—

"I suppose you are skipping all this to hear some news of the quilt and I may as well tell you first as last. When I got home I found the Fair was deferred till the 10th of November and that my quilt would not be considered a quilt if it was not finished, and two or three said it would look so much better if it had a border. I was discouraged, for I had so much to do and was more than half sick and had neither silk nor velvet for a border, so I concluded not to send it to the Fair. Now I think I hear you exclaim, 'Foolish child to spend all summer for nothing!' but I wasn't a bit and I will tell the rest of the story. My neighbors all saw how the case stood and thought if it was finished it would take the prize, so they brought all their pieces of silk and thimbles. Gus got some more velvet and turkey red to line it, and red ribbon to bind it and lo! it was done. The border was pieced in points alternate of silk and velvet. It went to the Fair and took the first prize from twenty-five quilts! There were some there with more pieces and some that looked prettier as they hung, but none bore examination so well as mine. I did not think mine looked so pretty there as it did at home, as it hung so high that it looked dark and small. The prize is a very handsome basket worth about $15.00."

The survival of the fittest was the rule in those rugged, strenuous days. "The white plague" claimed many a victim, especially among the women who lived in airtight houses heated by the deadly airtight stove — successor to the unconscionably open fireplace.

The common phrase of the time was, "she just went into a decline and pined away," or "she had the galloping consumption and died." The nature of the disease was so little understood that the first step taken was to shut the victim up in rooms still more hermetically sealed from the health-giving fresh air outside, and to torture the sufferers with plasters, and dose them with strong drugs. After writing about the quilt, Mrs. Burley continues: —

"My cough has been getting gradually worse since I came home, and about three weeks ago Dr. Boone examined my lungs. He says that my left lung is perfectly sound, but there is an inflammation of the bronchial tubes of the right lung, or congestion, he calls it. Since then I have had a sorry time of it. I have been plastered, blistered and dosed till, as I told the doctor yesterday, 'I thought the remedy much worse than the disease.' Did you ever have a tartar emetic plaster? If you did, you know how to pity me for I have one on all the time and sometimes three at a time, on my breast, side, and back. Every three hours I take a dose of ipecac and paregoric. So between drowsiness and sickness at my stomach all the time, I am not very interesting, and you may feel thankful that you are rid of my company. Notwithstanding what Hatty says about exercise, the doctor will not let me even hold the baby or poke my nose out the window, nor do anything like work. He has said nothing about my sewing, but I am growing downright lazy, so much so that I do not even darn my own stockings. I really do not believe I have my wits more than half the time as I take so much paregoric."

A few months later, in February, 1849, she writes to her father-in-law, the last letter of hers in the series: —

". . . I am about half sick all the time and feel so stupid that it is almost impossible to do anything. The only thing that I feel like doing, you and the doctor deny me. I do not feel well enough to go out often; I get tired reading; it gives me a pain in my side to write; you will not let me sew, and here I have to sit and fold my hands and rock all day — which is the hardest work of all. I have gotten so used to the rocking-chair now that anyone might take me for one of the Smith family (if you do not understand this, Harriet will). I wish I had one of the girls here this winter to keep me company. Gus can never leave the store till nine or ten o'clock in the evening and I get so tired of sitting here alone.

"This winter I have been plastered, blistered, cupped, taken ipecac every two hours for weeks and now I am in the stocks. Some time ago Gus wrote to Dr. Fitch of New York (the great consumption doctor) about me, and yesterday came a box from him containing twenty-one bottles of medicine, four boxes of pills, shoulder-braces, back-supporters, inhaling tube, pamphlets, directions, etc.

"Now, I am in for a siege. I am afraid I shall find the remedy worse than the disease. I suppose you will say, 'Serve you right, no school like experience: you must let sewing alone, bed-quilts particularly.' Whatever is the cause, I 'pay dear for the whistle.'"

The wordless hiatus between this and the next in the series dated May 23, 1852, from Mr. Burley to his half-sister, Miss Harriet M. Gale, tells its own story. Once more he is a bachelor, alone, working out his destiny in Chicago, only this time in much greater material comfort than when he arrived in 1837. He no longer has to practise sang-froid when plucking a hair from the stew, or cope with the crude conditions of fifteen years before: —

"Dear Sister:

"Here I sit in my new quarters with a window open looking up Clark Street upon a crowd of promenaders, who are all out to enjoy one of the very fine afternoons of the season. The bells are just ringing for evening service. My rooms (parlor and bedroom) are on the corner of Clark and Lake streets, fifth story, with two windows on south and three on east side, being about the pleasantest in town. The front room is carpeted with the blue and white.

"Our city is and has been for some weeks quite full of strangers, many of whom have been attracted by the land sales. And both railroads, being now completed to the city, are bringing large additions, making everything appear lively and very materially increasing business. I have found an abundance to do since my return. Arthur seems also to be very busy. . . .

"Say to John that the strides of Chicago are enormous, its increase is astonishing. The streets, hotels, everything is filled to overflowing and business, tho' now dull, has been very large. It seems impossible to conceive when or where it will stop. The improvement astonishes even the old settlers. Our city has been filled with men of note and wealth from the east, many of whom have been buying property and taking stock in our railroads. . . .

"Our Fourth of July passed off without any fuss in particular. On Tuesday last we had a procession and eulogy in honor of Henry Clay and it was the largest and most imposing thing of the kind ever gotten up here. Your humble servant was one of the marshals and had the pleasure of being in the saddle during four of the hottest hours that need be. The procession moved from Michigan and Wabash avenues and State Street on to the West Side and back, and then on to the North Side to public ground opposite Mr. Ogden's, where the eulogy was delivered by Lisle Smith. The stores were all closed and many hung in mourning. The bells were all tolled and guns fired during the moving of the procession. . . .

"Charles[1] has been elected to the important position of Foreman of the Hook-and-Ladder Company. . . ."

[1] A brother.

III

A NEW HOME

Letter of Mrs. Leander McCormick

A complement to the preceding chapter, which gives a glimpse of some of the outward aspects of life in Chicago, is this artless, engaging, garrulous letter written by the late Mrs. Leander McCormick on arriving here in 1838.

No family is more thoroughly identified with this city to-day than the McCormick family, descendants of the three Virginia brothers, Leander, Cyrus, and William. They are leaders in the industrial, social and philanthropic life of Chicago. Their name is known in every country on this globe where harvests are sown and gathered. The incomes of the great fortunes that have come to them through the world-famous business, which for so long bore their name, and through wise investments, have been spent with the same ability as the fortunes were made. Charities, local and foreign, civic institutions making for music and art, educational enterprises, have all been benefited by McCormick aid; while the most magnificent of the Medici princes was not better known to the art dealers of his time than are, or have been, some of the McCormicks of to-day. The "little Hall" referred to in this letter was the late Robert Hall McCormick, whose collection of the works of famous English portrait painters from the time of Van Dyck down to Watts and Rossetti is said to be one of the largest and most complete in this country. He also delighted in collecting curios, tapestries, rugs, furniture, and other objects of art. His house on Rush Street was crowded with interesting, valuable examples of the art and handicraft of ancient and modern times. He had made and published for private circulation a really beautiful illustrated catalogue of the best of his possessions, but it is safe to say that he took no deeper satisfaction in the ownership of his treasures than did his mother in her "beautiful flowered red and green carpet," her "dozen cushioned mahogany chairs," and her "twenty-four-dollar card-table in the parlor."

Nothing more completely epitomizes the growth of Chicago than the contrast between this first home made by the Leander McCormicks and the many and beautiful residences in and near the city of their adoption now built and occupied by the descendants of the three brothers. It is such sharp contrasts, such swift developments from simple beginnings to sumptuous fruition within the span of one lifetime, which have made the name of the city of Chicago famous the world over.

To be inscribed on an hotel register as coming from Chicago, no matter what your real financial status may be, is to be accepted immediately as having the wherewithal to pay your way and something over. But familiarity with the fact does not diminish the wonder of the accomplishment so emphasized by this happy young wife and mother of 1838:—

"*Chicago, December* 3, 1838

"My Dear Sister Martha Ann:

"We arrived in this city nearly two weeks ago, after having a very pleasant and safe journey from Rockbridge.

It was twelve days from the time we left Pa's till we reached here, and we could have come in seven days if we had not been detained on the way, and if we had been so fortunate as to have taken a swifter boat for crossing Lake Erie. But we happened to get into a slow boat, and were three days crossing the lake, while other boats came over in one day. That was the most unpleasant part of our trip. Leander and myself were both seasick, and I had Hall[1] to nurse, so that I was worn out and tired of that part of the trip.

"Since we have been here, we have been boarding at the Sherman House (the finest hotel in the City), until the first day of this month. On that day we commenced housekeeping. We are very nicely fixed indeed, and are very much pleased with our new home and friends so far. I would be so glad if you and Ma and my friends could see how well we are fixed for housekeeping.

"I have drawn off in a careless manner the plan of this house which I will put in the letter. Our furniture is all new and of the best quality. Beautiful flowered red and green carpet in the chamber and parlor, and when the folding doors are open, the stove in the chamber will heat both rooms. One dozen cushioned mahogany chairs for the two rooms, beautiful bureau in the chamber, and a twenty-four dollar card-table in the parlor. I would like to have a sofa and a pretty lamp in the parlor, and think likely we will get them before long. The stairs are carpeted and the passage floor has oilcloth on it. The dining-room is not furnished except with nice chairs and tables; my dishes and

[1] R. Hall McCormick, later one of Chicago's well-known citizens and art collectors.

eatables are kept in the pantry. There are three rooms up stairs, one finely furnished for Cyrus,[1] the others will not be furnished till we get our boxes of beds and bed clothes.

"*December* 10, 1838

"It is one week to-day since the above was written, and I had concluded not to send it, but as it will save me some trouble of writing it over, I will add a few lines more and put it in the post office. We are all very well at present, and very much pleased indeed. This city contains twenty-thousand inhabitants, but it does not compare with some places of its size, not even with Lexington with regard to buildings. The houses here are nearly all frame, but quite large, and some very fine brick buildings. I don't think the people any more fashionable or gay than they are in Pa's neighborhood. Mr. and Mrs. Hamilton and family are our most particular friends, and they are as friendly with us as any of our old acquaintances in Rockbridge. Mrs. Hamilton is from Kentucky, and she seems to look upon us as kinfolks.

"A great many Yankees here. Mrs. Hamilton does not like them much. She says that we must have a Southern society, and let the Yankees, Germans, Irish, French all alone. The people here seem to be from all quarters of the globe. We will soon have as many acquaintances as we want, and of the best in the city.

"Leander and myself have brushed up considerably. He

[1] Cyrus McCormick, the founder of the great company now known as the "International Harvester Company."

has bought a new suit, overcoat and all. I bought a very fine velvet bonnet in New York for $3.50. It is prettier than any I have seen here. A milliner here said that it would have cost $8.00 in Chicago. It is cherry color with plume and ribbon of the same color. I bought a small cloak the other day for $11.00. I have two women at present. The kitchen woman is the best I ever saw, either white or black; she is so good that she leaves nothing for the house woman to do except nurse, so that I will give up the house woman and get a little girl for a nurse.

"The white servants here are greater workers than the blacks in Virginia; they do everything you tell them to do and do a great deal better than black people. The white woman that we have is better than any black woman I ever saw. She keeps everything in order and perfectly nice. I have everything here that anyone could wish to make me happy, except my relations, and I live in hopes that I will see some of them here next summer.

"They have most excellent markets in this place. We can get the best of meat of every description for four cents per pound, such as sausages, venison, beef, pork and everything except fowls, they are very high-priced. We can get most excellent apples and dried peaches, also cranberries, which I am very fond of. The people here cook very differently from what they do in Virginia. Here they live on tea, cold meat and bread, crackers and cheese, pastry and cakes, and Irish potatoes for supper and breakfast. They never have a single meal without potatoes.

"Do excuse this letter, if you please. It looks so badly that I would not send it, but as I have written so many little particulars, I think I had better send it.

"You must write soon, and give me all particulars as I have done. Leander sends his love and says that he will write to James in a few days. My best love to him also.

Your affectionate sister,

"HENRIETTA."

"To MRS. MARTHA A. HAMILTON,
"Covington, Alleghany County,
"Virginia."

IV

THE FIRST CHURCH WEDDING IN CHICAGO

By Mrs. Arthur B. Meeker

During the month of September in the year 1845, I arrived in Chicago on board the old steamship, *Constitution.* We landed at the foot of State Street. It is difficult to imagine that this was the only means of reaching the city from the East, except by the big canvas-covered wagons, known as "prairie-schooners." It is also a bit taxing to imagine our Chicago River with green, sloping banks on either side. The front yards of some of our best homes ran down to the sedge-grown water's edge. After spending one whole week on the lakes coming from Buffalo and another week before that in the packet boats on the Erie Canal from Syracuse, not to mention a long coaching trip through the Berkshires, it was with a feeling of having very nearly encircled the globe that we arrived at the American Temperance House, on the corner of Lake Street and Wabash Avenue. This hostelry was one of the few inns here at that time and harbored temporarily many an eastern new-comer. After a survey of the small number of available houses, a desirable one was found near the northeast corner of Lake Street and Michigan Avenue. The grounds of this house ran down to the lake; the waterworks were on the corner, our house was next, and on the other side of us lived the then mayor, R. K. Swift. Other residents of this block included Isaac Cook, James Peck, and Frank Sherman.

The lighthouse which stood on the south side of Rush Street and about one hundred feet west of it was cared for by James Long. One of my great delights as a child was to climb its long, circling stairs with his daughter Clara to see the great light turned on.

Fort Dearborn, as many old Chicagoans know, did not stand where the tablet which faced Rush Street bridge for so many years commemorated its site, but east of that, on the other side of Michigan Avenue, its grounds running to the river as well as to the lake.[1] In 1845 the Fort and its whole enclosure were deserted and served principally as a playground for children.

On the northwest corner of Michigan Avenue and Lake Street was a very large, vacant field which was usually filled with camping parties; whole communities migrating from the East to the West. It was a common sight to see a long line of prairie-schooners drive into this field, with cows tied behind the wagons. There they would unload for the night. There was always mystery and charm about their evening camp-fires, and we hovered as near as possible on the outskirts of these fascinating groups.

The greatest excitement was the arrival of the weekly boat from Buffalo. Sometimes it brought people who had stopped behind until their more adventurous relatives had tried the new country. These boats also brought many supplies and our only news from the outside world. In those days the great West Side as we know it now, did not exist; and even the North Side seemed like a separate town because there were only one or two bridges connecting the

[1] The tablet was placed about where the southwest corner of the stockade once stood.—*Editor.*

two sides of the town. Our chief means of communication with the other side of the river was the old Rush Street ferry, a flatboat affair, carrying about twelve passengers, which was drawn back and forth by a rope worked hand over hand.

Lake Street was our one and only shopping street until Marshall Field built his shop on State Street shortly before the Fire. Washington Street was always called Church Street in those days, as the First and Second Presbyterian, the Methodist, Baptist, Unitarian and Universalist churches were all on this street. A block farther south was Trinity Episcopal Church.

I first attended Miss Moore's school, which was on Lake Street near Michigan Avenue. Miss Moore eventually married Mrs. Henry King's father, Mr. Case. Later I was sent to Mrs. Gaylord's school on State near Madison Street. The year before I was sent east to the Utica Female Academy, I attended the Gleason School on the West Side. This could only be reached by walking over the Madison Street bridge and about four blocks west, at that time quite a country stroll. Needless to say we always brought our lunch with us.

The town crier will always be remembered by those who lived in his day. He was a colored man, and when he stopped at each street-corner, ringing his big bell, crowds would gather to hear whose child was-lost. Very often it was my cousin, William B. Walker. This would happen especially often in circus time when there was little doubt as to where we might find him.

Up to 1856 the only way one could go as far south as Eighteenth Street, unless one owned horses, was by the old stage down State Street. Arrived at the southern terminal the horses would rest many hours before returning. This trip was made only twice a day. It was a common sight to see poles stuck in the mud in the road with the sign, "No bottom here," nailed to them.

Until my marriage in 1856, the few social affairs we had were extremely simple. I can remember the afternoon sewing societies at the churches. After our work was done, we were joined by our brothers or men friends and had an old-fashioned supper together. Then there were early evening parties when we danced a little and sang, always ending with a supper. This consisted usually of chicken salad and scalloped oysters.

In the winter time we frequently had sleighing parties which made their way over the snow-bound earth up north to the old Lakeview House—which seemed miles distant at that time—where we danced and a hot supper was served.

While east at boarding-school, I met my future husband. Our marriage took place September 24, 1856, in the La Salle Street Baptist Church. This building was afterward taken down brick by brick and, carefully rebuilt, now stands on the West Side. The hour for the marriage service was set at eight o'clock in the evening. Being the first church wedding in Chicago I remember that it excited a good deal of interest and curiosity. The church was, in consequence, crowded with people.

Preceding me up the aisle, when the wedding procession entered, were my two bridesmaids, Miss Alice Meeker and Miss Clara Thomas, on the arms of our two ushers, George C. Walker and Frank Van Wyck. Miss Meeker was dressed in blue silk, while Miss Thomas was in yellow. Following them I came on my future husband's arm. I was dressed in white silk, with a white tulle veil. As we approached the altar our bridesmaids went to the left, while our ushers turned to the right. Behind us in a semicircle stood my entire family. My great concern all day had been the non-appearance of the Rev. Dr. Howard, who was to marry us. An accident on the railroad had so delayed his train, that he only reached the Church just as we were starting down the aisle. My joy was complete when I discovered him waiting for us; I was very fond of him.

A supper was served afterwards at our home, only intimate friends, besides the family, being present. My uncle, Cyrus Bentley, objected so strongly to my going away the first night after I was married that I was obliged to stay at home, much to my annoyance. The next day my husband and I started for Clinton, Iowa. This was as far west as the railroads were built at that time, and as we were going east to make our home we felt that it was our last chance to see the West for a long time. We took our bridesmaid from the East, Miss Meeker, with us, and also one of our ushers.

After spending six months in the East, my husband and I returned to Chicago and for some time lived on Ontario Street. At this time everyone was devoted to dancing and it was one of my greatest pleasures; but I was soon to be deprived of it as it created such a disturbance in the Baptist Church, to which we belonged, that I was brought up before the Board of Deacons and told that I must decide between the Church and dancing.

From the beginning of the sixties the Civil War stands

out most prominently in my memory. Everything was at fever heat during those early years of the war. Colonel Ellsworth and his Zouaves will always be remembered by Chicagoans of that time, nor can anyone who was then alive forget Jules Lombard when he mounted the Court House steps and sang *The Battle Cry of Freedom,* before the ink was dry on the manuscript. This famous song was written by George Root, of Chicago. Crowds gathered in the street before the Court House and soon all were singing it.

The beautiful Crosby Opera House, with its openwork horseshoe of boxes, was a great addition to our social life; and Kinsley's restaurant, next door, was one of the best-known and most popular places of its kind in the city. Bryan Hall, where the Grand Opera House stood later, was our one hall for public entertainments. Here were held our Sanitary Fairs.

In closing this brief memoir, I will enumerate a few of the families living in Chicago when I first arrived: Judge Mark Skinner, George Snow, Charles Follansbee, the Hadducks, the McCaggs, William B. Ogden, Mahlon D. Ogden, John H. Kinzie, J. A. Smith, the Pecks, the Haynes, Silas Cobb, the Buchers, L. C. P. Freer, I. H. Burch, Dr. Levi Boone (our most prominent doctor besides being mayor of the city), and my uncle, Cyrus Bentley.

Much of this memoir has been written on a journey from Chicago to Santa Barbara. Crossing the Arizona desert we have passed many prairie-schooners, filled, I fancy, with families who have left their homes farther east to better themselves in the Great West, just as did those other families in the early days who journeyed westward to Chicago.

V

GLEANINGS FROM A FAMILY MEMOIR

By Joseph Turner Ryerson

[Even as long ago as 1882 the dramatic quality of Chicago's swift rise from primitive conditions to a position of world importance was keenly realized by her citizens. It was this realization by the late Joseph T. Ryerson that prompted him to write for his family his impressions of Chicago and a few of her prominent citizens as he first met and knew both when he arrived here in 1842. Not the least interesting part of his narrative is his description of the methods of travel in those days. From this valuable memoir Mr. Ryerson's son, Mr. Edward Larned Ryerson, has allowed me to cull the following chapter.—*Editor.*]

About the first of October, 1842, at the age of twenty-nine years, after a varied and not entirely fortunate business experience in Philadelphia, I thought it was time for me to seek some new field for my efforts, and determined to follow Horace Greeley's advice, "Go west, young man, go west." On a few hours' notice, I was on my way to the then Far West to seek my fortune. I left my old home in Philadelphia, a sad-feeling and sober-minded young man, not having any certain destination, Pittsburgh being my first stopping point. I travelled by rail from Philadelphia to Columbia, Pennsylvania, and thence by four-horse mail-coach to Pittsburgh over the Allegheny Mountains. The Pennsylvania Canal from Philadelphia to Pittsburgh was then in operation (it was abandoned some years ago in the interests of the railways) and there were through passenger boats. As they were slow, I preferred the mail-stage, although a long and wearisome ride of nearly two days packed in with nine passengers was my portion.

I remained in Pittsburgh a few days and then took the stage again for Cleveland — an eighteen-hours' ride. Thence I took a side-wheel lake steamer — there were no propellers on the lakes then — to Toledo. So favorably was I impressed with Toledo's geographical location and its coming advantages from the opening of the Wabash and Erie canals, that I meditated a settlement in Toledo, provided I could make satisfactory business arrangements. On my return to Pittsburgh, however, my destination was suddenly changed by the proposition of an iron manufacturing house there to send me to Chicago as their agent with a heavy stock of Pittsburgh manufactures. I soon started for Chicago, a place I had scarcely any knowledge of except as a broken-down, speculative town on the western shore of Lake Michigan and on the edge of the great prairie nearly surrounding it. Retracing my steps to Cleveland, I took a boat around the lakes to Chicago, where I arrived November 1, 1842. I put up at the old Tremont House, a wooden building on the southeast corner of Lake and Dearborn streets, where I boarded for four years, day board, at $2.00 per week, for which I received, as they say, "three square meals" a day of the fat of the land, which was in abundance, good and cheap. The hotel was kept by Ira and James Couch. My sleeping quarters were over my store.

Chicago, at that period, was broken down through wild land speculation, the stopping of work on the Illinois-and-Michigan Canal, and the panic of 1837. Many of the inhabitants had left and the town contained only 6,500 people. Navigation being near its close, the streets were comparatively free from the activity usually prevalent during the autumn months, but I could discover from the teams loaded with farm products, entering the city from all directions, that there was a good prospect for a respectable-sized city in time, and a fair chance for a young man to settle down to hard work and grow up with the town and its people.

The winter of 1842 set in early. We had, on November 19th, a heavy snow-storm, and there was good sleighing all over the country until the following March. Chicago merchants used to make journeys on runners as far as Galena for trading, returning with loads of lead, shot, and other merchandise. The business of the country with Chicago far and near was done largely on sleds. It was a very severe, cold winter.

I started on March 25, 1843, for Philadelphia on a stage-coach, arriving about evening at Michigan City, fifty to fifty-five miles from Chicago. Finding a heavy bed of snow on the ground, we changed to a stage-coach on runners, wrapped ourselves in our buffalo robes, our feet being incased in buffalo shoes, and composed ourselves for a "long winter's nap." We changed from coach sled to wagon-box sled and open sleigh at times, and finally reached the then small town of Toledo, Ohio. We rested part of a day at Toledo, took a regular stage-coach and jogged along towards Cleveland. We arrived at Cleveland towards evening. I put up over night at the best hotel there, the American, and started the next morning by stage for Pittsburgh, making the journey by stage from Chicago to Pittsburgh in seven days and nights. After a day's delay at Pittsburgh, I took stage again over the mountains, most of the time being the only passenger. The road was cut through snow, in some places five to seven feet deep. I arrived in Philadelphia in ten days' travelling from Chicago.

Our usual route at that time between Chicago and the East, during the season of lake navigation, was by steamboat around the lakes to Buffalo, by rail to Albany, and by steamer to New York,—occupying six to eight days, according to weather on the lakes and the necessary calls of the boats at ports along the way. The lake passages in the summer seasons were very pleasant. The boats were large side-wheel steamers, with cabins and state-rooms all on deck. The saloon, stretching from bow to stern of the boat, with state-rooms extending the whole length on either side, was handsomely decorated, carpeted and furnished. There was generally a full load of passengers and in the evenings the saloon was handsomely lighted and cleared and, there being usually a band of music on board, the passengers amused themselves by dancing, singing, card-playing, and promenading outside of the saloon or inside until the time came to retire to their state-rooms.

I used to travel back and forth to Philadelphia and New York twice a year, sometimes via Buffalo and Albany, but generally by boat to Cleveland, thence to Pittsburgh and on to Philadelphia. On one occasion, however, I went from Chicago to Ottawa by stage; and thence on the Illinois and Mississippi rivers by boat to St. Louis, and again by boat on the Mississippi and Ohio rivers to Pittsburgh; thence by stage over the mountains to Philadelphia,—a very long and wearisome journey. This was in 1844, the season of high water on the western rivers, when the bottom lands for 400 miles were swept by floods and the country generally soaked from the long continued rains. As our boats passed down the Illinois River, we made landings at the second story of some of the warehouses on its banks, and, on arrival at St. Louis, found the river had been up to the second floors of the stores and warehouses on the levee and was then washing over the pavements in front of the stores.

As we passed down from the mouth of the Illinois River and along the Mississippi in the middle of the afternoon, the sun shining brightly, we came to the wide-spreading mouth of the Missouri,—a grand sight! That noble river came coursing down with its overloaded volume of water in a wild and rushing torrent, struck the Mississippi and annihilated it in a moment with a turbid body of water. Some of our Missouri passengers appeared overjoyed at the sight of the muddy stream and cried out for a drink. A bucketful was soon drawn up and they indulged freely in the thick and yellow water, as if it were the most delicious drink in the world.

When I came to Chicago the sand-bar at the mouth of the river had nearly disappeared and the shore of the lake south of the harbor was about 175 feet from the east line of Michigan Avenue. For some distance south the land had been washed away by the lake. At the point on the lake where old Deacon John Wright at one time had a large garden with fruit and other trees, east of Michigan Avenue opposite the southwest corner of the Avenue and Madison Street, the land had nearly all been carried away by the action of the waves, and a few years later this garden had entirely disappeared. I recollect on one occasion a severe storm on the lake which washed away one-third of the width of Michigan Avenue. The City and owners of lots fronting on the Avenue were compelled to protect the land from further encroachments.

The settlement or town of Chicago first began on the North Side, near the foot of Rush and Cass streets on the river. In this locality speculation in land ran high. The house of the American Land Company, afterwards purchased and occupied by William B. Ogden as a residence, stood alone on the block bounded by Erie, Rush, Ontario and Cass streets. I was told on reliable authority that the block south of it was sold for $40,000 at that early day and some years later was bought by E. J. Tinkham for $5,000. About the same time the block west, known as the Magee block, was purchased by Magee for $5,000. I paid, soon after I came to Chicago, $100 per front foot on Cass Street for property 150 feet deep. The block north brought double this amount after the Fire. These facts show the ups and downs that have occurred in north-side real estate within the forty years from 1842 to 1880.

Speculation ran high on the North Side, because it was considered more eligible for business and residence, the South and West sides then being low, wet prairie-lands, and no one dreaming that the city level would or could be raised by three successive ordinances about ten feet above its original level. Whole blocks of stores and massive buildings were screwed up to grade. In one instance the half block extending from Clark to La Salle Street on the north side of Lake Street, by one movement of 6,000 screws, was lifted above six feet,—a feat of mechanical operation the country had never heard of before. The business of the block went on as usual during the operation; not a pane of glass was broken, nor were people aware of the movement, so gradual was the process. About all the heavy and permanent buildings of the South Side, including the large, five-story brick Tremont House, were screwed up in this way, business going on without interruption. In places the sidewalks were four to six feet above the roadway with steps at the corners. At every street-corner in the business portion of the South Side pedestrians went up and down stairs. Until the grade of the city was raised, there was no possibility on the South Side of having any cellars or basements under buildings. If a hole was dug in the ground a couple of feet, it would fill with water seeping through the wet soil. If a descent of a few feet was made, water from the river would come through.

Drainage at that early day was a difficult problem. The streets were the natural soil, and in continued rains or in the spring season when frost was coming out of the ground, they were, in places, seas of mud of unknown depth. One would frequently see an abandoned wagon in the mire and a sign board set up, "No bottom here." I had personal experience of this once on South Clark Street, opposite the Court House block, when on a Sunday afternoon, going to church, my hat being carried by the wind into the middle of the street, I sank knee-deep in the mud in regaining it. Once in a while you would see ladies and children seated on buffalo robes going to church in a cart to avoid the mud. Arriving at its destination the cart would back up to the church door and unload.

The city fathers about this time were struck with a bright idea in the way of sewerage engineering. The surface of the ground was so level that the water would not run in any one direction, and to accomplish surface drainage it was ordered that ditches should be dug on the sides of the streets running towards the south banks of the river. However, when one of the periodical rises in the water of the lake came, the water ran back into the city instead of out of it.

Another experiment, for fire prevention purposes, was the laying of wooden conduits from the river up into the business portion of the city below water-level, with wells at the corners, out of which water was pumped by hand-engines; but these wells got stopped up and were a failure.

When I came to the city, the Chicago River was a small stream, whose clear water was used by those living on its banks for house and culinary purposes. It ran within its natural banks, which in many places were covered with grass. On the main river were a few docks for warehouse and shipping purposes, but the branches were almost entirely free of improvements. There was an old wooden bridge across the river at Clark Street. The bed of the bridge rested on a scow float which was swung about by a rope wound on a windlass to accommodate passing vessels. A similar bridge crossed the South Branch at Lake Street. Later on, a rope ferry with a scow was installed at State Street, and a short time subsequently another rope ferry was placed at Rush Street. In winter the main river and its branches were used for sleighing: I once followed the South Branch on the ice in a sleigh until nearly lost far out in the prairie. The main river from Rush Street to the forks of the stream was used on winter afternoons as a race-course, where with sleigh and bells the speed of the native nags was tried out.

North Water Street used to run along the river from the North Branch east to about the foot of Cass Street, where it intercepted Kinzie Street, now occupied by railroad tracks. The great hotel of the early days of land speculation was the Lake House, quite a large, four-story brick building, destroyed by the great fire. It stood on the northeast corner of North Water and Rush streets. On the river, across from the Lake House, stood the wheat storage and forwarding warehouse of Newberry & Dole. (Oliver Newberry of Detroit and George W. Dole.) I think Julian S. Rumsey was a clerk with this firm at the time I brought letters of introduction to it.

In 1842, the south pier forming one side of the harbor extended out into the lake about a thousand feet from the present Rush Street bridge. The lighthouse stood on the bank of the river just west of the present south abutment of Rush Street bridge; the lighthouse tower and the keeper's house were built of stone. The south pier used to be a favorite walk on summer evenings and on Sundays, and also a swimming place at times. We used to go down on the lake shore opposite Dearborn Park, [1] on the warm summer evenings after the stores were closed, about ten o'clock, for a swim before going to bed.

Old Fort Dearborn, then abandoned, was at the east end of River Street, surrounded by a high picket-fence. The whole fort was built of logs, — officers' quarters, blockhouse, magazine, and other buildings. Michigan Avenue abutted on the Fort grounds and was not extended north

[1] Where the Public Library now stands.

to the harbor for some years. When Major Charles H. Larned, — my brother-in-law through my marriage to his sister, — was ordered to Chicago on recruiting service after the Mexican War, he made his headquarters in the officers' barracks at the old Fort, and during the winter assembled a large company of ladies and gentlemen in the old military apartments. This was one of the social affairs of the season. It was at this party that the "German," the now popular dance, was first attempted in a simple way under the leadership of Captain von Schneidau and his wife, late of Stockholm, Sweden. He was once attached to the court there, and had come to this country to seek his fortune.

On the northeast corner of Clark and Randolph streets stood, in 1842, the City Hotel, a three-story brick building, kept by Jacob Russell. This was the crack hotel of the town and was supposed to be just a little "extra" in the way of a hotel, where the higher-toned travellers put up. An old one-story brick court house, about thirty by eighty feet, stood on one corner of the public square on the southwest corner of Clark and Randolph streets, in the basement of which, in the west end, was the Recorder's office, while in other portions of the basement were the clerks' and other offices. It was sometimes used for concerts and exhibitions. I once saw Tom Thumb there in after years. It was lighted by candles or oil lamps, and was a pretty rough-looking place, including the bench for His Honor, the Judge. It was in this courthouse that Judge Buckner S. Morris, Judge Mark Skinner, Judge Hugh T. Dickey and others held forth, and all the legal profession practiced law.

Of the large wooden warehouses, built for the storage of

grain and the receiving and forwarding of merchandise, there were, on the South Side, the Reed warehouse, occupied by Bristol & Porter; on the dock at the foot of State Street, Charles Walker's warehouse; on the block west of State Street, James Peck & Company's warehouse; on the dock at the foot of Dearborn Street and west of there between Dearborn and Clark streets, Humphreys & Winslow's and D. D. Stanton's warehouses; and west of Clark Street bridge one more, which was occupied by Russell & Company. The elevator power in all these warehouses was supplied by a horse, sometimes on the first floor, though in some warehouses the horse was elevated for life and put to work in the loft. Of course, these grain elevators were small affairs compared with those of the present day. The wheat was unloaded from bags out of a farmer's wagon at a small hopper on the front of the building.

The first large steam elevator that was ever built in Chicago for handling grain from railroad tracks was on the North Side, on the river west of Wells Street. It was built by George A. Gibbs and E. W. Griffin of Gibbs, Griffin & Company. Gibbs told me that people thought he was crazy to undertake such a thing and that it would not pay. A year or two later George Steel, a Scotchman, built another elevator just west of Gibbs, Griffin & Company. He sold out to Wesley Munger and George Armour. Munger had owned a small mill at Waukegan, which had burned down, and George Armour had been a contractor on the canal. Both were at this time men of moderate means, but their early development of the grain-elevator business made for them both great fortunes.

The other business buildings of Chicago were devoted

mainly to the selling of goods and to trade in one form or another. They were generally built of wood in the "balloon" style on account of cheapness and the speed with which they could be erected. They were one and two stories high, occupying lots of twenty feet front mostly on South Water and Lake streets. The dwelling-houses on the South Side were near at hand on the north-and-south streets. These were small frame houses, a story or a story and one-half to two stories high, often covering a good deal of ground, convenient, snug and neat inside, and easily kept in good order and attended to. Servants were either not obtainable or, for the sake of economy, were dispensed with. Nothing but stoves were used for heating, and wood was the only fuel. This cost about two dollars per cord, and a Norwegian man would saw it twice, split it and carry it into the shed, for three to four shillings a cord — or thirty-two and one-half to fifty cents.

About 1849 I bought of John P. Chapin, of Chicago, the northwest corner of Wabash Avenue and Madison Street for $2,050 cash. About the same time I bought of Edward J. Tinkham sixty-five feet on Ontario Street, one hundred feet west of Cass Street, two hundred and eighteen feet deep to Erie Street, for $1,600, intending both these lots for residence property, one for myself and one for my brother-in-law, Dr. Rutter, and his family. The Doctor chose the Wabash Avenue lot as the better location for his profession, and I conveyed the corner lot, twenty-five by one hundred and fifty feet, to his wife; of the Ontario Street lot I conveyed twenty-five by one hundred and fifty feet to my maiden sister, Mariette Ryerson, and twenty-five by one hundred and fifty feet, to my other maiden sister, Ann Catherine Ryerson. On the last described lot I built for my sister, Ann Catherine, the owner, the first three-story brick dwelling ever built in Chicago, at a cost of $5,000; and it was also the first house in the city with a double front-door and vestibule. It was twenty-five feet front and about fifty feet deep, with stairs in the rear, dining-room and kitchen beyond on the same floor, and a good cellar under all. It was a Philadelphia style of house, the plans having been drawn in Philadelphia. This house was the best dwelling erected up to that time (about 1850) in the city, and was the object of much curiosity and comment because of its size, general appearance, and the spaciousness of its interior.

There were no public buildings in Chicago in 1842 except the small one-story Court House on the northeast corner of the public square, and the old log jail surrounded by a high board fence on the northwest corner of the same square. There were no public halls or meeting rooms for amusement or other purposes, except the hall on the third floor of the saloon building on the southeast corner of Clark and Lake streets. There was a small wooden theater on the west side of Dearborn Street between South Water and Lake streets, where, about 1843, I saw the play of *The Stranger*, by some native artists. It was a pretty rough and dilapidated place. In a corner of the building was a small saloon kept by Ike Cook, at that time a well-known character in Chicago. He was a good-natured and well-behaved man, who in the political days of Senator Douglas was a strong adherent of "Little Doug.," as he was called. It was Ike Cook who remarked on a certain occasion at a Douglas meeting: "Gentleman, I tell you, truth squashed to earth will rise again." On the same occasion Frank Sherman, once His Honor, Mayor Sherman, said, "I only hope in these remarks to facilitate business!" Sherman owned the Sherman House and from him the hotel took its name.

In the way of concerts, I recollect one got up by the Unitarian Church in the winter of 1842–43 and held in the east hall of the saloon building. The overture (to something) was by the following performers: Charles Burley, who played in the Unitarian choir, violincello; Edward J. Tinkham and C. B. Nelson, flutes; a man by the name of Collamer, violin; and at the piano, I think, was Mrs. Dr. Stewart, while her sister, Mrs. Harrington, the wife of the minister of the Unitarian Church, was the vocalist of the occasion.

There was no regular music in town for dancing. At parties, after the refreshments had been served, sometimes John H. Kinzie would play dance music on his violin for the young people; and now and then a Mr. Nicholson, living on the southeast corner of Rush and Ontario streets, would do the same thing. On rare occasions Mr. Kinzie would go through the Indian "pipe-dance" for the pleasure of the company. The dances were all the old-fashioned square-dances.

Society at that early date was very simple. It had to be, everybody being poor. The style of dress was plain and inexpensive; silks and satins were the exception among the ladies, and I doubt whether a lady's dress for a party cost more than from five to ten dollars, for it was mostly what they called "white tarlatan" adorned with some bright-colored ribbons. Everybody had just as good a time, however, and enjoyed the entertainments as much, as if velvets, satins and silks, diamonds and other jewels had abounded

The parties usually began about half-past seven or eight o'clock, and "the ball broke" generally about eleven or twelve o'clock; when there was no dancing it ended at ten or eleven o'clock.

In later years we indulged at times in sleighing parties. We would send word to a country tavern, some ten or twelve miles from the city, hire a number of double sleighs and take a violinist along. Then when we arrived we would have a dance followed by a good supper, and after supper more dancing: it was often two o'clock in the morning before we reached home. These very pleasant occasions were always chaperoned by some married couples.

The only literary association in the city was the "Young Men's Association and Library." It had a small room in the third story of the saloon building where its meetings were held and its few books were kept. This was Chicago's first attempt at a library. An occasional lecture was arranged by the members of this association. In later years it was reorganized under the direction of E. B. McCagg, Edwin C. Larned, F. B. Cooley, myself and others, when a new course of lectures was inaugurated. These were delivered in the State Street Hall, a new assembly room, the first lecture being given by George William Curtis, of New York, on "Alcibiades," a character which Mr. Curtis treated in his finished and elegant style of oratory. After Mr. Curtis, came Bishop Alonzo Potter of Pennsylvania, on "The Character of George Washington," a good, moral, fatherly kind of address, which he closed with the remark, which we often repeated afterwards, "If you want to be as Washington was, you must do as Washington did."

Some years later the Chicago Historical Society was

founded with the idea of forming an historical library of general character. To house it, a good building was erected on the northwest corner of Dearborn Avenue and Ontario Street, which included a comfortable little hall for lectures, capable of holding three or four hundred people, while below were necessary rooms and a spacious library on the second floor.

In 1842 and '43 the Catholics had a small one-story frame church on the southwest corner of Wabash Avenue and Madison Street, which was later moved to the rear of the lot and turned into a school-house to make room for the brick church of St. Mary, which was burned in the great fire. On the southeast corner of Clark and Washington streets, was the frame Methodist Church; on the same site a few years later they built a brick church which was also destroyed in the great fire. On the north side of Washington Street, about midway between Clark and Dearborn streets, stood the neat frame church belonging to the Unitarian Society of which the Rev. Mr. Harrington was pastor. On south Clark Street, between Washington and Madison streets, stood an old, one-story church, the First Presbyterian, the Rev. L. F. Bascomb, pastor. On La Salle Street, on the southeast corner of Washington Street, was the First Baptist, an old one-story frame building. On Randolph Street, about a hundred feet east of Clark, stood a neat, new modern church, the Second Presbyterian Church, of which the Rev. Robert W. Patterson was pastor.

On the north side of the city at the southwest corner of Cass and Illinois streets, stood the original St. James's Episcopal Church alone in its glory. It was a small brick building in the Gothic style, quite simple in its exterior. The interior was remarkable for a mahogany pulpit and altar screen built at a cost of $2,000. The first rector of this church was the Rev. Isaac W. Hallam. The new St. James's was built on the southeast corner of Cass and Huron streets and the old brick church was sold to the Presbyterians. The great fire later swept away the comparatively new building, the tower alone remaining standing.

In continuation of church memoranda, I might say that the south-side Unitarian Society divided the value of its Washington Street property, giving to its west-side church a portion and the rest to the north-side church which was then under the ministry of the Rev. Robert Collyer. The Unity Church congregation built a neat frame church on the northeast corner of Chicago Avenue and Dearborn Street, where I remember hearing Ralph Waldo Emerson preach one Sunday morning.

The Fourth Presbyterian was the first church of that denomination started on the North Side. Prominent among its members were Messrs. Wadsworth, Woodbridge, Hoge, Dorman, McCormick, Mason, Miller, and others, under the Rev. Mr. Richardson, pastor. Their first meeting-house was built on the east side of North Clark Street, between Illinois and Indiana streets. This was several years later moved to the southeast corner of State and Illinois streets, at which time the Rev. Dr. Rice was pastor. They moved later into a new brick church on the southeast corner of Cass and Indiana streets, the old church being turned into a sales-stable for horses and carriages. Both the old and the new churches were destroyed in the great fire.

For some years there had been another Presbyterian church in existence, the Westminster Church, on the southeast corner of Dearborn and Ontario streets, under the charge of the Rev. David Swing.[1] These two churches were found to be in too close proximity to each other, so they united as one church, the Fourth Presbyterian, under Professor Swing, in the new stone church built after the Fire, on the northwest corner of Rush and Superior streets. Professor Swing retired from the Fourth Church and in later years became a noted independent preacher.

The Rev. Dudley Chase, son of the Right Rev. Philander Chase, first Episcopal Bishop of Illinois, founded the Church of the Atonement, as the first Episcopal church on the West Side. It was built on the northeast corner of Peoria and Washington streets. The Church was reorganized afterwards by Bishop Whitehouse and became the Cathedral of Saints Peter and Paul.

The first theater with any pretensions to respectability was built by John B. Rice, at one time mayor of Chicago, and representative in Congress from the Chicago district, a man of good character and good sense, and much esteemed as a citizen. This theater was built about 1846 on Randolph Street east of Clark. Later Mr. Rice built a larger theater on Dearborn Street, where the Rice Block now stands, which was finally made over into stores and offices about the time McVicker built his theater before the Fire. The Crosby Opera House, built about 1862 or '63, and said to have cost $400,000, equaled anything of its kind in the United States.

In the Randolph Street theater the best people were to be seen. All the noted actors and singers of the day appeared, and Italian opera was produced there.

[1] David Swing (1830–1894) was called to the Fourth Presbyterian Church in 1866. In 1874 he was tried for heresy and acquitted, but, as a consequence, resigned his pastorate and withdrew from the Presbyterian ministry.—*Editor.*

There is much talk nowadays of Chicago's variable climate. The changes in weather when I came in 1842 were just as frequent and as violent as they are now. The only difference I can see is that the atmosphere seems to be more cloudy or darker. When the city was small, with no manufacturing, very little coal was used. There was scarcely a boiler in the whole town. No steam, no engines, no steam tugs, and wood was the only fuel, so our atmosphere was beautifully clear and pure, and was one of the delights of life. There was no sewage in the river; there were no packing-houses or anything of the kind. The lake winds and the prairie winds and the water were all free from pollution, and Chicago, at that early day, was a good place in which to live. It was rarely very hot in summer, and, however cold the winter might be, a stout, large, air-tight, sheet-iron stove, with a chunk or two of wood in it, would keep us warm night and day.

About the coldest weather I ever experienced in Chicago was the long, bleak winter of 1842 and '43, and again in January of 1864, when the thermometer marked 30° F. below zero in and about Chicago. The night of January 2, 1864, there had been a very heavy snow-storm, and the morning of the 3rd opened intensely cold and with a heavy gale blowing the drifting snow in every direction. My wife's sister, Mrs. Samuel Greeley, died that day. I wanted to get a carriage to take my wife to the house, which was on Hinsdale (now Chestnut) Street, near Wells. The livery-stable man would not send a carriage out, because the weather was so bitter. He let me have a cutter, however, one horse and plenty of buffalo robes, in which I managed to drive my wife up to her sister's house and return to the stable as quickly as possible. On the same night the regiment in barracks at Wright's Woods, opposite the forks of the Graceland and Lakeview roads, broke camp and started for the city to save themselves from freezing to death. In the morning some of them were seen straggling down North Clark Street and all the sleighs and horses that could be gathered were sent up to get them into town.

Before railroads began operating out of Chicago, there was quite a furore for plank roads to overcome the bad condition of the dirt roads,—turnpikes, they were called, made from mud thrown up from the side ditches in the spring and during the rains. These new roads were made of planks about three or four inches thick and a foot or so wide, of the required length, laid on stringers and spiked down. There was the Milwaukee Plank Road, the Northwestern, the Southwestern, and the Blue Island Pike roads, all toll roads. When railroads came into operation they were abandoned.

The first piece of wooden block pavement put down in Chicago was the original "Nicholson" on South Wells Street, between South Water and Lake streets. Samuel S. Greeley, a civil engineer, laid this initial stretch of wooden-block pavement; it was a good, honest job and wore well for years. The patentee, a Mr. Nicholson of Boston, had never been able to do much with it. Chicago soil was well adapted to it, and from its introduction here has come the extensive use of this kind of pavement in many cities of the United States. Mr. Greeley really made known the pavement for the patentees, and about the first thing the patentees did was to part with a large portion of their interest and deprive Greeley of the benefits justly due him in its introduction in the West.

Among the early residents of Chicago, whom I knew, was Walter L. Newberry, whose name is perpetuated by the Newberry Library. A few years after I came to Chicago he married a Miss Clapp of Lenox, Massachusetts, and lived in what was called the Hunter House, on the southeast corner of Illinois and Rush streets. Afterwards he built a house on the northeast corner of Rush and Ontario streets, where he lived until he died. His death occurred on a steamer going to Europe. He left a widow and two daughters. The death of these heirs released his large fortune for use in founding the reference library which now bears his name.

Another old resident was Justin Butterfield, an eminent lawyer who came from western New York and owned the half block on the northwest corner of Rush and Michigan streets, adjoining John H. Kinzie's property. His residence was a two-story frame house, double front, with a large garden. His eldest daughter married William S. Johnston, and the youngest daughter, Ada, married a Mr. White. Old Justin Butterfield was said to know more law than any man in Illinois and could refer to book and page from memory. He was a rough and surly man in manners, as a general thing, and never noticed anyone in the streets, unless it might be some professional friend or client.

He was said to be a man of wit, quick at repartee and cynical, but certainly he was not an agreeable man to deal with. It was related of him that when he was defending Joseph Smith, the Mormon, at Springfield, the court room being crowded with ladies, Mr. Butterfield opened his address with these words:—

"I rise to defend the prophet of the Lord, surrounded by his angels."

John H. Kinzie, son of old John Kinzie, the first white settler in Chicago, was one of the early residents I knew well. Kinzie's Addition was named for him. He lived in a two-story brick house on the northeast corner of Cass and Michigan streets, with barn and garden. There was nothing remarkable about John H. Kinzie, except that he was one of the old inhabitants. I think that in 1842 and '43, he was the registrar of the Land Office, his office being on Kinzie Street near State. I brought a letter of introduction to him and presented it there. Mrs. Kinzie was a woman of intellect and influence. Their daughter, Nellie, married a Mr. Gordon of Savannah, Ga., and a son, Arthur, commanded a colored regiment during the Civil War. There was another son, George, who was in the regular army. The Kinzie house was a headquarters for Episcopalians, Mr. and Mrs. Kinzie being chief pillars in St. James's Church. She was the author of *Wau Bun*, a book which gave an account of the early days of Chicago and Illinois. Kinzie's estate was small. He generally held some public office. He died in Chicago during the Civil War.

On the block bordered by Rush, Erie, Cass and Ontario streets stood William B. Ogden's residence, a large, double, two-storied, conspicuous house, with portico and columns and broad steps. There were stables, outhouses, and greenhouses. Originally built by a land company, it was sold to Mr. Ogden during the panic of 1837 and 1838. Mr. Ogden was a very pleasant man socially. His manner was genial, attractive, and gentlemanly, and his conversation intelligent, reflecting the power of keen observation — altogether he was a very agreeable bachelor. He was also a man of great ability; clear-visioned and far-sighted, a projector on a large scale. I knew Mr. Ogden well. He was always courteous and pleasant, and on several occasions did favors for me for which I was very grateful. In about his seventieth year, he married a Miss Arnot, a maiden lady of Elmira, New York. He died a year or two afterwards at his country place near New York City, "Boscobel," leaving a widow, but no children.

On the northwest corner of Dearborn and Ontario streets, in a long, low frame house, lived Isaac N. Arnold, a lawyer. On this corner the Chicago Historical Society building now stands. Mr. Arnold was a man of acknowledged ability in the law; was a member of Congress from the Chicago district; an honest, patriotic Republican, and a friend of Abraham Lincoln. He wrote several books on historical subjects, among them a life of Lincoln.

Gurdon S. Hubbard was, after John Kinzie, I believe, the oldest settler in Chicago. He came from Middletown, Connecticut, but had been in the northwest country since boyhood. He was a widower when I came to Chicago. He had one son, Gurdon S. Hubbard, Jr. His second wife was his cousin, a daughter of Mr. Hubbard, who lived on the northeast corner of Dearborn and Ontario streets. Henry Hubbard, the father of Mrs. Herbert Ayer, was a son of the same Mr. Hubbard. I knew Henry Hubbard very well, having hunted deer with him and others along about 1844 and '45 in the "sag timber" twenty miles below Chicago. Henry Hubbard, or "Hank" Hubbard, as he was called, married a daughter of Judge Smith. She was a sister of Mrs. Dr. Boone and Mrs. Stephen F. Gale. Gurdon S. Hubbard married a second time, about 1850. He was a pork packer when I arrived in Chicago, his establishment being next door to my store on South Water Street, near Clark. He was a man of iron constitution. He told me that he once walked seventy miles in one day from early morning to candle light and beat some famous Indian walkers across country. He was always a pleasant, genial man, — a good citizen and much respected. He had much to do with the Indians in his early life as a fur-trader, and now and then when we were neighbors on Indiana Street, some of his old Indian friends when in town would come to see him.

On Cass Street, between Huron and Erie streets, lived the McCagg family. I first knew Mr. McCagg as a storekeeper on Randolph Street, not far east of Randolph Street bridge. Afterwards he entered into partnership with John S. Reed in the lumber business. Ezra B. McCagg, the well-known lawyer, was his son. Another son went to the Civil War with a Chicago battery, contracted a disease and died. His name is recorded with others on the Soldiers' Monument in St. James's Church vestibule. He had two daughters, one who married Andrew Brown of Evanston, and another, Miss Caroline McCagg. E. B. McCagg's first wife was the Widow Jones, a sister of William B. Ogden. They had one son, Louis McCagg.

Another old resident was Monsieur Canda, father of Mrs. Humphreys and Mrs. Payson, and also of the first Mrs. William Norman Campbell. He owned a large plot of ground on North Wells Street, where he was living when I first came to Chicago in 1842. I made the acquaintance of his daughter, Miss Canda, later Mrs. Humphreys, about 1844 in New York, when I called upon her with a mutual friend to get some trifle she wanted to send to her father in Chicago. She was a very agreeable young French lady.

She came to Chicago the same fall after my return here, and married David Humphreys a year later.

In 1842 the city had about 6,600 people and the population did not increase until the resumption of work on the Illinois-and-Michigan Canal. There was really but very small increase in population until the railroads reached Chicago and began to build west from the city. Chicago's location demanded railroads and they came as a necessity. Chicago had not had any better start in a business way than several other lake towns. It had five or six grain storage warehouses of moderate capacity, and fair stocks of goods in the hands of active, energetic traders, who were always ready to buy whatever farmers had to sell and to pay for them in goods or cash, but there was very little capital in the town in 1842. Most of the merchants purchased their goods in the East on time twice a year, and about all the money to buy wheat was furnished by the Wisconsin Marine and Fire Company Bank, of which George Smith was the head and Alexander Mitchell, of Milwaukee, the cashier. The rate was twelve per cent per annum on drafts or bills of lading consigned to the Bank's agents at Buffalo, and Smith, on the proceeds going to New York, charged merchants two and one-half per cent exchange in New York, which really cost him nothing; while his agents handling the stuff between received their commission on sales of the produce. It was in this way that Smith, backed by Scotch capital in Dundee, made his money and laid the foundation of his large fortune. Then too, he commanded the Galena lead trade through his bank there under direction of James Carter.

In those quite distant days in Chicago the comparatively

small circle of business and professional men, and others of note, were generally well acquainted with or known to one another, and whenever there was a social gathering there would be a good deal of mixing in. Every man in those days stood on his own merits. There were very few conventional restrictions on society. There were really no rich men, although there were a good many people possessed of land who were really land poor. Each one seemed to have but one object in life and that was to strive for the main chance, the means to live and get along, so that in this respect all were very much on a level. There were, however, some people better educated, more cultivated, of more intelligence, than others and, as a matter of course, these were more agreeable to meet in a social way; but there were no purse-proud people, nor any fashionable and exclusive, for the simple reason that the people were all poor and everyone was disposed to respect his neighbor. Vice, wickedness and crime were comparatively unknown. Chicago was not a fertile spot at that time for amusements of a public character. There was not a restaurant in the city, nor what is now known as a saloon. [1] If one wanted a drink, about the only place he could get it was the small, simple bar in the public room of such hotels or farmers' taverns as there were here then. Chicago in the forties was really a "one-horse" town and had not begun to step forward towards metropolitan proportions and surroundings, — with all the attending evils of a great city.

[1] Written in 1882.

VI

OUT OF THE PAST

By Mrs. William Blair

I first saw Chicago in 1854, when I came here a bride. It then boasted a population of 75,000, which we thought a large city compared with the 5,000 when my husband took up his residence here in 1842. My first impression was: How very low! How very flat! How very muddy!

When I think of the earlier Chicago and the influence of environment, I ask myself whether hills and mountains are essential to romance and especially attractive to brave and chivalrous spirits.

We recall the historical novels that center about the rugged banks of the St. Lawrence, the Heights of Abraham, the Château of St. Louis or Frontenac, which read like the social life of a new Versailles in a new France; or we look back to the hill-country of our own New England, where many of us have seen, in old Colonial homes, much to excite the imagination. What have we to compare with such settings of social life? Let us gather up what we may.

Our prairies, we grant, are low and generally level, but they are not without beauty. In the early days their *flora* excited enthusiastic admiration. "Flower oceans," they have been called, and the green swell of the rolling prairies contributes to the fitness of the simile. Of our admiration for our ever changing and ever beautiful inland sea, it is not necessary to speak.

And when we turn to the men who made Chicago, even if they were not born on our soil, or cultivated and developed here, we feel that they created a community which enables us to call ourselves "citizens of no mean city or state." While we may not say "Chicago is Illinois," as the French say "Paris is France," yet all must acknowledge the dominating influence of our city in the State.

Whenever I have heard some of the pioneers of Chicago, by my own fireside, relate their early experiences, I have thought that the courage in surmounting obstacles, the indomitable perseverance in overcoming difficulties, contempt for hardship, were the same in essence — whether exercised by soldiers in war, in mountains or wildernesses, in the Old World, or in the New — as these men exercised in the sloughs and quicksands of our own Prairie State.

Judge Grant Goodrich said of Gurdon Hubbard, in an address before the Historical Society, after rehearsing some of his acts of heroic endurance and self-sacrifice, at the imminent peril of his own life, to save another, "In ancient Greece or Rome the memory of such deeds would have been perpetuated in bronze or marble and glorified in historic song." The Chicago Spirit, of which we hear much, is not a rhetorical vaporing, or of recent birth. It has been with us from the beginning.

For several years of its early existence, Chicago was simply Fort Dearborn and the trading establishment of John Kinzie. "Only this and nothing more," save perhaps a few huts, inhabited by half-breeds, and the wigwams of the Pottawatomies.

The early social life of Chicago was influenced greatly by events that mark our financial history. From 1833 to 1837, the city experienced unparalleled prosperity, owing to the prevalence of "the western fever," when thousands were flocking from the East to secure homes in the West.

The superior advantages of Chicago were being exploited; the most alluring reports of the character of the soil of our State, its productiveness and the facility for making farms on our prairies, were circulated far and wide. Soon both capital and credit were enlisted. Money, owing to unlimited bank issues, was abundant, and loans to any amount were effected with the greatest ease. The building of the Illinois-and-Michigan Canal was the Panama event in our early history. The sales of the city lots donated by the State for the benefit of the project were epochs in the financial world that served to increase the speculative fever. The high tide of speculation was reached in 1836. The turn in affairs came the following year, and in 1837—the year the city was incorporated — occurred one of the greatest financial panics that has ever afflicted our whole country. It was a period, generally, of protested notes. In Chicago, it was a season of mourning and desolation. Real estate in which all had invested was greatly depreciated — in fact, could not be sold at any price. The depression continued until 1839–40. Everybody was poor, and at the social gatherings of those days, a writer says, "the costumes of both men and women were of a bygone age."

There were but one or two private carriages, but the condition of the streets in winter was such that a dray was a safer vehicle than a carriage.

No merchant of the present time can realize the money troubles in the forties, or the blessings now of a stable currency.[1] All western bank-notes were then at a discount, which varied from day to day. There were also hundreds of counterfeit notes in circulation. A necessary equipment for every store was a copy of *The Bank Note Detector*, issued monthly in New York, which gave the present value of all bank-notes and described counterfeit paper. This was consulted in nearly every trade where money was paid. This experience was repeated in 1857, and I remember waiting at the counter in Carter's, our leading dry-goods store at that time, while my bills were passed upon as to their genuineness and their value. On the counter, also, was a bottle of nitric acid with which to test coins.

Many people, after the collapse of the real estate boom in 1836, went back East, or to Galena, where the lead mines were doing well, or to the new town of Milwaukee, which attracted numerous immigrants.

The position of Chicago, however, was too favorable to permit the city very long to be seriously affected by any calamity, however great. Her citizens returned to early habits of industry and economy; her business men called into requisition all their experience to build up their injured credit, and to restore their business to a safe and permanent foundation.

Some years ago I spent a delightful hour with Mrs. Gurdon Hubbard talking over early days. She arrived with her father's family in 1836. At that time everybody was rich. There was much elegant dress. Fashions were peculiar and school-girls wore low-necked frocks and slippers to school, even when there were no sidewalks. The school taught by Miss Willard was near the present location of the

[1] The population of Chicago in 1840 was 4,479.

Sherman House. Many of the girls came from the north side of the river. On South Water Street they had to cross the slough on a plank. Mrs. Hubbard recalled this incident: One day, as the girls were coming from school, they met on this plank a number of Indians, who, with heads erect, looking neither to the right nor the left, brushed the young girls off the plank into the slough.

At Rush Street there was a ferry, but at Dearborn Street a drawbridge, which was used by the school-girls. It was drawn up by a windlass and chain, which would often catch and furnish a convenient excuse for being late at school. Since Chicago began, the river has been the scapegoat for many a tardy mortal. Extravagance in dress in those days was encouraged by the system of long credit which prevailed. Everything was charged, and unfortunately little was paid for when the general failure occurred the following year.

Mrs. Stiles Burton also told me interesting incidents of the early days. She explained to me why, in the first year or so of my life in Chicago, I so frequently heard allusions to Warrenville and Geneva. I did not understand their relation to Chicago. The farmers in that region had come from the eastern part of Massachusetts at an early day and naturally brought families with them. The daughters had become attractive young ladies; while Chicago men, both business and professional, were generally young bachelors. There were very few young ladies in Chicago. When the sessions of the County Court met in Geneva — the county seat of Kane County — the young lawyers, Norman B. Judd, Judge Hugh T. Dickey, Thomas Hoyne, Judge John Dean Caton, and others, attended the sessions, followed by a greater or lesser number of young business men interested in the cases. It was always an occasion for a dance and the farmers' pretty daughters were gathered in.

There were seven sisters in the Warren family, who lived in Warrenville, near Geneva. Later, one was married to Silas B. Cobb. Another, Mrs. Jerome Beecher, is well known for her many charities. Mrs. Stiles Burton met her "fate" on a horseback ride — the popular pleasure of the day. Chicago bachelors who wished to show some politeness to a young lady visitor invited her for a horseback ride.

In going to dances in those days, or rather evenings, the gentlemen walked, wearing high boots on account of the mud, exchanging them for slippers at the house. The young ladies sat on buffalo robes spread in the bottom of two-wheeled carts, which were backed up to the doors, when strong arms lifted the fair freight from carts to front halls.

An address by Isaac N. Arnold on the presentation of a portrait of William B. Ogden to the Chicago Historical Society gives an interesting picture of early days here. Speaking of the old Lake House, the principal hotel, corner of Kinzie and Rush streets, Mr. Arnold says: —

"It faced across the river towards the neatly kept and brightly whitewashed stockade, pickets, and buildings of old Fort Dearborn. The river was spanned at this point by a rope-ferry and on the south side of the river was the military post, with its grass plot, shaded by the old historic honey-locust, and within it stood the granite boulder, which, tradition said, had been the Indian 'Stone of Sacrifice and Death.'[1] The river was then a clear, trans-

[1] After a half-century in the Arnold garden, this stone now rests in the Chicago Historical Society rooms.

parent, running stream, its grassy banks fringed with trees and flowers.

"Toward the east, the grounds of the old Kinzie house, the home of the father of John H. Kinzie, sloped gently to the river. The banks were grassy and the broad piazza was pleasantly shaded by four large Lombardy poplars. The young ladies of those days were accustomed to the saddle, and horseback riding was a common amusement. There was a fine natural forest between Clark and Pine streets, north on the lake shore, and along its grassy paths lay fallen and decayed trees. Over these we practiced our horses and Indian ponies in leaping. Few now living can recall those gay scenes, but those who can will not have forgotten the almost unequalled beauty of a daughter of Colonel Whistler, nor those black-eyed, dark-haired Virginia girls, nor the belles of mixed French and Indian races, who united the graces and beauty of both. And I am quite certain none who was so happy as to participate in those rides will have forgotten that rosy-cheeked, golden-haired lass, the most fearless and graceful of all, whom the Indians in their admiration called, '*O-go-ne-qua-bo-qua*' (The Wild Rose)."

This was Mrs. Skinner, the wife of one of Chicago's most eminent jurists and mother of the late Mrs. Henry J. Willing, the late Mrs. Ambrose Cramer, and the Misses Elizabeth and Frederika Skinner, and grandmother of Mark Skinner Willing, Ambrose Cramer, Jr., and Mrs. J. G. McClure, Jr. I have been told of the special admiration of a young chief who gave her a silver ring and wished to marry her.

Mr. Arnold gives us a picture of the house of William B. Ogden, the first mayor of Chicago. He writes:—

"There is not to-day (1884) in our wealthy and luxurious City — there never has been in fact — a residence more attractive, more homelike, more beautiful than that of Mr. Ogden, which, with all its treasures of art and books, was destroyed in the great fire of 1871. The house stood in the center of a block bounded by Rush, Cass, Erie and Ontario streets. On it was a fine growth of maple, cottonwood, oak, ash, cherry, elm, birch, and hickory trees. In the center stood his double house built of wood. A broad piazza extended across the south front. A large conservatory and fruit houses added to its beauty and comfort."

In this house of generous and liberal hospitality was found no lavish or vulgar exhibition of wealth. Here were refinement, broad intelligence, kind courtesy and hospitality. Here all prominent and distinguished strangers were welcomed and entertained and here, too, the humble and poor, if distinguished for merit, culture or ability, were received. Among the guests entertained in this home were Martin Van Buren, Daniel Webster, Henry J. Tilden, William Cullen Bryant, Miss Harriet Martineau, Fredrika Bremer, Margaret Fuller, Ralph Waldo Emerson, Wendell Phillips, Charlotte Cushman, and Charles Lever, the Irish novelist.

In 1854, my first winter in Chicago, our ways were not yet all made smooth. Lake Street was the only paved street and that was only "planked" and was in bad condition. Along the lake shore, which was sandy, it was always dry, but the sand was so deep and heavy that carriages plowed their way as slowly as through the prairie mud not more than a couple of streets away.

There seemed to be a change of climate about 1854, if I

may believe what was then told me. There was more snow and much colder weather than formerly. In the winter of 1855, President Hitchcock, of Amherst College, the noted geologist, was invited by the Y. M. C. A. to give a course of lectures on geology. He was our guest during his stay in the city. The cold was so intense and Metropolitan Hall at the corner of Randolph and La Salle streets, the Auditorium of those days, was so poorly heated, that during two of his lectures he wore his overcoat and leggings, looking like an Arctic explorer. One evening the gas failed from frost — a not infrequent occurrence — at the beginning of the lecture and the hall was dimly lighted by lamps and candles.

Furnaces were not common in private houses and, in our parlors, we warmed ourselves one side at a time before the grate fire, and our "hot faces were steaming, the while we were freezing our backs." My first home, a three-story-and-basement brick house, was at No. 111 Wabash Avenue, now part of Stevens' dry-goods store, then a quiet residence district. Our church, the Second Presbyterian, stood on the corner of Wabash Avenue and Washington Street. Our friends and neighbors on either side in our block, were J. H. Dunham, Dr. Rutter, the Stephen Gales, Judge John M. Wilson and others, while across the street was the home and garden of Judge and Mrs. Mark Skinner.

I attended many delightful parties, as they were then called, that winter. My sister-in-law gave one to introduce me. It was no small task to give a party in those days. First of all, your very formal invitations must be written in a fine, feminine hand, and next, they must be delivered in person, lest some should be lost. The mail was not thought of, and it was some time before it was considered quite safe or even polite to trust such an important matter to a messenger.

The caterer, who kept a small shop on Lake Street, could be depended upon for little else than ice-cream. His sign proclaimed proudly that this commodity could be furnished "at all seasons of the year." Your cakes, a prominent feature of the table, and whatever else you desired, must be prepared, not by a chef, but by your plain, willing cook, with yourself as first assistant.

In the early days, our food supply was varied and abundant. The prairie teemed with game, so that we had prairie-chicken, partridge, quail and other birds, and venison also, while from the lake we drew delicious fish, lake trout, white-fish and perch.

In fresh fruit we were deficient. Only berries were abundant. The larger fruits were all brought around the lakes from Buffalo.

I remember our long and disagreeable drive, with mud often to the hubs of the wheels, the afternoon before a party, to a village called Cleaverville, somewhere between 35th and 39th streets, east of Cottage Grove Avenue, to the only florist known, where we could buy flowers. Flowers were rarely seen at an entertainment in the winter and our friends expressed surprise at seeing them on the parlor mantels on this occasion.

The people of that time were delightful, so wide-awake and intelligent! The young men were educated, energetic, and high-principled. Where there was not a surplus of young ladies, I can testify that young matrons did not lack for attention. There were so few young ladies that it was quite common for married ladies to have some young woman friend from the East spend the winter or part of it with them. I remember that it was a common question, "Do you know what young ladies are expected here this winter?"

When we moved into what was for over fifty years our home at No. 230 South Michigan Avenue,[1] there was but one other house in the block, a one-story-and-basement brick, and in the block north there was but one house (the Clarks'), which was the beginning of Terrace Row. We felt ourselves quite in the country. One of the familiar sights was the "lowing herds which wound slowly o'er the lea," attended by the cowherds, who for years drove them, morning and evening, to and from the open pastures farther south on Michigan Avenue. Every self-respecting family kept a cow.

The basin of water between the narrow park and the railway was much used for boating.

I would like to refer to a small, but charming, literary club organized in the late fifties, at the home of Mr. and Mrs. Walter Neef — a house of delightful social culture. Mrs. Neef was a sister of the late Mrs. R. W. Patterson. Mr. Neef was chosen president of the club. We met Saturday evenings at each other's homes — about twenty members, ladies and gentlemen. At the close of the evening simple refreshments were served. The members were the Burches, Bentleys, Farnums, Judds, Farwells, Havens, and a few young ladies and gentlemen. We wrote no papers; the literary part was chiefly selected readings. I remember one Christmas Eve two ladies read Dickens' *Christmas Carol*, which was new at that time. But we had, even then, aspira-

[1] Where the Congress Hotel and Annex now stand.

tions for cultivating our dramatic tastes, different members taking part in reading expurgated plays. There were none to laugh at us but ourselves.

My large parlor, sixteen by twenty-four feet, was the scene of numerous delightful occasions. The memory of many of these is now like the dim outline of old daguerreotypes. There were two or three benefit concerts for local charities. I recall one for the building fund of the Home for the Friendless, especially promoted by Mrs. Joseph Medill. The music was given by the very popular singers Clara Louise Kellogg and Annie Louise Carey. The gentlemen who sang with them were Castle and Campbell or Tom Carl. Another interesting evening was an annual meeting of the Historical Society, before they had a building. The address of the evening was given by Dr. Charles H. Ray, at that time editor of the *Tribune*.

But to consider society with its present-day definition — one author says, "We had nothing worthy of being called 'society' until after the great fire of 1871." Another says, "Not until the Columbian Fair of '92." I have no means of knowing when it was organized, but I remember some things that would have hindered a large organization of this kind during the first thirty years of our city life, besides those hindrances that have been already mentioned.

In 1854, there were but two or three benevolent institutions established in Chicago — Mercy Hospital and the Catholic and Protestant Orphan Asylums. If one should try to count the large number of institutions and societies "ministering to all the ills that flesh is heir to," established during the last fifty years, he would realize how very busy a great many men and women have been — especially women.

During our four years of Civil War our women were much engrossed in work for the comfort of our soldiers at the front — sewing, knitting socks, and scraping lint for the wounded. Later they worked for the great Sanitary Fair, in which Chicago led the way and set the fashion for eastern cities. In this grand and successful effort, Mrs. A. H. Hoge and Mrs. Mary Livermore were leaders. After the war, Mr. Lincoln presented medals to these noble women.

Six years later, on October 9, 1871, came the great fire. The churches were open daily that winter to feed the homeless and to distribute clothing to thousands who had not a change of any sort. The Michigan Avenue front of the block between Congress and Harrison streets, where my home was, was the boundary line of the devastation of the "Big Fire," and also of the great fire of three years later. I was asked to open my parlor as a distributing center for new clothing intended for those who had been driven from homes of every comfort, until they should have time to look about and in some way provide for their needs. For six weeks I received and distributed clothing, some of my friends coming in to assist me — among them our well-remembered, generous-hearted Jessie Bross Lloyd.[1] The experience of those weeks will never be forgotten.

Among the many memories of sixty-four years of social pleasures, of hospitalities in homes whose doors are forever closed, I treasure those of that most gracious hostess, Mrs. Norman B. Judd, who on account of her husband's various official positions, always entertained distinguished strangers; of the generous hospitality of Mr. and Mrs. J. Y. Scammon; of the charming host and hostess, Mr. and Mrs.

[1] Daughter of Governor Bross and wife of Henry Demarest Lloyd.

G. P. A. Healy; of Dr. Rutter, where we met Judge Stephen A. Douglas, when he first brought home his beautiful bride; of the cordial and frequent entertainments of Judge and Mrs. Skinner, of Mr. and Mrs. Henry W. King, and of Mr. and Mrs. E. W. Blatchford, will always be delightful recollections, as will be the dignified home of Mr. and Mrs. W. H. Brown, where, with a small company, we met Mr. and Mrs. Lincoln, and Mr. Hannibal Hamlin, the Vice-President, just after Lincoln's first election to the Presidency.

Mr. Lincoln chanced to walk from the dining-room into the parlor with me, where we sat on a sofa for a little time, and I remember my embarrassment in finding myself conversing with one for whom I already felt unbounded admiration. His simplicity and cordiality were very apparent. I recall his standing back to back with Doctor Robert W. Patterson, to see which was the taller!

I remember, too, an interesting visit with Judge Stephen A. Douglas, the political opponent of Mr. Lincoln. It was on the deck of a Mississippi steamer that he entertained a little group of us with the recital of his recent visit to Russia, where he had been received with distinguished honors, being invited by the war-Emperor, Nicholas I, to review with him the Russian army.

We met General and Mrs. U. S. Grant, soon after the war, at Mrs. Judd's. Notwithstanding the great success that had crowned his career, the grave face and taciturn manners reminded me of the stories told me in my girlhood of Napoleon by an old man who in his youth was an English sailor, and was on the ship that carried Napoleon to St. Helena. I remember his picture of the great Emperor sitting immovable on the deck for hours every day, with elbows on his knees and head resting on his hands. But this, as Kipling says, "is another story."

I recall a gentlemen's dinner that we gave when the guests of honor were Hugh McCulloch, Secretary of the Treasury under Lincoln, and called the "Father of the Greenback Currency," and Speaker Colfax, afterwards Vice-President.

One evening at the Brown's, after the war, we enjoyed a visit with Mrs. John H. Kinzie, author of *Wau Bun,* and her daughter, Mrs. Gordon of Savannah (Nellie Kinzie), granddaughter of John Kinzie, Chicago's first white settler. Mrs. Gordon told us a story of Sherman's entry into Savannah, when he was "Marching Through Georgia," and her attempt to illuminate her home, frustrated by other members of her family with Confederate sympathies.

Out of the dim past they come before me — the dear friends of those early, golden days. In Memory's hall, in my inmost heart, I entertain them still.

VII

AS I REMEMBER IT

By Mrs. Joseph Frederick Ward

The words "Old Chicago" bring to my mind a vision of joy and gladness. The Chicago of my youth was a green and flowery place — a place of gardens and trees and birds and grass and charming homes — of sandy beach and dashing waves, with a sense of youth and of the beginnings of things all about us.

The region about the river was always devoted to business — River and Canal streets, South Water and all the docks. Randolph Street had wholesale places and leather and hardware. Lake Street was our shopping street; there T. B. Carter, whose children live among us, had the first dry-goods store, and Henry Willing, a boy then, later member of the firm of Field, Leiter & Company, would carry your packages home for you on foot. The first deliveries by wagon were considered very grand. There, later, Potter Palmer had a store, and was always about it himself — would stop and chat while you tried on your new coat, and would perhaps cheapen the price.

On State, between Lake and Washington, was the market, with a red brick market-house in the middle of the street, and here on market days would come the farmers from the prairie farms, their wagons piled with the marvelous fruits of the virgin soil, their wheels thick and clogged with that same virgin soil which neither corduroy nor plank roads could quite subdue. The Court House, standing where the County Building now does, was in the center of a green square with a high iron fence about it. A number of churches faced it around the square and the whole place had a rather reserved and solemn air.

The lake shore was a sandy beach, and at Van Buren Street there was a place where horses could be driven in to drink and wagon-wheels could be washed. There were several places where the young people could rent rowboats to go on the lake. When the Illinois Central Railroad was built, piles were taken out of the railway breakwater and patches of white made to show us where we could go through to the open lake.

The streets of the young city were frightful, with deep mud and holes and many places marked "No bottom." A frequent sight was a cart stuck fast and abandoned. I remember one such cart deeply imbedded in the mud just in front of McVicker's Theater. The sidewalks were of uneven planks, with frequent steps up and down, but the homes were charming, a favorite style of architecture being a square building with a hall through the middle and a white-pillared veranda. All had gardens with fruit trees, overflowing flowers and an abundance of shrubbery. All had fences and gates, I do not know why, as all our cows were driven away out to Twelfth Street, were watched and driven back at night. We were a very primitive people; we knew everyone or at least knew who they were; the men called each other by their first-names and frequented the family grocery of a Saturday night to talk politics and discuss business. R. H. Countiss' grocery, on the corner of Clark and Van Buren, was a very favorite meeting place. Mr. Countiss' son has been, I believe, president of the Chicago Stock Exchange.

The churches were great factors in social life. The Sunday School Picnic and the Church Social were events. Creeds and rules were also of more importance and more rigidly observed. For instance, little girls in those days wore pantalets. These could be embroidered or braided or hemstitched. They were stiffly starched and grandly flopped and rattled about their white stockings and cross-tied slippers. A great disturbance arose in the First M. E. Church because the minister's wife trimmed her daughter's pantalets with lace, and also, herself, went the length of wearing a plain gold watch on a black ribbon. It almost dismembered the Church.

Everyone even then had a most joyous faith in the future of Chicago, although it was feared at one time that St. Charles, a far older place, would surpass it and become the metropolis of the West. If one possessed any real estate at all, that one's fortune was considered made.

When Washington Irving wrote the *Knickerbocker History of New York*, he began at the creation of the world to get a really good start, and in this little personal history I also will start a little back of my remembrance.

In 1835, my husband's father and mother came west from Massachusetts, intending to invest here and stay, if they liked it. They were offered twenty acres within the then narrow limits of the city for two thousand dollars, but the place was such a mess and medley of mud, shanties, and Indians, that they declined the offer and returned to live and die in Massachusetts.

That same year a young man,[1] a scion of the Governor Wentworth family of New Hampshire and a graduate of Dartmouth College, arrived in Chicago. He had very little money, but in some way became possessed of a lot on La Salle Street between Lake and Randolph, built a printing-office, called it Jackson Hall, and began to publish a daily paper which he named the *Chicago Daily Democrat.* He was six feet six, or more, in height, and was very generally known as "Long John Wentworth." In 1837, having been elected to Congress, he wrote my father, David M. Bradley, then just out of his 'teens and an old schoolmate, to come and run the paper while he went to Washington. My father did so and in 1839 went back East, married, and brought my mother to Chicago. They boarded at the old Sauganash Hotel, and, among other fellow guests, were Mr. and Mrs. Augustus Garrett. Mr. Garrett was at that time mayor of the town. I do not know what his business was, but in some way he made the money with which later Mrs. Garrett founded Northwestern's Theological School (Garrett Biblical Institute).

In 1841, having then one child, my eldest brother, my parents purchased a piece of land, one hundred feet on Jackson Street, running through to Quincy. It was between State and Dearborn, but Dearborn at that time was only cut through to Monroe. Jackson was a fairly wide street, but Quincy was a narrow lane called "Printer's Alley." My mother declared, if she had to live way out there, she did not wish to turn her back on the town. So for her benefit the lane was widened to a street, and, having a great admiration for John Quincy Adams, she named

[1] Hon John Wentworth.

it Quincy Street. After the death of Mrs. Charles Rowe's mother, Mrs. Samuel McCarty, some of the Chicago papers told of this street naming as being due to her. It really was my mother's achievement, however. Mrs. Rowe's early home was on the corner of Adams and State streets where Peacock's jewelry store now is. After her father's death, however, Mrs. Rowe and her mother did live for two years in a house belonging to my father, next door to us. There was a little stream running from Quincy to Jackson between our place and State Street — a little, muddy, swampy stream, and Mrs. Rowe and I used to wet our feet and soil our dresses trying to get the cattails and blue flags that grew there. When the high building that stands there now was being built, they found that same little stream and were obliged to build a special miniature aqueduct for it before they could put in their foundations.

To return to 1841 —

After my parents had sold twenty-five feet on Quincy Street in order to have a neighbor, their home was built out on the wide prairie, the tall prairie-grass waving all about it, just where the Lyric Theatre now stands, and just east of the Great Northern Hotel. It was a lonely place and when, after the evening meal, the waste bits were thrown out of the kitchen window the prairie wolves would come under the window and dispose of them.

When my brother was two and a half years old, he was lost one day, and it being such a wild place and many Indians about, there was great excitement. A friend on horseback, seeing the tall grass between Quincy and Jackson, Clark and Dearborn streets waving a little in a long line, rode in and found the child. The grass grew far above his head. All this was scarcely eighty years ago.

In 1840 Chicago had 4,479 inhabitants, almost all Americans, and largely from the New England states. I was born in 1844. Among my earliest joys was visiting the *Democrat* office. Being in every respect a genuine, old-fashioned country town, people sent my father, as editor and publisher, everything from turkeys and big pumpkins to sofas and refrigerators. On his birthday the management of the Tremont House, our best hotel, sent him his birthday cake and we children marvelled at the "David M. Bradley —Chicago Daily Democrat" in the icing. I simply adored the printing-office. The paper's great Norwegian engineer, Ole Gulicson, would set me on his shoulder and go about oiling the one engine, singing meanwhile Norse Sagas; or I was lifted high on one of the presses, and the great ink-rollers and flapping paper-carriers lunged at me; or I watched the marvelously quick hands setting type; or I found good company in the office — my father, of course, and Mr. Wentworth often; also Stephen A. Douglas, Owen Lovejoy, Dr. Evans (afterward Governor Evans), Orrington Lunt, Dr. Charles Dyer, and many another then famous Chicagoan whose name would be meaningless now. Mr. Douglas being very fond of children, I often found a seat on his knee. My mother early put a stop to these joys, but I could still swing on the gate and watch and count the "prairie-schooners," or "Forty-niners," go by on State Street. Trains passed of twenty, thirty, or even forty of the great ribbed wagons, drawn sometimes by mules, sometimes by horses, and sometimes by oxen — often a mother and baby in the wagon and a troop of barefoot boys and girls trudging beside, all cheerful and full of enthusiasm. "We'll get thar," "Pike's Peak or Bust," "Reach it or die," and "Plenty of gold in the world I'm told — on the banks of the Sacramento," were familiar legends scrawled on the wagon-covers.

From that same gate in the cholera year I watched eight funerals in one afternoon in half a square. It was a dreadful time. Everyone left the city who could, even some of the doctors fled. A member of our household, Miss Clara Martin, having an errand at a neighbor's, found all the doors open and the lower rooms deserted, and, hearing groans above, discovered there the master and mistress of the house, alone and deserted, in the agonies of cholera. She stayed and nursed them until they were safe, and then devoted herself to that work, nursing rich and poor to their recovery or death, until at last she came back to us and was stricken herself. Forbidden the room, I climbed upon the arm of a chair and, when the door was opened for the doctor, saw her lying there black and shriveled like a mummy. She lived, however, and knew a good old age. Although the sanitary condition of the city must have been frightful, and I remember no effort to improve it, the cholera finally left us.

Slavery and its conditions dawned early on our childish minds. I must have been five or six when one evening, needing the help of a woman in the neighborhood, my nurse took me with her on the errand. The negro woman, Aunt Charlotte, had bought herself, one husband and one son — husband and son were both worthless — and she often remarked in the most heartfelt manner: "Catch me ever buying another nigger!"

We found her house dark, every shade drawn. "Charlotte can't be at home," said my nurse. At that the door was softly opened and Charlotte's hand drew us inside. The door was shut and a candle lighted. There side by side on the floor lay sixteen of the most wretched objects in sodden sleep. They were fugitive slaves, caked with mud, scratched and torn with briers, and showing through their rags marks of the most brutal ill-treatment.

"I sure thought you was them catchers 'till you spoke," whispered Charlotte, and, "Poor things, I must wake them at two in the morning and start them on their way."

I never forgot that sight. On State Street not far from us lived a man who had been born free, and had bought his wife's freedom. They were almost white, industrious and happy, and had twin girls two or three years old. Professional slave catchers found out in some way that these children had been born less than eight months after their mother's freedom. They reported this to her former master, who immediately laid claim to them. One afternoon two men in a wagon stopped at her door and asked for a drink of water. As she went into the kitchen to get it she heard a struggle and rushed back to find they had thrown her children into the wagon and driven off. She flew after them, clung to the back of the wagon and dragged her children out. A crowd collected, the kidnappers were forced to go for a constable and a warrant. Meanwhile the little girls were put into a rowboat and rowed far out into the lake. A steamboat starting for Canada that night was as usual searched for fugitive slaves before it left its dock, but it found that little boat out in the lake and carried the children to safety. Those same girls came back after the war, educated young women, and taught successfully in the Freedmen's schools. All officers of the law were by oath obliged to help return fugitive slaves; all private citizens were liable to fine and imprisonment if they gave the latter aid. But Chicago was not a good place from which to get a slave returned; public sentiment was against it. The sheriff one morning received a letter with orders to arrest a woman quite white, who was both beautiful and educated, who, having been purchased by someone in New Orleans, had run away. Ten minutes after receiving it he met that girl in the street and recognized her. As he passed, he said: —

"Go at once to such a number on such a street." It was Dr. Dyer's office, and he was the head of the "Underground Railroad" of the State. A few minutes later the sheriff met my father.

"Go to Dr. Dyer," he said, "tell him to have that girl stain her face, cut her hair, dress in boy's clothes and leave the city inside of two hours or I will have to arrest her."

There was only one reason for which beautiful slave girls were sold in New Orleans; this girl was saved. You can scarcely imagine how the facts of slavery filled our daily lives. The papers had long lists of advertisements for fugitives, often described as branded on the hand, with back showing recent whipping, or ridged with old marks, or otherwise giving evidences of ill-treatment.

Being a wooden city we had many fires. Our fire-engines were pumped by hand and we had a volunteer fire company. All the sons of all the best families belonged to it, and ran to the fires. Standing three or four on each side, they worked the pump, or else did valiant things with the hose. A fire was almost a social event. The first steam fire-engine was a marvel; it was called the "Long John," and I believe was presented to the city by Mr. Wentworth. Wise old heads were shaken over the first paid firemen. It was prophesied that there would be no more enthusiasm, no more heroism.

We had many Indians in those days. They brought in furs — for Chicago was quite a fur center — also buffalo robes and maple sugar. There was always a fringe of them in the back of the church, and we saw them constantly about the streets, grave and silent in their blankets and moccasins. They certainly were neither dirty nor drunken.

We also had a town crier. We met him one night coming along, a crowd of men and boys about him, as he rang his bell and called, "Lost! Lost! Lost! Little girl seven years old!" He frightened me almost to screaming when he stopped us and swung his lantern in my face to see if possibly I was that little girl, and several of the men and boys scratched matches and also took a look at me.

Having weak eyes, I was not allowed to learn even my letters until I was eight years old. Then I began to attend a school which I cannot quite locate. It was so near the lake that the boys brought water from the lake in a pail and passed it around to us in a tin dipper, sometimes placing a frog in the pail to scare the girls. It was near the river, for at recess we wavered between playing in the sand and wading, or going up to Fort Dearborn, the blockhouse of which was still standing, and talking to a one-legged soldier who always sat at the door holding his musket. We used to bring him apples and oranges, but he never said anything to us except that we couldn't go inside. From this school I went to "Sawyer's Female Seminary," on Clark Street between Monroe and Madison. This was in the heart of the residence district. Emma Bigelow, afterwards Mrs. Milton Wilson, lived in a very pleasant home just across the street, while the Pecks, Ferdinand Peck's family, were two squares south. This school was afterwards sold to Mr. Grover, moved to Wabash Avenue and became the Dearborn Seminary.

There was a remarkable singing-school attached to the institution, which was housed in a wooden building with a Greek front. This school was taught by a strange genius named N. Dye. We practiced and performed wonderful cantatas, to the admiration of crowded audiences.

My brother attended "Snow's Garden City Institute for Boys." This stood on Adams Street not far west of State; part of the Fair covers the ground now. William Liston Brown and the late Daniel H. Burnham were fellow-students there.

We had the primitive liking for grand names and loved to call our city the "Garden City." We had Garden City hotels and restaurants, and banks and saloons. Later, people not knowing what Chicago was in its youth, have explained the name as referring to the German market gardens that were afterward so numerous. From these schools we went to the High School and had the honor of belonging to the first class in the first Chicago High School that ever existed. It was on the West Side, on Monroe Street, a few squares west of the river. Madison Street bridge was building and we crossed the river on an old-fashioned ferry, with a flat bottom and a post at each end through which passed a rope, by which the ferryman pulled us over. We found this method of crossing delightful. The High School gave us a stiff course of three years. We graduated in great glory at Metropolitan Hall at the corner of Randolph and La Salle streets. There never was a grander occasion — there never could be a grander occasion than that was — the city fairly crowed over us. Three of our number, however, dying within six months of various brain troubles, the course was lengthened to four years and greatly simplified. That ended my school days. My brother went East to college, but we had lost our father, and our mother could not be left alone. It was a shocking case, to begin school at eight years old and finish before fifteen. The women's clubs of to-day would have taken it up, but serenely unconscious that anything dreadful had happened, I went joyously on, educating myself in all sorts of ways with all sorts of results. The point is that fifty years ago there was nothing in Chicago for a girl after the High School, although for the boys there was the old Chicago University, which later died a natural death and was noted only for its telescope.

The city grew steadily larger and lost its charm. Alas! it was one of those unfortunates that lose their beauty with their first youth. Business pushed the homes back from the center; the old homes became boarding-houses and went to seed, or had store-fronts attached. People bought and built farther out and horse railways came into being. Dr. Dyer, whom I mentioned in connection with the "Underground Railroad," was the first to buy and build beyond Lincoln Park, then the city cemetery. You had to go the whole length of the cemetery to reach his home. Now, Dr. Dyer was a joker and a free-thinker. "David," he said to my father, "I know you have often been anxious about my soul. I can assure you that I have at last secured a happy home beyond the grave."

Many bought great estates and built beautiful homes in

beautiful grounds; among them the Clarks, the Egans, the Hart L. Stewarts, and others. Some of these homes survived for years, crowded among meaner houses, with a dignity and charm all their own. John Wentworth owned a great piece of land extending southwest of Thirty-First and State streets, on which a race course was in operation until after the Civil War.

Although primitive, we were not quite uncivilized. We had our Public Library, a Mechanics' Institute, a Philharmonic Society under the leadership of Hans Balatka, and always McVicker's Theatre. There all the old stars appeared, and little Mary McVicker, as "little Eva" in *Uncle Tom's Cabin,* brought tears to all eyes. Mary was afterward the wife of Edwin Booth, the great tragedian. We had many lecture courses and listened to Horace Greeley, Henry Ward Beecher, Bayard Taylor, the incomparable Wendell Phillips, John B. Gough, the great apostle of temperance, Susan B. Anthony, and Mrs. Lippincott, better known as Grace Greenwood.

I went, when perhaps ten years old, one night with my father to a concert where besides Madame Parodi, Madame Strakosch and other stars, was a little girl about my own age. She wore a short, pink silk dress ruffled to the waist, and had great black eyes and long black braids, and sang like a bird. It was Adelina Patti. She was a naughty little girl and would not sing at all unless Ole Bull led her out and stood by her while she did it. I have heard her since more than once, but never enjoyed her as I did that night.

Before the Pacific Railroad was built, the city was crowded with young men — graduates of eastern Colleges and others, who had come West to make their fortunes. Girls were in great demand and went into society far younger than they ought. We attended many a function where there were seven men to every girl. As soon as these young men owned even a small portion of Chicago real estate, they considered their fortunes made, and were ready to propose marriage on the slightest provocation — so every girl was a belle in those days.

Dwight L. Moody was a picturesque figure in the city. I taught in a Sunday School in which he was interested. He actually washed and dressed the children and personally conducted them to the school. Many of the stories told of him are apocryphal, but he really did put his hand on the arm of a stranger going into a basement saloon, and say, —

"My friend, you are going straight to Hell."

"Just my luck!" the man answered.

He did get up in service and announce that he had just become engaged to Miss Emma Revell and could not be depended upon to see the girls home from meetings any more. However, he developed as the city did, and it was not many years before that city was building a great temporary auditorium to hold the people who wished to hear him speak.

The Ellsworth Zouaves were also most picturesque. They were all, I think, sons of good families, and Captain Ellsworth was a fine drill-master, with ideas of his own in regard to what a Zouave should wear. We all attended their exhibition drills, and watched them go through marvelous evolutions in their still more marvelous uniforms. Captain Ellsworth took them on a grand tour through the East which was a great success; the illustrated papers were full of their pictures and they were admired and applauded everywhere they went. After their return, one of them, calling on me, said, —

"I have a button for you."

"A button?" I echoed.

"Yes," he said, "the girls fought for our buttons in every city, but I saved three for the girls at home and one is for you." I am afraid I was more amused than appreciative and afterward I was glad I did not accept the gift, for he was the only one of them all who did not serve his country when war came. Instead he drilled troops at Richmond for the Confederacy.

The Republican Party came into being while we were at High School, and everyone, Whig and Democrat, who was anti-slavery joined it, and all shouted for "Fremont and Jessie"; Fremont's wife, Jessie Benton Fremont, having taken a strong hold on the popular fancy. Of course, we were defeated.

In 1858 came the famous Lincoln and Douglas debates. I heard both men, not in debate, but on different evenings. As I was only fourteen and we were a party of young people in Judge Lemoyne's office across the way, what was said made little impression on me. The crowd and torches, the illuminated balcony of the Tremont House from which they spoke, the contrast in looks and manner between the men are all that remain in my memory. This was the only time I ever saw Mr. Lincoln alive.

In 1860 the Prince of Wales (the late King Edward VII), then about eighteen years of age, visited Chicago. The city simply went mad over him. My sixteen-year-old, republican soul revolted; I was ashamed and I said so, that free-born Americans should make such a fuss about a commonplace English schoolboy. John Wentworth was mayor at the time — he had almost as incurable a habit of being mayor as Carter Harrison — and of course he entertained the Prince. When he sent me a note asking me to make a fourth with the Prince, Mrs. Wentworth and himself, in a drive about the city and a reception afterward at the Tremont House, I rose to a height of consistency never afterward reached and declined the honor, and thus lost my first, last and only opportunity to hobnob with royalty. Afterward we had another and different mayor and another and different visitor. The visitor was King Kalakaua of the Hawaiian Islands. He was received with a band of music and a speech, then this mayor said, —

"Come on, King, let's go up to the Tremont and have a wash-up."

In those far off years we had great trouble with our money. Our National Banking system was not yet established and private banks issuing bank-notes were far from reliable. At one time rent and other debts were paid in bundles of bills each with a strap about it, saying these were worth eighty-five cents, or sixty-five cents, or even less, on a dollar; it was a mathematical problem to find out if one had the right amount. These must be spent quickly or they would grow less, for the banks took them only at a discount, and shops and stores had notices posted:

"Wild Cat money taken only at this morning's quotations."

In 1860 the Convention was held that nominated Abraham Lincoln. The Wigwam in which it was held was built in rather rough fashion on the corner of Market and Lake streets. It was on the third day of the session that my mother and I reached the door at eight o'clock in the morning. There were no entrance tickets and the plan was to let in a small portion of the crowd, shut the door and when that portion had gone up a rather narrow stairway, open it again and let in another contingent. Alas! I was let in and my mother was shut out; I was forced up the stair a little and there was small chance of my finding her again in the crowd. A man named Peter Page, a rather prominent Chicagoan, had charge of the door. I saw that his head was just within my reach. I hesitated not an instant, but beat a tattoo on his shining silk hat with my parasol and demanded my mother.

"Let that lady's mother in," he commanded the doorkeeper, and she was let in. The crowd took it up outside and long after we were in our seats we could hear the shout, —

"Let that lady's mother in!"

We found good seats, and young and thoughtless as I was, and amused and flushed by my little adventure, I felt almost at once that it was a serious and momentous occasion. The air was fairly electric with the great questions and the tremendous issues at stake. The preliminaries had been finished and the platform accepted on the previous days. The platform stated that Congress had no right to interfere with slavery in the States where it existed, but that the Republican Party opposed definitely its being admitted into the Territories. The balloting began almost at once. Men were stationed at the skylight and down the roof to announce the votes as quickly as possible to the crowds in the streets. At first the favorite sons of different States received votes; then it settled down to a struggle between

Abraham Lincoln and William H. Seward. New York and her following stood by Seward valiantly, yet the votes swung into place fast for Lincoln. To the very last, the New York chairman's call rang out, "Seventy votes for William H. Seward;" and when it became his duty to make the choice unanimous, he did it with choking voice and tears streaming down his face. The great place rang with cheers and outside pandemonium reigned, yet I think everyone was half joyful and half frightened; it was such a critical time that it would not do to make a mistake. The nation's very existence might depend on what was then done. Many of the best and wisest thought Mr. Seward's ripe and skilled statesmanship was needed, and others, that Lincoln alone had the moral courage for the time. Events proved these latter to be right, but Mr. Lincoln was not well known out of his state; in the East people asked, "Who is Abraham Lincoln?"

This was my first convention, but not my last; I was present at the great scene in Crosby's Opera House when Grant was nominated by acclamation. I was in the Exposition building when Conkling made his great speech for a third term for Grant, beginning: —

"If you ask me where he hails from,
My answer can but be:
He hails from Appomatox,
And the famous apple tree."

The applause was tremendous, but a few minutes later he unfortunately said: "Show me a better man!"

"James G. Blaine!" shouted a man in the gallery.

The place went mad with applause; Senator Hoar beat with his gavel and the band played its loudest, and it was funny to see the instruments move apparently soundlessly, while the human voice was all that was heard. The applause only ended with exhaustion and the Convention nominated neither Grant nor Blaine, but James A. Garfield. I was also present at the Auditorium when Benjamin Harrison was nominated.

But to go back to 1860 —

Events came fast after Lincoln's election. We were shopping when we heard of the firing on Fort Sumter, and the news was accompanied with the advice to buy cotton-goods as they would rise in price, which they did to an unheard-of height. There were at once many enlistments for three months: that would, of course, be long enough to settle the matter. We were at the Des Plaines Camp Meeting when we heard of the first battle of Bull Run, and Bishop Simpson preached such a sermon as only times of great disaster can bring forth.

After that it was war and nothing but war. Our friends all enlisted; we despised them if they did not. At first the enlistments were for nine months and then for three years or the duration of the war. Chicago was a camp of construction, and regiments came marching in from all of the States north of us. Camp Douglas, south of 31st Street, was thick, at first with tents, and afterwards with wooden barracks, and was soon crowded. J. J. Spalding, whose family lived in Evanston, raised a company and was made Captain. We with other friends went to the camp and gave the company a grand luncheon and presented him with a sword. To other companies we helped give flags. We went on some such errand to another camp north of the city, Wright's Grove, I think, and were the guests of Lieutenant-Colonel Bigelow, Mrs. Milton Wilson's brother, and of Captain Edward Whitehead, brother of William H. Whitehead, of Evanston.

Nothing was spoken of but the war; nothing was done except in reference to it. We worked hard, scraped lint, tore and rolled bandages, made hospital garments, tied comforters, knitted stockings and mittens, put up fruit and pickles and jelly, all for the soldiers. We held great Sanitary Commission Fairs lasting a week, two weeks, or even three weeks. One of these fairs was in the Illinois Central Station at Randolph Street when the building was new and before it was used as a station. It is difficult for anyone who sees that building nowadays to believe that it was ever new. The last of these fairs was in session when the war closed. It was there I first saw General Grant. He looked tired and bored and finally took refuge from the crowds that pressed upon him, in the booth where I was busy. We girls were all alert, we gave him a chair and fanned him and brought him glasses of water and lemonade. When he finally recovered and left us, he gave some flowers he was carrying to one of the girls and she kindly divided them among us — I kept my share for years.

But the end of the war was long in coming and our souls fainted within us. Men grew scant among us and the mourners went about the streets. You of to-day can realize how horrible it was to know that the armies were fighting; to know that thousands were dead or dying, wounded or prisoners. We soon learned to wish our friends dead rather than prisoners. We dreaded to see the papers, yet could not rest until we knew the latest news and scanned, with sinking hearts, the lists of dead and wounded. It was a desperate time and wrought in us a desperate and passionate patriotism. Then came the time when George Root wrote war-songs, and Frank and Jules Lombard sang them on the Court House steps, and hundreds enlisted in a day. Ah, those war-songs! They may seem trivial now, but they meant much to us then. There was one with a simple refrain, with a foolish little repetition in it: —

> Brave boys are they,
> Gone at their Country's call,
> And yet — and yet, we cannot forget
> That many brave boys must fall.

It went sharply to our hearts. It was cruel to sing: —

> We shall meet — but we shall miss him,
> There will be one vacant chair.

So many families had those vacant chairs!

It changed us, of course. No one could live through all that and be the same. It may be that those four years of strain and stress and horror are in a measure responsible for the nervous temperaments of the generation following us.

Camp Douglas ceased to be a camp of construction and became a prison. We saw the prisoners march in, seven thousand of them, looking most miserable. They occupied the barracks built for the soldiers and a high board fence was put up to enclose the place. We were very good to those prisoners; we sent fruit, jellies, and other provisions for their hospital, and much clothing for their wear.

The clergymen of the city took turns in holding services for them. One Sunday, Dr. Eddy (Mrs. Tallmadge's father) had preached and there was much interest manifested by his audience. He closed his sermon and gave out a hymn. There were no hymn-books except for the preacher and for the young people who were there to serve as a choir, so the custom was to read a verse and then sing it. He read: "Show pity, Lord, O Lord, forgive;" the next line was, "Let a repenting rebel live." He was quick enough to read it, "Let a repenting sinner live," but it was evidently familiar, for there was a chuckle and a ripple of laughter, and every vestige of serious attention vanished.

The Chicago preachers of Civil War times were a band of strong men; among them were Matthew Simpson, Dr. Robert Patterson, Dr. W. H. Ryder, Dr. T. M. Eddy, O. H. Tiffany, and Robert Collyer. It is a roll of honor.

It was, I think, in 1862, that we were on the porch one evening with some friends, when a troop of cavalry turned off State Street, came to position in front of our house, and were there put through the manual of the saber, sharp and quick, to be addressed in very strong language by their commander, after which they turned about and went jingling down State Street. A friend said, "I did not know there were so many soldiers in the city, everything has been rushed to the front; there are hardly enough left to guard the prisoners." We thought little of it, and after our friends left us, we closed the house and went upstairs. Then came a ring at the bell and a voice, "Every man go at once to the Armory and be armed, the prisoners are out and armed." Our household had no men. The messenger went on his errand down the street and presently all the men in the neighborhood went hurrying off to the Armory. We changed our thin summer dresses for dark walking-suits; we gathered up a few things in hand-bags, turned out the lights and sat in the dark, stunned and stupid with fear, and waited. Suddenly there was a volley of musketry — another — a third — then cannon — then all was still. It seemed ages before a neighbor returning told us what had happened. The fence-posts had been sawed beneath the ground in one section so that, with a push, that part of the stockade fell. The prisoners came forth in force, well-armed and in some show of order and discipline. To their surprise they faced a regiment in line, waiting for them. The rebels fired; the soldiers answered; the regiment opened right and left, disclosing a battery. The prisoners were warned to retreat; they answered with another volley. Then the cannon spoke; the prisoners threw down their arms and fled back into the prison and all was over.

The next day the Confederate officer who was to have taken charge was found in a house half a square from us, where it chanced my small brothers had played with the boys of the family all the day before. He was in woman's clothes and had not destroyed his orders which were: to take command, to burn the city, to seize what shipping they needed, burn the rest, then sail through the Lakes and out the St. Lawrence, doing all the harm they could by the way. If they reached the ocean, they were to proceed to Charleston or some other port and break the blockade. It was a fine plot, except that someone betrayed it. If Governor Yates had not been able to rush a regiment and a battery to Chicago, there seems to be no reason why the scheme should not have succeeded. A number of Chicago's prominent families, who were responsible for arming the prisoners, left the country that night and did not return until the war was ended.

At last came Lee's surrender, closely followed by the assassination of President Lincoln. I saw the sad procession as he was borne through our streets, and every loyal heart was filled with deepest grief. We went at midnight to show our respect for the dead, as he lay in state in the broad hall of the old Court House. There was a curious silence over the city; many had chosen that same hour for the sad duty. Softly we climbed the long flight of steps and paused where he lay at rest from his cares and sorrows. General Sheridan stood at his head and General Logan at his feet. Many were passing, and deep sorrow was on every face. As we reached the top of the further steps we looked down on two or three hundred men with torches and music-books, and as we looked they began to sing a requiem for the dead. The night, the men's voices, and the quiet dead made an impression that remains with me still.

We saw the rebel prisoners depart for their home, strong and hearty, and much better dressed than when they came. Then our prisoners came home, some of them from Andersonville. I hope you may all be spared such a sight. The rest of our soldiers also returned. There had been some anxiety as to the result of disbanding at once so large an army, but, without a ripple, they dropped back into their places as citizens.

Chicago grew — Irish, Germans, and Scandinavians flocked in. The Bohemians came and formed a city of their own. We joyously laid down miles of wooden block pavement, and tried to adjust our levels. Michigan and Wabash avenues and State Street became level, but if you stepped west off State Street, you would walk a few hundred feet and go down six steps, a little farther you would go up two or three, and then down again. It was like New York's famous sky-line. Every man decided for himself what the ultimate level of his street would be and arranged his building and his wooden sidewalk accordingly. It was very inconvenient, especially in the hoop-skirts which were the fashion during the war and for years afterward. Every woman wore them, even my little six-year-old sister was caged in her tiny hoop. The highest sidewalk I knew was on Jackson Boulevard between Dearborn and Clark streets (about where the Union League Club now is), and is connected in my mind with an Indian girl, the only beautiful Indian girl I ever saw. I was walking on the low side of the street, where the board walk was level with the roadway, and I saw her coming toward me on the high side in her moccasins and blanket, with her free, easy stride. She had something she was greatly pleased with; she drew it out and smiled at it and put it back in her bosom, only to take it out and smile at it again. A young man passing held out his hand for it; she gave it to him readily enough. It was her picture and he kissed it. I never saw such a blaze of wrath. She snatched it from him and, with one swing of her arm, sent him flying off the edge of the walk to fall eight feet to the roadway below, while she went her way without one look to see where he went or how he fared.

The side toward the street of these erections was not boarded up, but open, and papers drifted in and stray dogs and cats and tramps made their homes there. I suppose no place was ever so ugly as was a large part of Chicago at that period. The business part in the center of town was built chiefly of brick and stone. From State to the lake and quite far south there were more or less fine homes, many built of the white limestone which came to be characteristic of Chicago and which we called Athens marble. Terrace Row on

Michigan Avenue, a really fine block of residences, was our idea of true magnificence. We were very proud also of our Crosby's Opera House, although it did come to be raffled off at five dollars a ticket. It was there we had our first real Grand Opera. And there we listened to wonderful oratorios with Parepa Rosa, Annie Louise Carey, Myron Whitney, and Brignoli for soloists. The North Side, from Clark Street to the lake and down to a few streets from the river, was full of charming residences, and Wabash as well as Michigan Avenue on the South Side, was lined with delightful homes.

My husband and I were boarding on Michigan Avenue near Hubbard Court at the time of the Fire. It was Sunday evening. We had just returned from church. When the fire bells rang a friend said she had never seen a fire, so she and her husband and I and mine went to watch the conflagration. It was already a great blaze, and being among old wooden buildings, it spread fast, a fierce wind from the southwest carrying forward the flames. Our husbands soon hurried us home and went back; we did not see them again until daylight. In the meantime the waterworks burned, the gas-works had blown up, and half the city was destroyed. It was frightful — just the old idea of the Day of Judgment. The night was light as day. The wind carried before it great blazing pieces of roof, or building paper, or shingles; they flew flaming through the sky. The space inside our gate was filled with women and babies, and one man badly burned, to whom we carried food. The part between the sidewalk and the street was crowded with people, the few things they had saved huddled about them. The sidewalk was also thronged with men and women fleeing south, carrying whatever they could. One very well-dressed woman dragged a trunk along by a rope tied to a handle. Another woman sat guarding her household goods and we saw an expressman drive up and begin to load them into his wagon; she protested and we found he was stealing them. Then everybody tried in vain to help her, until a neighbor with a revolver threatened to shoot the robber, when he drove off with what he had already secured. We were told frightful stories of thugs and robbers, and at intervals we heard explosions. The city was under martial law, and there being absolutely no water after the destruction of the waterworks, General Sheridan, in command, was blowing up houses in an attempt to stop the fire. The wind and flame acted like a blow-pipe; it took just fifteen minutes, so fierce was the heat, and so strong was the wind, to burn to ashes a solidly built block of brick and stone.

The people about us began to move south and we were told that in ten minutes our block would be in flames, — but it did not come to that. The Wabash Avenue M. E. Church stood on the corner of Harrison and Wabash. Next to it was a broad excavation for another building and a great pile of sand. Our pastor was a stalwart man. Gathering a group of young men about him, he began to cover every exposed part of the Church and to smother every small flame with the sand. When General Sheridan saw they were having some success, he ordered every house for a block around blown up, and so succeeded in stopping the progress of the fire southward. The church was taken for a post office the next day and never saw another service.

On the North Side all but one dwelling was consumed. At last,, late on Monday afternoon, the wind stilled and the welcome rain came down. Many stories were told of how the people took refuge in the tunnels and were almost suffocated, how others ran into the lake as far as they could and kept throwing the water over themselves to cool the heat, until rescued by rowboats and carried out to ships and steamers; how hundreds found refuge in Lincoln Park and little ones came into the world that night under the trees in the rain, who, but for the Fire, would have been born in the lap of luxury. That night there was no light in all the city. Our fathers, husbands, and brothers patrolled the streets armed, while we quaked with fear within doors. Tuesday morning my friend and I started with some clothing for a church that was full of the homeless. Hearing shouts, we looked up the street and saw some people trying to throw a man out of a fourth-story window. We were told he was caught starting a fresh fire, but we fled around the next corner and never knew what further happened.

There was no credit for anyone, and it was astonishing how little money people had in their pockets. It was nearly a week before money could be obtained from the banks. We were not allowed to use kerosene and there were so few shops left unburned and so few candles in them that only four could be sold to one person. Our only water was brought in barrels from the lake.

When the vaults of the banks were opened, after four days' cooling, a large part of the bank-notes were found baked to a brown crisp. These were sent to Washington, where experts estimated their value and sent back new bills.

The Horse Railway Company had built a new car-barn near 22nd and State streets. It had never been used, and there Field and Leiter opened a store. Mandel had a small establishment on 22nd Street, but no one bought anything except to make clothing for the sufferers. All the world rushed to our relief. Tents and, afterward, rows of wooden cabins were hastily put up; everything was done by widespread charity and sympathy. It is true that St. Louis, Milwaukee, and other cities shouted aloud and printed in their newspapers that this was their opportunity to take to themselves Chicago's trade, but these were exceptions.

It was a strange winter. When we looked across the ruins and counted our losses, everyone joked; it was so great and universal a disaster, there was no other way to bear it. There were calico balls and all sorts of entertainments, all for the benefit of the relief and aid societies. I heard Ole Bull play in a hall on 22nd Street where the stage alone was lighted, and that with candles. It was a blessing to hear Ole Bull under any circumstances. With his grand figure, his noble head and beautiful white hair, he came forward, gave us a bow of old-fashioned courtesy and a benign smile, lifted his violin to his shoulder, laid his cheek against it, closed his eyes and filled the world with music.

I heard Charlotte Cushman read *Henry the Eighth* with much the same scheme of lighting. However, we soon had gas and water once more, and life began to be less strange to us.

The work of clearing away and rebuilding was undertaken with great vigor and much good cheer. With that rebuilding my tale ends. Old Chicago passed in that smoke and flame and on the wings of that mighty wind, and it exists now only in the memories and hearts of those who loved her.

VIII

LONG AGO

BY MARY DRUMMOND

As a foreword to my personal knowledge of Chicago, a few extracts from a letter from my father, Thomas Drummond,[1] to his father in Maine, may be of interest. At the time the letter was written he was twenty-four years of age, and had recently been admitted to the Philadelphia bar. The letter is dated Chicago, May, 1835, at which time he spent a week in the city which later was to be home. He was staying at the old Sauganash Hotel, near Market and Lake streets, kept by Mark Beaubien. He speaks of it as "the best hotel in the place, with prices equal to the New York and Philadelphia hotels, but frequently destitute of beef, butter, and milk."

He writes of the "young Giant of the West," and of the unparalleled rapidity of Chicago's growth: —

"Two years ago there were but forty inhabitants; and now it contains a population of nearly or quite three thousand. It is no uncommon thing for real estate, to the value of forty or fifty thousand dollars, to be sold in one day. Lots that last fall could be bought for a thousand dollars, cannot now be purchased for seven times that amount."

[1] Judge Thomas Drummond, one of Chicago's most distinguished jurists.—*Editor.*

In speaking of the buildings he writes: —

"The main object seems to be to erect a house or store, but of what kind is a matter of small consequence. Most of the buildings are therefore of wood and put up in the slightest possible manner. . . . The river, though narrow, is deep, except at the mouth, where there is quite a bar formed by the washing in of the sand, and where they are now building piers which are to remove it, and Chicago will then have a fine harbor."

His first experience with Indians seems to have left a most unpleasant impression on his mind, for he writes: —

"There is a large number of Indians encamped in and about the town and arrangements are being made to remove them beyond the Mississippi, several agents of the general government being here for that purpose. The tribe, or such as I have seen, probably one hundred or one hundred and fifty, are ill-featured, ill-formed, and there is nothing noble about them. Their love for whisky seems incurable. Last Sunday morning they found a cask in the street, broke it open, and, with scarcely one exception, got drunk. They cut a curious figure in the street, many of them naked or with a piece of cloth around the loins. In walking out towards night, in the company of a gentleman, we found one of the poor wretches lying in the water, nothing but his head out — and that in the mud. A large number of men were sitting around, apparently regardless of his situation; even his wife, when we pointed out his perilous position, only smiled. I took hold of him and awoke him, for he was sound asleep. Having recovered a little from his drunkenness, he succeeded in getting up. When he came up the bank he was saluted by a laugh from his friends. He staggered along to a fire which was near and sat down. He was as miserable a spectacle as you can conceive; the idiocy of drunkenness in his face, which was, besides, covered with mud. He took off his shirt, which was wet and dirty, and his wife went quietly, picked it up and carried it to the river and washed it. This same wife had an infant in her lap and, though so careless about its father, seemed to manifest all of a mother's love for her child. Many of these Indians appear to be rich, most of them have horses, and many are very gaudily apparelled, but altogether, I cannot look upon them with anything but disgust."

In speaking of the natives of Chicago in the early days, he says: —

"The tone of moral sentiment among the great mass of the people seems to be lamentably low. I have been introduced to many professional men, and most of them are shockingly profane. They are great card players. The other evening at the hotel there were no less than three whist tables in the common sitting-room, though I did not notice that there was any gambling. There is much frankness of manner certainly, but little or no polish. Their knowledge of books is small, conversation, in which they excel, being their principal talent. Their tremendous profanity I dislike very much. It is so unusual to hear a gentleman in the East do more than swear a little. Here it appears to be an admitted point that there must be an oath to every sentence, and the more far-fetched and strong, the better.

"There are few women compared to the men, and it

seems to be understood that a man must go East to get married. This has long been a military post,[1] and the garrison grounds are prettily situated. I have become acquainted with some of the officers, who appear to be agreeable men. It is almost impossible to obtain servants here, and the wife of the man who keeps the house where I lodge is obliged to clean the floors and make the beds herself, and the landlord attends to us at the table; which would be considered a great hardship by a landlord or landlady at one of our city hotels in the East.

"The temperance reformation has not effected much here in the West, at least in this part of it. Brandy and whiskey are set upon our table every day at dinner, and it is as much a matter of course to ask a friend to drink a glass for old acquaintance' sake as it once was in the East. I saw no glasses of brandy upon the dinner-table until after I passed Utica. Since then it is universal at all hotels where I have stopped. There is a scene passing in the room adjoining mine which is characteristic of the country: Three gentlemen are there drinking champagne and telling stories, and every now and then a round oath falls upon my ears. Though the swearing seems to be confined to one, yet he makes up for the deficiency of all the rest. And this much for western men and manners!"

My father, being appointed Federal Judge in 1850, found it necessary to remove his family from Galena to Chicago in 1854. Thus it happened that in September of that year a very youthful and unnoticed personage, aged eight, be-

[1] Fort Dearborn was built in 1804; destroyed by Indians on August 16, 1812; rebuilt in 1816, and was finally demolished in 1856. — *Editor.*

came a resident of the "Giant of the West." My father took us to the old Lake House, which stood by the river on Rush Street, and with this hotel are associated my first recollections as a resident of Chicago. It is a bit humiliating to remember that on our arrival, our great city made no impression on my mind, while the good crackers and milk for our tea, the playing on the floor in Mrs. Henry Farnham's room, and the fact that Georgie Kinzie, having injured something in the large parlors, was not allowed to play there with the other children, are the only incidents which are firmly fixed in my memory.

We soon moved to a little frame house on Wolcott Street (now North State Street), between Erie and Huron streets. There was no other house in that block on Wolcott Street except a tiny cottage, inhabited by a kindly Irish washerwoman, Mrs. Dorsey, and her two little girls, with whom I became great friends. Often of late years, as I wait for the State Street cars on that corner, I try to picture it as it was sixty-five years ago, when it was a vacant lot surrounded by a board fence; and it comes vividly before me as it looked in that snowy winter of '54 and '55, with the drifts piled to the top of the fence. I think it remained a vacant lot until after the Fire, and was used as a croquet ground where many a battle royal was fought out among the champions of that decade, Kitty Goodrich and Will Scudder ranking high on the list of players. Vacant lots were common in those days, and many were the cross-cuts we children took in walks and runs.

The next year we moved to Dearborn Street, remaining on the same square, and so it happened that my home life in Chicago was spent on the block bounded by Erie and

Huron, Wolcott and Dearborn streets. In our early years our daily horizon is apt to be exceedingly circumscribed; add to that the fact that our own feet, and those of our good friends, the horses, were our only means of transportation, and it is easily seen that of necessity my childish memories are largely limited to the North Side.

On the South Side we did not often go beyond Madison Street. Lake Street was our shopping street, Palmer's[1] hose and jewelry store, the grandeur of "Ross and Gossage," with its black lions guarding the entrance west of Clark Street, and almost all the other retail stores of those days being found there. Many south-side families, the Judge Mark Skinners, the Dr. David Rutters, the J. Y. Scammons, the Highs, Chapins, Clarks, Brosses, Carters, Bentleys, Dickeys, Farnhams, Fleetwoods, Blackwells, and numerous others, were household names, but it seemed a long way to their homes. Trinity Church, on Jackson Street, was "miles away," and when James Bowen, whose daughter Jennie was my schoolmate and friend, moved to Twelfth Street, we almost felt it an eternal farewell.

The North Side was "home," and a lovely, homelike place it was. The large grounds, and beautiful shade-trees about so many residences gave a sense of space, rest, flowers, sunshine and shadows, that hardly belongs nowadays to the idea of a city. There was great friendliness, and much simple, charming living. While in new places the proportion of scholarly and professional men and cultivated women is generally not so large as in older cities, in early Chicago it was greater than usual. The more ambitious and energetic among eastern young men of the first half of the

[1] Potter Palmer.

Nineteenth Century were keen to move to what was the "out west" of their generation.

Some of the homes stand out clearly in my mind. On Michigan Street (now Austin Avenue) and Cass Street, across from the old St. James's Church, of which they were stanch supporters, was the homelike place of Mr. and Mrs. John H. Kinzie — a low house with pleasant rooms, standing in a large yard, with many trees scattered here and there. On the porch of this old house Mrs. Erskine, the little "Tinie DeWolf" of those days, remembers being swung in the hammock one day by Arthur Kinzie, when she caught sight of a company of Indians coming through the gate. She screamed and ran to bury her face in Mrs. Kinzie's lap, but found her quite undisturbed by this not uncommon occurrence.

Many were the pleasant meetings in the parlors of the "Kinzie House," when Mrs. Kinzie at the piano, and Mr. Kinzie with his violin, would play for their guests to dance. I can remember a cap of Mrs. Kinzie's with pink ribbons, which appealed to my childish taste, and how I tried to induce my mother, a much younger woman, not yet forty, to wear pink ribbons!

Old St. James's Church across the street, was a brick building with a square tower, square pews in the galleries, and four large square pews with tables in the center for books, in the rear of the church. Ours was one of the gallery pews and we little people, sitting on small chairs in the front of the pew, found it a most interesting place, as we had a fine view of the congregation. The Sunday School was in the basement, and I well remember being taken there with my sisters, who were to be put in Mrs. Kinzie's class, while

I belonged in Mrs. George W. Dole's infant class. From the Sunday School we had to go outdoors to reach the church, and one rainy Sunday, Mary Newberry,[1] who was a veritable goody-two-shoes that day with her new shoes, refused to expose her treasures to the wet. So down she sat on the steps and took them off, trotting up to the church as a barefoot girl. Dr. Robert H. Clarkson,[2] the well-beloved rector of this church for so many years, with his poetic nature, warm sympathy, and keen sense of humor, can never be forgotten by the large circle in and out of his own church, who loved and honored him.

Not far from the river also lived Edward K. Rogers, and Judge Grant Goodrich; and on Indiana Street (now Grand Avenue) were many pleasant homes, among them those of George B. Carpenter and Mr. Hathaway. Over between Clark, Illinois, Dearborn and Indiana streets, stood the old North Side Market, where the men of the families often took their market-baskets in the morning, while the "virtuous woman" stayed at home and "looked well to the ways of her household." A pleasant place was the old market, with the big doors opening to north and south, and with stalls on either side, where meat and fish and crisp, fresh vegetables and fruit were displayed. To-day South Water Street offers more variety, but the old market, clean and cool and roomy, was far more tempting. On the corner of Ontario and Clark streets stood the brick house of Mr. and Mrs. William F. DeWolf, with a broad flight of steps leading up to a pillared porch, a style repeated in Mrs.

[1] A daughter of Walter L. Newberry, whose fortune founded the Newberry Library.

[2] Afterwards Episcopal Bishop of Nebraska.

Dodge's white frame house (afterwards the home of W. H. Bradley), on Ontario and Wolcott streets.

On Ontario and Dearborn streets stood the Arnold cottage, occupied by Isaac N. Arnold and his family until they moved to Erie and Pine streets, the family home until 1914. After the Arnolds moved from Ontario Street, the cottage was occupied by Samuel H. Kerfoot and family, who moved from Maryland to Chicago in 1849, going first to the Sherman House and afterwards living on or about Ohio and Ontario streets. In 1856 they moved north to their well-known place "Dawn," in what was then known as Lake View. This residence was the scene of many good times, as were also the homes of John Valentine LeMoyne and Dr. Charles Dyer, north of the city, and of Thomas B. Bryan at Cottage Hill, now Elmhurst.

Miss Alice Kerfoot remembers how, in her childhood days, General "Joe" Stockton and his companions would put an organ on a hand-cart and "go serenading," and also, how they would get a big bob-sled and drive from house to house picking up "the girls," giving them no time to "prink," and then drive out to "Dawn" for a dance; and how one night a heavy rain came up and carried off the snow. One of the bob-sled horses had to be saddled and ridden to the nearest livery stable four miles away to fetch the town "hacks" to convey the guests to their various homes. The company had breakfast at the Kerfoots', as candles and lamps flickered yellow in the light of the coming day, after which the party drove down through what is now Lincoln Park and was then a dripping, sodden, melancholy cemetery. It was indeed a long journey from "Dawn" to daylight when the weary revellers reached town!

Miss Kerfoot also tells a story, learned from her father, of a basket-picnic on July 4, 1849, which was considered then a great expedition into the wilds. Mr. Kerfoot and Dr. Swope, then Rector of Trinity Church, being the best horsemen of the company, headed a procession of citizens from the Sherman House, marching to "the woods" on the North Side, said woods being where the Cyrus H. McCormick and Isaac N. Arnold houses afterward stood, on the block now bounded by Rush, Huron, Erie streets and North Michigan Avenue.

Between Ohio and Ontario, North State and Cass streets, stood, in the center of the block, the brick gabled house of H. H. Magie, father of Mrs. Lambert Tree, grandfather of Arthur Tree and great-grandfather of Ronald Tree. The house was full of beautiful things brought from abroad, among which was the celebrated "Nydia," by Ball. Back of the residence were many currant and gooseberry bushes, which made an impression on my mind. Directly north, on the corner of North State and Ontario streets, surrounded by large trees, stood the low, brown cottage of the George B. Meekers and Mr. Meeker's sister, Mrs. Scudder, and a block east, between Ontario and Erie, Cass and Rush streets, stood the charming home of William B. Ogden and his brother-in-law and sister, Mr. and Mrs. Edwin H. Sheldon. This was a large, white frame dwelling, surrounded by fine trees. The rooms were spacious and delightful, the dining-room, with its windows opening on three sides, being one of the most beautiful rooms in Chicago. In early days Mr. Ogden's housekeeper, Mary (afterwards Mrs. Henry Wischmyer), was a local celebrity, and few were the north-side people she did not know. Her tea-biscuits were renowned, and her invitations to "help yourself often" were rarely refused.

In the large parlors of this pleasant home one night in the sixties, a clever little performance caused much entertainment, both to actors and audience. Not the least of the fun was the program. The "Grand Opera," *The Lovers*, was presented for positively one night only, with Signorina Eleanora Wheeleretta (afterwards Mrs. A. C. McClurg, mother of Ogden McClurg), the "famed cantatrice, whose recent triumphs have set all Europe in a furore," as prima donna, and Signor Guglielmo Emersonio Strongini (General William E. Strong), as Prince Almanzor. The other parts were taken by Fräulein von Schneidau, Signora Drummondini, Signor Giacomo Kelletto (James Kelly); Signor Samuellino Jonstonio (Sam Johnston); Signori Enrico DeWolfo and Edwino Sheldoni (Henry DeWolf and Edwin Sheldon). "The management," we are told, "takes pleasure in announcing that the remarkably large chorus is in perfect order, and the costumes have been imported especially for this occasion." Also that "the management has with the utmost difficulty secured the services of the renowned Directeur Musical, Carlo Iones"—this "renowned directeur" being Caroline Ogden Jones, to whose bright mind and musical knowledge was largely due the entertaining little "opera."

A member of this household from her early girlhood until her marriage to Eugene Jerome of New York in 1867, was Pauline von Schneidau, probably one of the most beautiful girls Chicago has ever known. Her father, who belonged to a noble Swedish family, came here with his wife from Wisconsin in 1844. Mr. von Schneidau, owing to pressure of circumstances, became a daguerreotype artist, — I think the first in Chicago, — and some of his old pictures still remain to show his skill. His wife dying in 1855, the little Pauline became a member of the home of those good and kindly friends of her father, Mr. and Mrs. George W. Dole. Afterwards, just before her father's death in 1859, she moved to the home of William B. Ogden, Chicago's first mayor.

Another beautiful girl, Rose Howe, was often, with her young sister, "Frank," a guest of some of the old families, the Arnolds, DeWolfs, Scammons, and Ogdens. They were daughters of Francis Howe. Their mother, a highly educated woman, was a descendant of a French grandfather and a French and Indian grandmother, which romantic circumstance, added to the fact that the elder daughter so strongly resembled Faed's picture, *Evangeline*, made them most interesting personalities to us all.

East of the Ogden house, between Rush and Pine, Ontario and Erie streets, stood the brownstone house of Walter L. Newberry, whose fortune founded the reference library that now bears his name. The Newberry residence was placed on the southeast corner of the lot, and, oddly enough, after the Fire the ground on this corner was never broken for building until the erection of the little shops now occupying it. On the northern part of the square was the garden, and here grew yellow roses and fragrant Madonna lilies. As this family was one of the few that often visited Europe, the house held many lovely things, but nothing more beautiful than G. P. A. Healy's portraits of the two daughters of the family — Mary, with her dancing blue eyes, fair hair, and face so full of vivacity; and Julia, with her dark hair and splendid gray eyes. The loss of these pictures in the fire of 1871, particularly the one of the younger daughter, attired in a simple white dress, with a string of bright red beads about her neck, is something I often mourn, as I also do, the beautiful portrait of Edwin H. Sheldon with his children, "Ed and Fanny," (the latter the late Mrs. William Fitzhugh Whitehouse).

Anent the question of going abroad, I remember a story once jestingly told of a party at the Newberrys', when it was claimed that those who had been abroad twice were welcomed in the parlor; those who had been once were received in the dining-room; those who had hopes of going were relegated to the hall, while those without hope were out on the porch.

Mrs. M. Tiernan, now living at Evanston, but whose pleasant home in those days was on the southeast corner of Rush and Ohio streets, opposite that of George E. Stanton, tells of an incident during the Civil War which happened at one of the Newberry parties to her brother, General Joseph Stockton, and which furnished much amusement to him and to that delightful, fun-loving family of Stocktons of which he was a member. He was at home on a furlough, and Mrs. Newberry, who considered him a bit of a lion, introduced him to a lady guest as, "the brave and gallant Colonel Stockton, of whom you must have heard."

The truth-loving lady, seemingly fearing that silence might give consent, frankly answered,—

"No, I never did."

Those who knew General Stockton will understand his enjoyment of this.

Mrs. Tiernan also remembers another of the Newberry parties being distinguished by the presence of three brides, Mrs. Colonel Graham, Mrs. Henry Miller, and Mrs. Stephen A. Douglas,[1] the latter dressed in a "simple white dress, low-necked and short-sleeved." Later Mrs. Douglas became the wife of General Williams and lived many years in Chicago.

North of the Newberrys, in 1854, was "the Arnold's new house." Well do I remember its vegetable and flower gardens, and the joys of the juicy stalks of rhubarb "served on the spot." In this large house, strangely enough, where there was so much ground, there was a basement dining-room. There were at that time not a few subterranean dining-rooms and they were difficult of access at parties. There was a story that made me regard my clever schoolmate, Louise Goodwin, daughter of Stephen A. Goodwin, with deep admiration. She and her escort were going downstairs to supper at a party at John N. Jewett's on Ontario Street when the youth quoted in Latin, "*Facilis descensus Averni.*" Much to his surprise his clever companion continued in Latin, "*Sed revocare gradum, hoc opus, hic labor est.*" Bright school-girls were in evidence in those days as well as in these.

The Arnold house made its first deep impression on me because it was the scene of my "introduction into Chicago society," the occasion being the birthday party (Valentine's Day, 1854) of the eldest daughter of the house, Miss Katherine Arnold, who, honored and beloved, is still well known in Chicago.

Dr. Brainerd's Milwaukee-brick house on the corner of

[1] The mother of Mrs Walter Farwell, of Chicago

Rush and Huron streets was the scene of my second "ball," and I remember feeling properly dressed for the occasion in a long-sleeved, high-necked, blue merino gown. Dr. Brainerd was probably Chicago's most able surgeon at that time, and his daughter, Julia, became one of our most gifted and delightful musicians, though perhaps not ranking with Annie Tinkham (afterwards Mrs. James Anthony Hunt).[1] On Huron and Cass streets, diagonally opposite each other, were the homes of the Julian Rumseys and John Reed. Few locations in Chicago have remained so long the home of one family as has that of the Julian Rumseys, the house being rebuilt after the Fire on much the old lines of the earlier building, and having been lived in ever since by the children of the original owners.

On North Clark Street, opposite Washington Square, was what was perhaps the handsomest place in the city, the home of Mr. and Mrs. Ezra B. McCagg, occupying fully two blocks, well planted with noble trees. The driveway wound through the beautiful grounds from the southwest corner of the lot to the north end, where stood the delightful house. Among its many attractions perhaps the fine library counted first. A large, stately room, lined with books almost from floor to ceiling, was the *sanctum sanctorum* of Mr. McCagg. Mrs. McCagg,[2] a social leader in the best sense of the word, and the Misses Jones, her daughters by a former marriage, made this home the center of everything charming, simple, and refined in social life; and many were the happy times enjoyed there — delightful dances, musicals, private theatricals, *et id omne genus*, — but no elaborate

[1] Mother of Mrs. Ralph Hamill, of Winnetka.

[2] A sister of William B. and Mahlon Odgen

suppers, late dances, or other harmful forms of entertainment.

Just north of the McCagg place stood the dainty little house of those two charming daughters of Mr. Canda, Mrs. Humphreys and Mrs. Payson, with their attractive French ways and gay music. To have these two sisters play their delightful duets for a little dance was enough to make the heaviest feet "light as a feather." East of Mr. Canda's came the house of Mr. Mahlon Ogden, which escaped the Fire but afterwards gave place to the Newberry Library. This was the home for many years of two other charming sisters, Mrs. Ogden, one of the noblest and most beautiful women Chicago has ever known, and her delightful sister, Mrs. Wright, afterwards Mrs. J. Y. Scammon. All the three "Ogden families" were celebrated for their hospitality, and it was a rare thing when their homes were not full of guests and their carriages overflowing with friends and neighbors.

There was no lack of good public amusements in the fifties and sixties, with North's and McVicker's theaters, and Metropolitan, Bryan, Smith and Nixon, and Farwell Halls, as their scene of action. Two of my sisters kept scrap-books of their programs, and from these I glean many items of the "gay world" of that time. The first record is a program of *The Witch's Daughter*, given by Mrs. Julia Dean Hayne at the Chicago Theater in 1855. The boxes sold from three to five dollars, other seats at from twenty-five to seventy-five cents apiece. There was a notable concert in 1857 with the Great Western Band, Messrs. Ahner and others, as attractions; packages of five tickets for one dollar being for sale at Higgins Bros. and Well's shoe stores. There were concerts of the Chicago Musical Union, with Mrs. Emma G. Bostwick as soprano; Mrs. Mozart in concert; Mme. Johannsen in *Child of the Regiment;* Mr. Hans Balatka and the Philharmonic Concerts; Parodi in *Ernani;* Carlotta Patti and Gottschalk (with tickets at twenty-five to fifty cents!).

"Little Adelina Patti" first sang in Chicago as a child, at the Tremont House, before we moved to town, in 1854. The giving of one opera under Mr. Balatka's direction, I remember caused us quite a feeling of triumph for our city on one occasion. A foreign visitor of those days, Colonel Lichtenheim, thoroughly posted about operas, was talking over those that had been presented in Chicago. He seemed much surprised at their number and at last exclaimed, "I know there is one you have never seen, *The Czar and the Zimmerman.* Great was our joy to be able to reply that we had, and we felt deeply grateful to Mr. Balatka for having enabled us to say so.

In 1859, at McVicker's, came Strakosch with his opera troupe, Mmes. Colson, Cora de Wilhoest, and Strakosch; and Messrs. Squires and Brignoli as stars. This was the first appearance here of Brignoli — that wonderful tenor whose voice, to my mind, has never been equalled. There being no phonographs in those days, this statement cannot be proved, or disproved, but I doubt its being contradicted by those who heard him and who have heard our later tenors, Campanini, de Reszké, Caruso, and others. Good opera seasons in 1863 and '64 at McVicker's brought Lozini, Susini, Adelaide Phillips, Cordier, and Tamaro; while in 1858, *Uncle Tom's Cabin* at North's Theater; in 1864, Frank Aiken in the *Ticket of Leave Man,* at Wood's Museum; and in 1867, Joseph Jefferson in *Rip Van Winkle*; and Edwin Booth and Mary McVicker in *Romeo and Juliet*, indicate that the theatrical side of the amusement world was provided for.

On April 20, 1865, occurred what was probably the most important event in Chicago's operatic history, when Crosby's Opera house was opened with *Il Trovatore* as the opera, and that inspiring soprano, Mme. Zucchi, as Leonora; and Massimiliana, Morensi, Bellini, and Colletti in the other rôles. It is cheering to see in the newspaper account, that the opera house and the opera seemed to be more important than the audience and the costumes thereof.

That opera season lasted a month, and great was the pleasure it gave. The newspaper description of the house itself speaks of "the blue and gold, the artistically chiseled figures, the beautifully carved pillars of white and gold inclosing the proscenium boxes, the crimson and gold curtains of these, the beautiful frescoed chariot of Aurora sailing through the clouds, the mellow moonlike light emanating from above and throwing its pale shadow over the beautiful faces of our Chicago houris."

Alas, that the great fire deprived Chicago of what, despite the hyperbole of the foregoing account, was a really lovely auditorium. It was my good fortune to be present that opening night and the charming effect of the white, gold and blue coloring, the lightness and grace of all details, made a deep impression on every one. Of course the dressing of the "Chicago houris" was such as to do honor to the occasion, though little attraction nowadays could be found in the fashions of the sixties.

There were numerous entertainments with local talent. On a program of the second graduating exercises of the

Chicago High School in 1858, I find the names of Albert G. Lane, Charles V. Kelly, and H. F. Chesbrough. In 1865, for the benefit of the Sanitary Fair, "the young ladies and gentlemen of Chicago" presented *The Loan of a Lover*, *Perfection*, and *Poor Pillicody*. Well do I recall a play, *The Little Treasure*, given by our then young people, in which Miss Clara Gage, now Mrs. Edwin Clarke, gave a most charming impersonation of the title rôle.

In 1863, a company of ladies and gentlemen from Detroit, with Mr. and Mrs. Richard Stors Willis at their head, repeated in Chicago for the benefit of the Soldiers' Northeastern Fair, a program of most beautiful tableaux, which they had given in Detroit. This was quite a "society event," and one of great interest to me as, Mrs. Willis being my mother's cousin, she and Mr. Willis were our guests and it seemed to me almost like being "behind the curtain" at a play!

War times brought many such entertainments, giving a touch of brightness in the shadows. Numbers of the young men had gone, some never to return. The city was full of patriotism, flags flying, war-songs filled the air, with the Roots as composers and the Lombard brothers as singers.

Before the war, came the Lincoln-Douglas campaign, with the great meeting at the Wigwam, and party feeling running high. A night when the "Wide-Awakes" serenaded my father with their marching-song, "Ain't we glad we joined the Wide-Awakes! joined the Wide-Awakes! down in Illinois, — Lincoln boys we, Lincoln boys we, . . . " seemed an exciting occasion to me. My last sight of Mr. Lincoln was when, after his nomination, he came to St. James's Church with Isaac N. Arnold. When, in 1865, he next came back, we watched the solemn procession that bore his body through the streets of our mourning city. I have few personal memories of him, but I recall his walking, at my father's request, under the chandelier in our parlor, to see if his tall head would hit it. War times brought the great Sanitary Fair, and our women were quite as busy with making bandages and scraping lint, as were, recently, the women of to-day for our friends across the seas, and for the American Army and Navy.

One sad feature of those days was the severed friendships. Some of our southern citizens were "copperheads," and a copperhead was *persona non grata* even to his best friends. But the southerners who stood by the Union, like the Bryans, and Clarksons, "grappled their friends anew with hooks of steel."

The great meetings at Bryan Hall, April 18–24, 1861, and April 9, 1863, at all of which my father presided, were enthusiastic occasions; and the list of speakers and contributors for war funds includes most of the well-known names of the city: Julian S. and George Rumsey, Solomon Sturges, William D. Houghteling, Orrin Lunt, Dr. Brainerd, Dr. N. S. Davis, Gurdon S. Hubbard, Judge Van H. Higgins, Samuel Hoard, Edwin Tinkham, and others.

Another ante-war memory is of a little upper room in a brick building near Rush Street bridge, where he who was afterward Colonel Ellsworth — a slight, alert figure, with gallant bearing — drilled his Zouaves. It was a sad "fortune of war" that brought his death in the very beginning of hostilities. While his military career was too short to make his name widely known, in Chicago, at least, it should never be forgotten.

An important part in the lives of our youthful citizens was played by our schools. On the South Side, "The Misses Lane and Baker's," and the Dearborn Seminary, are the ones I best remember. On the North Side, the school of Mrs. Whiting and her daughter, Miss Mary, was the place where many of the "young ideas" of that generation were trained. Mrs. Lewis' School, on Indiana Street, was the principal school then. Everyone loved and admired Mrs. Hiram Lewis and her daughters, Anna and Mary (afterwards Mrs. Otto Matz). The older girls with Mrs. Lewis, and the little ones with Miss Anna, were fortunate. (Miss Mary took charge of music lessons only.) Then there was Misses Saunders' school where, I remember, the Marys—Mary Adams, Mary Wadsworth, Mary Murray, Mary Howe, and myself—outnumbered Queen Mary of Scotland's, Marie Seaton, Marie Beaton, and Marie Carmichael. Later on, Mrs. Newall (afterwards Mrs. Kate Doggett), had a school which some of us attended. Then there was Mr. Snow's school for boys on Huron Street, and here I remember seeing Louis James,[1] who was always getting up plays, act *Bombastes Furioso* with a fire that gave promise of the name he won on the stage later. In a letter from Mrs. Nellie Kinzie Gordon to Edward P. DeWolf, she says that Louis James assured her he made his début as an actor in her father's barn! The Ogden School, a public school, took many pupils from the private schools. Then came M. Berteau's French school on Cass Street near Erie.

The physicians of those days, Drs. Brainerd, Freer, Blaney, Herrick, Davis, Small, and others, were a close part of our family lives; while the many fine lawyers, Messrs.

[1] Later, one of America's best-known comedians. —*Editor.*

I. N. Arnold, Edwin C. Larned, S. A. Goodwin, Van H. Higgins, E. B. McCagg, J. Y. Scammon, Judge William Beckwith, Mr. Blackwell, and Leonard Swett, made a bar of which one might well be proud.

One of our "institutions" was New Year's calls, when those on the "distaff" side of the family either hung out baskets to show they were not receiving, "or decked themselves in gallant array," ready to receive the masculine portion of the community who sallied forth, on foot or in carriages, singly or in groups, to give their New Year's good wishes. Sometimes the refreshments served included wine, but this was considered by some as "fast," and the results of so doing were not always fortunate. New Year's calls slowly disappeared, but they were pleasant, and the keeping and comparing of lists was always exciting. On those I have in my possession, appear the names of most of the "beaux and gallants" of the day. One New Year's, that dreadful January 1, 1863, when the mercury in the thermometer almost dropped out of sight, and the wind howled and the snow-drifts were deep, I remember plunging through the snow to carry to Dr. Clarkson a large card which, anticipating numerous calls, he had asked my brother to print, and which he expected to hang on his popular doorway. The legend it bore being, "Please walk in without knocking," my labor seemed quite unnecessary!

At Mrs. S. A. Goodwin's that same day, while the ladies, dressed in their best "bib and tucker," waited for the callers that did not appear, a carriage drove up and the driver brought in a small thermometer to which was attached the card of William H. Kerfoot!

Certainly so great a delight to old and young as the

Ogden skating-rink at the then foot of Ontario Street, near the lake, must not be forgotten. Here, those of us who were still at school, met after school and on Saturdays for the joy of ice-skating; and on the afternoons and evenings, when we had carnivals, it was a gay sight, with the many lights, pretty costumes, and graceful skaters. I remember one afternoon when we were all singing with the band, hearing a beautiful voice near me. I turned and saw, and heard for the first time, Mrs. George B. Carpenter, a recent bride, whose lovely contralto was a gift to the musical life of Chicago, brought through her marriage into that musical family, the Carpenters.[1] Their homelike brick house in Indiana Street must have heard many a "concord of sweet sounds."

Another institution of our day was the custom of sitting on the front steps, though even then there were those who rather scorned that democratic meeting place. But for those of us who did not rejoice in porches and large grounds, they had their joys, and many were the pleasant summer evenings which my sisters' friends, young men and maidens, spent on our front steps. In fact it was even possible for unconventional people like ourselves to carry out chairs, and sit on the board platforms built across the ditches that ran along each side the street, and on which carriages drove up to the sidewalks. My memories of a wonderful comet of that year are always associated with watching it from our platform. Our streets certainly had their "ups and downs" in those days. Under the board sidewalks and in the roadside ditches lived many rats who doubtless considered themselves among the city's "first families."

[1] The sons of this family, Captain Benjamin, Judge George A., Hubbard, and John A., carry on the family's musical traditions. — *Editor.*

The social clubs were an important element in our life. One was "The Grasshoppers," which consisted largely of southerners living at that time near Ashland Avenue, among whom were the Badgers, Kerfoots, Harrisons, Honorés, Rogers, Walkers, and Halls. This was the first of many such organizations, and got its name from the fact that the dresses of the ladies, as they passed to each other's houses through the high grass of the fields, were often covered with grasshoppers.

As I look back through the perspective of the long years since those early days, I try to bring before me the atmosphere in which we "lived and moved and had our being." We all realize our tendency when old to think that "the former days were better than these," and must guard against that; but, while to-day sees great improvements, social, moral, religious, and philanthropic, as well as material, in some things we can claim much for the past. Naturally, in a smaller city and with less wealth, there was more simple living. Of course there were "high teas," when our mothers and fathers were regaled with "pound to a pound" preserves, chicken salad, escalloped oysters, pound-cake, fruit-cake and all other cakes known to womankind; and where they played old-fashioned whist and chess, — but such things as the bridge-parties of the present day with women playing for money were indeed rare. At many of our parties, ice-cream and cake for refreshments were considered "an elegant sufficiency." The ladies' dressing also was simpler than it is to-day. Young ladies wore organdies and tarlatans for party-gowns, and it can fairly be claimed that, in spite of a few exceptions, the gowns were modest. I remember that our rules for the popular Sans

Cérémonie Club required afternoon dress, — which in those days meant high neck and long sleeves, — very simple refreshments, but good music, and home by twelve o'clock. Escorts were not to bring carriages for the ladies. These rules were for all the parties except the last one of the season, and in spite of them, never was there a more popular club.

Of course there was no "organized charity," as we know it nowadays, but there was much of that now despised "basket charity," when friendships were formed between rich and poor. Certainly there was at that time far less class feeling. Most of our young people who sought to be philanthropic worked through their churches, and the churches and religious observances seemed to enter more closely into our home lives than is the case to-day. Many were our "Mothers in Israel," who did noble work. Mrs. Joseph T. Ryerson, Mrs. Reynolds, Mrs. Hoag, Mrs. Clarkson, Mrs. F. B. Peabody, Mrs. W. D. Houghteling, and many others, were our "United Charities." Perhaps, however, the greatest change is in the way everything in that era centered in the home. No such article as, "The Passing of Mother," suggested itself at that time. Even fathers were a part of family life, and were expected to have a voice. There were no dinner-parties for young people; no smoking by the women; gentlemen, even, asked permission to smoke when in general company; hours were early, and it was rare to find wine at a party. "Square-dances" were popular, and at one time a program would have two to every "round" dance. Afterwards they alternated, and then the square-dances hid their defeated heads entirely.

Perhaps one thing that kept the home-ties strong was the

established "festivals," Christmas and Thanksgiving, which were always spent in the bosom of the family and added their happy associations to "the dearest spot on earth." It was a homelike, simple, friendly life we led, and those of us who look back on those decades as the "days of our youth," see them through the shimmering clouds that hang between us and them, and give thanks for the "good old times," while we bid "all hail" to the powers and opportunities of the present!

IX

FORGOTTEN CHICAGO

BY MADAME CHARLES BIGOT

THERE comes before my mind a little picture of which I can recall every detail: A small, cozy salon in a Paris apartment, Rue de Ponthieu, close to the Champs-Elysées; an open fire; a round table with a big lamp on it; our mother, surrounded by those among us who were old enough to understand, reading a long letter on thin paper, written very small, for in those far-off days postage was abominably dear and we were not rich. These closely-written pages came from over the ocean, from a town with an absurdly difficult name which we pronounced something like "Tchicaggo," and which was situated on a lake as big as a sea. How my elder sister and I listened, as to some wonderful tale, open-mouthed and wide-eyed! The letters were written by our father[1] who had left us for a venturesome journey into the unknown. They told of a hearty reception, kindnesses without number, unceasing work.

And this is how it all came about.

A most charming gentleman, who had become quite intimate in our Paris home and whose name is associated with the early history of Chicago, William B. Ogden, never wearied of talking about the prairie town, destined, he felt sure, to become a very great city indeed. It has become

[1] G. P. A. Healy, the distinguished artist.—*Editor.*

greater and richer and more important even than our visitor imagined it could ever be.

Our father had had a remarkably successful early career; he had been sent by Louis Philippe, first to Windsor Castle, with Queen Victoria's permission, to copy historic portraits; then to America to paint portraits of well-known statesmen for the Versailles gallery. He took this opportunity to collect an immense number of likenesses of orators and political men which he utilized in his great picture of Webster replying to Hayne, now in Faneuil Hall, Boston.

After the fall of his royal patron, the enormous expense incurred in the painting of this big picture, caused the young artist some financial embarrassment. The family was growing rapidly; there was always a baby in the house in those days. Two of the older children, both boys, had died in childhood, but the series of girls continued with alarming regularity.

Mr. Ogden, keen-eyed and shrewd, persuaded my father to go to Chicago, on a visit at least, and with true American hospitality opened his house to his new friend. It was from that house, at the head of which were Mr. and Mrs. Edwin Sheldon, brother-in-law and sister of the owner, that came the closely-written pages of thin paper. I suppose that we did not clearly understand everything they contained, but we were fascinated. Once the letter told of cold such as we had never imagined: "I stood," said the writer, "on the high steps of a house where I meant to pay a visit and the fierce wind, the cruel cold, made my old Roman cloak seem a mere sheet of paper." What sort of country was this, and how could one live in it without being frozen into a lump of ice?

But there were many other details which made us glow with anticipation for, almost from the beginning, we felt dimly that we, too, were destined to see that strange town of "Tchicaggo."

After a year came the long-expected summons. We were all to cross the ocean as soon as our mother could have the furniture boxed, get a few clothes made, and start on the lengthy and painful journey.

What were our first impressions of Chicago? They remain very vague in my mind.

As no home was yet ready for us, we were all received with open arms in the big, roomy Ogden house, situated in the middle of a garden filled with superb trees. I had just made my first acquaintance with Fenimore Cooper's romances, and I liked to imagine great, stealthy, soft-footed Indians lurking behind those trees, ready to swoop down upon us children — with rescue at hand, of course. Unless I am much mistaken, Mrs. C. Wheeler, an elder sister of Mrs. Sheldon, was then also at the Ogden house with her children, some of whom were about our ages. I remember especially Ellie, because she wore little low-necked frocks, a fashion I longed to imitate. Many, many years after, I saw her as Mrs. Alexander C. McClurg, a rare woman, whom I greatly loved and, later, most sincerely mourned.

Without any transition in my remembrances of these prehistoric days, I see ourselves installed in a tall shell of a frame house on Illinois Street, rather near Clark Street. My mother trembled when the furnace roared and sent up great blasts of heat. She felt sure the tinder-box of a house would burn up; and so it did — but after we had left it.

We had not long been in our new home when one morning at breakfast time, we noticed through the dining-room window, some strange and certainly unexpected guests on the porch. We went out to investigate and found ourselves face to face with real American Indians, men and women; among the last, I fancy, who ever visited this spot which was once the hunting-ground of their forefathers. These poor creatures carried no tomahawks and very gratefully accepted the meal my mother caused to be served to them. This really was an American episode, and my romantic young soul was satisfied.

It would be difficult to enumerate the kind friends who opened their homes and their hearts to the rather bewildered little troop of uprooted pseudo-Americans. My mother was English to the backbone and remained such to her last day, ever loyal to "her Queen," whom she somewhat resembled, and who was about her own age. As to the rest of us, we seemed, what Mr. McCagg later called, "blasted foreigners"; but we took to our new home with great zest after the first surprise had passed. In many of the families we quickly got to know there were boys and girls — especially the latter — with whom we were soon intimate.

Our best friends we found in the families of Judge Drummond, Judge Mark Skinner, and Isaac N. Arnold. And now that our hair has turned gray or white, they are still close and dear to us.

My mother was particularly fond of Mrs. Drummond, whose modest pecuniary position, borne with unswerving dignity and courage, recalled her own circumstances. Judge Drummond, a very remarkable man, was universally respected and admired. His foremost fellow-citizens were proud to be invited to his nice, comfortable and very simple home.

We, the older children, spent many a cheerful hour in that living-room with its worn carpet and faded armchairs. We enjoyed there some of the happiest, jolliest evenings I can remember. All of us, boys and girls, were as chummy as possible without — as yet — any thought of flirtation.

Then, for my sister and myself, came the question of school. Of course, our first education had been in French, though we had been taught some English too.

It was decided that we should go to a school kept by two highly-educated eastern ladies, Miss Lane and Miss Baker. This school was held in the basement of a church; of what denomination was the church, I have no idea. At any rate, during the week the basement was filled with the murmur of young voices. Of course, it was only a day-school. It was a very bare and ugly place, supported by wooden pillars. Rows and rows of small desks were occupied by the daughters of the "first families" of Chicago, that is, of the old settlers. I forthwith fell madly in love with Miss Baker, the younger of our two teachers, a pretty young woman, as I remember her, with very white skin and clear, rather cold, blue eyes. She taught English and encouraged my feeble efforts.

My sister and I used to attend school most regularly, generally crossing the river in a ferryboat at Rush Street, before the bridge was built. One morning, we boarded it as usual, I holding in my hand a theme for the beloved Miss Baker. Suddenly, there were cries of alarm; a steam tug was close upon us and the danger was great. Men shouted, women screamed; we remained close to each other, not uttering a sound, it seems to me. Luckily, just in time, the ferryman was able to lower the chain or cord and the tug passed by without upsetting us. But my masterpiece was lost in the very dirty water and I shudder still to think that we might have been drowned in that horrid, slimy river of long ago. When my brother grew up to the dignity of breeches and school, he was asked what was a river. He promptly answered: "A body of water that has a very bad smell."

Among the younger girls I noticed two, Minnie Burch and Sarah Farnham, who were always together. They were so natty, in their little short frocks and with curling hair that I regarded them with a curious sort of envy. When I was eight or ten, I never used to look as dainty as they. Sarah married an American. Minnie went to school at Fontainebleau. It had come to be a sort of home for the American girl, and she was married from it. Some years later, her first husband having died, she married his most intimate friend, M. Alexandre Ribot, who has made a great name for himself, was once very nearly elected President of the French Republic, and, during the great war, directed the finances of the country in a most masterly fashion. Madame Ribot has long been a very prominent figure in ministerial circles, where her charm and tact have made her a universal favorite.

Memories of other schoolmates flit before me, though only a few have remained distinct. But I see, especially, the room as a whole when I shut my eyes. In reality, my sister and I only remained at the Lane and Baker school about a year. I remember that the winter was a hard one, with blizzards and cruel cold, or else a thaw with such mud as we had never imagined, accustomed as we were to the clean Paris streets. But whatever the weather might be, we trotted off with our books under our arms. Our father, the kindest of men, was inflexible when he thought duty was involved. Personally, nothing stopped him when he had made up his mind to do a thing. And, what he could do, we were also forced to do. One day, I happened to be coming from school alone. The streets were in a terrible condition. In those days, the sidewalks were raised on high, I suppose for the better accommodation of thousands of the largest rats I ever saw in my life. Rickety steps led up to these sidewalks and, where the mud was deepest, a board was thrown across the street. Just as I put my foot on one end of such a plank, a great, coarse German put his on the other side. I had a strong sense of my personal dignity and it had been dinned into my ears that chivalry, supposed to have been banished from the old world, had taken refuge in the new, where my sex was held in high esteem. My dignity refused to yield. Chivalry, represented by this hyphenated American, held its ground — or rather advanced along the plank. We met in the middle. With a Teutonic curse, the man pushed me into the deep mud, and went on his way rejoicing, as though he had invaded a neutral country. I, poor tot, humbled and heart-broken, dragged my left leg, encased in filthy mud, as far as our house, where my mother consoled me, wiped away my tears — and washed me.

Among the stories of those times was the following: A man's head was visible above the sea of mud and kindly Samaritans proposed to throw him a rope that he might land in safety, at which he exclaimed: "Don't bother about me, I am riding a good horse." It must have been about this time that I had a curious adventure. I was a little intoxicated with the new liquor of liberty, and determined to go out into the world and see what it was like. Without saying anything to my mother, I sallied forth — probably it was a holiday, as I had no thought of school. At that period, from Illinois Street to Chicago Avenue the waves washed in where now stand great rows of houses and factories, and the lake possessed for me a singular attraction. I plodded through a wide sandy territory, where hovels were inhabited by a very queer population. Untidy women stood in doorways and looked at me askance; ragged children ran after me. I did not care. I was out for adventure. Soon, I reached the beautiful water's edge. I walked on good, firm sand. There were no evidences of the nearby town. Then came trees, many trees, to my mind a primeval forest. A forest had always had for me a peculiar fascination with its silence, broken only by rustling leaves, its depths full of mystery. Enchanted, I went on and on. What is now lovely Lincoln Park was a sombre tangle. I was absolutely alone in this new world, and if my heart beat a little faster than usual, that was added pleasure.

Only — only — from the dark woods suddenly emerged an ill-dressed man. He came toward me rapidly. Should I turn and run? Perish the thought! Besides, I knew that if he had evil intentions, he could easily overtake me. So I went on, but with less pleasure in my adventure. The man and I were rapidly nearing each other when — still from the woods — another man, an older one, came toward me. He looked severely at me:

"What are you doing here alone, little girl?"

"Just taking a walk."

"Well, turn around and walk home as fast as you can."

Meekly, I obeyed, internally most grateful to my gruff protector. At the sight of him, the young man had taken to his heels. When, at last, I reached the unsavory settlement by the water side, the policeman — for it must have been a policeman — was still following and protecting me.

I never boasted to my mother of my adventure.

Among the friends my parents had made were Mr. and Mrs. Thomas B. Bryan, who, in the late fifties, built a house and planted trees in a place derisively called Cottage Hill. The village now rejoices in the more appropriate name of Elmhurst, and nowadays, in 1919, we occasionally motor over to the old Bryan house, the same, but much enlarged. The trees are now magnificent, a veritable English park. Mr. Bryan advised my father to buy a little place just opposite — which he immediately did — and there established his young and numerous family.

It was a queer frame house, with a good many rooms, but so low of ceiling that when, one day, George Higginson came to call, he touched the ceiling with his hat, saying: "You are not very high up in the world here." I was silently indignant and looked upon our visitor as a very rude gentleman, for I, with my enthusiastic nature, took to country life — during the summer at least — most fervently. Besides the Bryans, we had but few neighbors. However, I remember pretty distinctly Mrs. Case, step-mother to Mrs. Henry W. King, and her small brood of children. But on the whole, our mother found this long sojourn in the country rather austere. We children had a governess, a nice

Maine girl of twenty-two — an advanced age, it seemed to us. I think her greatest recommendation was that she had a broken heart, which it was hoped might be mended in time. It evidently was, for later she was very happily married. It rendered her to us, the elder children, an object of much interest and speculation. We had a school-room fitted up on the second floor next to the billiard-room. Off this billiard room were tiny cells, occupied by the governess, my sister, and myself. To have a bedroom all to oneself seemed to us the greatest of luxuries, even though it might be about the size of a closet.

During this first winter, our one joy — and it was a great one — was to crowd around our mother and listen to her reading of anything and everything, poetry and prose, French and English. The days might be dull, with horrid arithmetic or what not, but we could always look forward to the evenings, when bedtime came ever too soon. And our young governess was as eager as we were ourselves. I think I have never heard anyone read better than our mother. In that way, she made Shakespeare and her beloved Byron familiar to us, as well as the best novelists. She read *Les Misérables* of Victor Hugo, which fascinated us . . . and how many other works!

Our parents soon understood that for my sister Agnes and myself some sort of instruction, other than that given us by our nice governess — who at least had learned some French from us — had become necessary. We were taken to a convent in western Virginia, highly recommended to my father.

This school period spent far from Chicago, with our holidays in the country, is quite out of my subject. Meanwhile, the war of Secession was going on. We, of course, were ardent northerners and there were many southern girls in the school. The nuns were forced to forbid any allusion to politics, else we should have fought the battles over again in our class-rooms. So, after one long stride, I must get back to Chicago once more, as a grown girl, when Agnes and I began to see something of society, in a very modest way, however, — very different from the "coming out" of the modern young lady, with its wealth of flowers, its innumerable engagements, its whirl and fatigue, ending at times in absolute lassitude — until one becomes, what is so gracefully called, a "back number," or is married. Nothing of that sort was the fashion in the sixties, at least so far as I can remember.

Let me try to see the past, as clearly as one can after such a lapse of time.

My father bought a house on Wabash Avenue, between Jackson and Van Buren streets. It was a frame house, originally small, probably, but to which numerous additions had been made, so that it was of rather singular construction, very deep for its width, giving us a large living-room, excellent for dancing. Unfortunately, during our long absence from Chicago, the friends we had made as children had grown up in their own way. We were now almost as much strangers as on our first arrival. Some of the girls we still knew and loved; they received us with open arms, and that was very pleasant. But we knew almost no young men. An experience of mine at that time has remained stamped on my mind with most unpleasant vividness.

A friend of the family who had a daughter, a little older than I, out of the goodness of his heart, asked me to accompany them to some big ball, given where, on what occasion, I do not remember. A ball — a real ball! I was frightened, but yet in a state of excitement and expectation. All the novels I had read, those of Miss Austen especially, turned on such events: the heroine generally met the hero at an "assembly," and great were the consequences thereof. But when I found myself in the midst of a crowd where I knew no one, I began to wish myself safely back in my little room, far from curious and unsympathetic glances. The young lady whom I had been asked to accompany was soon whirled away by a partner. By some chance a young man, whom I knew, asked me for a waltz, but ever, ever so far off. My friend's unfortunate father stoically sat beside me until I so earnestly begged him to leave me to my sad fate, that he did. Before long I was submerged by rows of chairs occupied by dowagers, utter strangers, who looked at me askance. I could have cried from sheer mortification and misery. Hour after hour of this torture passed. Meanwhile, I saw my one partner go by, evidently looking for me. I hid behind a stout lady. Anything, rather than to be found in my forlorn condition; I felt sure that I had grown ten years older and ten times plainer after this ordeal. Since then my pity for wall-flowers has grown apace.

Before very long, however, we made our own friends and our circle was enlarged. My father, more popular than ever, saw his studio always filled, and my mother's quiet, gentle grace in receiving his friends, old and new, made of our home a center. Little by little, my sister Agnes and I, not only went to parties, but helped our parents to receive. In these days when the smallest entertainment is adorned by masses of flowers from the fashionable florist, where there is rivalry as to the newest gowns, when balls have to be given at hotels or halls, because one's own drawing-room is too small to contain the innumerable guests, and where everything is regulated according to a well-established, rigid and somewhat monotonous method, these informal receptions of ours would seem singularly provincial. But we enjoyed them and they became popular among our friends. Someone opened the piano and we had many a gay waltz or polka, long before the "Boston" became the rage — that poor, graceful Boston, now so forgotten and superseded by queer dances, not always very proper to my old-fashioned mind. We always wound up with a Virginia Reel, as in old Sir Roger de Coverley's time — just think of it! Often we would go to each other's houses without any invitation at all and, as soon as a few couples had assembled — quick! the piano was opened and we had an hour of delightful dancing, in our every-day clothes. We also got up private theatricals of a primitive kind, which greatly amused us, if not the spectators.

Our way of living differed greatly from that of the present day. As my father's work was chiefly in the morning, we had a regular old-time American breakfast, with meat, potatoes, cakes, and so forth. The dinner was at two o'clock. At seven, we had supper, or "high tea," as it was called, the coziest and most elastic of meals. Constantly some friend, or friends, would drop in. There was plenty for all: cold meats, hot biscuits, jellies, cakes, tea. It was a simple sort of life, but a singularly pleasant one, it seems to me.

Then, often in the mornings, we would go and chat with our girl friends, the Drummonds, the Skinners, the Arnolds, the Brainerds, the Newberrys, and others. In the last named family there were two really beautiful daughters, Mary and Julia. Both of them died young. Their fine house was in the midst of a superb "yard," occupying a whole block, bounded by Rush, Pine, Erie and Ontario streets, shaded by magnificent old trees. Chicago in those days fully justified its name of the "Garden City." This household was kept up in a somewhat European style, though even there, I do not think that there was a butler. The fact that Mary had her own suite of beautiful rooms rather awed me, but we were very good friends all the same. Some years later, we saw them again in Europe, where they were much sought after. But their young lives were embittered by the fear of falling a prey to fortune-hunters, and they turned aside from many a suitor who, very likely, saw, not their fortune, but themselves.

Another great house, most luxuriously comfortable, opened its doors to us: that of Mr. and Mrs. Ezra B. McCagg, which also stood among great trees and beautiful flowers, on Clark Street where now are the Walton apartments. When my father first came to Chicago, the McCaggs were abroad. On their return, Mr. McCagg absolutely refused to make the acquaintance of that "Frenchified artist," who was being lionized by everybody and about whom all the women were making such a fuss. But he did finally meet the "Frenchified" painter and very soon succumbed to his charm. They remained intimate friends to the last.

I have now come to the age of wide hoop-skirts, of war horrors, and of heroism, of a more dignified Chicago, where, however, frame shanties still held their own by the side of tall, marble-fronted houses, very grand and somewhat coldly uniform in style. The North Side kept its beautifully shaded streets and was still very rickety as to sidewalks. Michigan Avenue had become the fashionable residence quarter. Our Wabash Avenue retained its look of suburban beauty, with its two rows of fine trees and its frame houses, low, but comfortable. The sidewalks, however, were a terror. One still had to climb four or five crazy steps held together by huge nails; these often caught the lowest hoop of our voluminous skirts. Many were the falls we endured. These same hoops were a source of annoyance and of shame too, as, in order to scramble into a carriage we always had to be preceded by the extended skirt or to let it go up unblushingly behind. But carriages were rare in those days. I suppose that there must have been some sort of public conveyance, but I cannot recall it. How we covered the great distances between our different homes, I do not remember. I suppose that we were better walkers than we now are. We have grown lazy, thanks to the street-car, to the taxi, or, frequently, to the automobile or "electric" of our well-to-do friends.

Meanwhile, in spite of war and apprehension as to the future, my father kept very busy. Among his sitters at this time was a very pretty girl, one of Chicago's belles, who, in spite of her beauty, sometimes ventured to improve on nature. My father looked upon this as disloyal rivalry: paint against paint. One morning, the young lady arrived with so high a color, that much embarrassed, he said: "My dear child, you must have walked too fast, you are so flushed that I must put off the sitting until to-morrow — when I beg you to come in a carriage." At the following sitting, she was less "flushed."

At times my father went here or there, professionally. In

Washington, Lincoln sat to him for the fine portrait which, with many others, is in the Newberry Library. Generals Grant and Sherman, and Admiral Porter also sat to him. He was then meditating the picture called, "The Peacemakers," which showed Lincoln, Grant, Sherman, and Porter on the *River Queen*, discussing the conditions of peace. This picture was destroyed when the Calumet Club, to which it belonged, was burned to the ground.

The great excitement of those years was the building and opening of Chicago's first opera house. Even as I reflect upon it, I cannot quite make out why the excitement should have been so universal, as well as so intense. Of course, it was a justifiable subject of pride to our young town to possess as fine a theater as could be found in the eastern cities and, as I remember it, the house was not only large and commodious, but very harmonious in all its details. These, however, were minor considerations. It was built, not by a company, but by one man, a society man, Mr. Crosby. He had a great fortune, of course, otherwise, he could not have built the Crosby Opera House. According to my remembrance of him, he was neither handsome, nor fascinating. There were many men in Chicago, even then, richer than he proved to be, but they dwindled into insignificance in his presence. I do not pretend to solve this mystery. It was so, because it was so. He possessed a fine turnout, with two high-bred horses that he drove himself. The palpitating question of the day was: "Whom is Mr. Crosby going to take out?"

It was the fashion in those primitive times for young girls to go out with young men, even to the theater or to balls. When my sister first came out, a very well-known society man asked her to go to the opera with him: "Thank you," she said, "but we are all going with Papa." At which he stared at her in amazement, and when it was understood that we were "Frenchified" enough never to go anywhere without our parents, the amazement turned to something like indignation. This was one of the things which, in our society life, was singularly against us.

Naturally, when the time came for the opening night of the Crosby Opera House, at which we all assisted, public curiosity was on tiptoe to discover who was the fortunate belle who would be brought in by the hero of the evening. It was Miss Mattie Hill, a remarkably beautiful and stylish girl, whom, in advance, we dubbed Mrs. Crosby. But Mrs. Crosby she never became. It seems to me that the opera given on that occasion was *Martha*, and beautifully given it was, with Clara Louise Kellogg, Brignoli, Susini, and others in the cast whose names escape me. The old-fashioned music, light and graceful, — long before the Wagner craze and certainly long before the Strauss madness, — was a delight to this unsophisticated audience.

Mr. Crosby's extraordinary triumph came to a sudden collapse, how or why, I have never understood. I suppose his great venture had ruined him.

At about the same period, a big bazaar, The Sanitary Fair, was held by society women for the relief of the war victims. We helped in one of the booths. General Sherman, fresh from his Georgia raid, was in Chicago just then and was the hero of the moment. My father and he were devoted friends, and later his daughters and we became quite intimate, especially during the Shermans' stay in Rome. So he patronized our booth and gave us many of his military buttons, which we sold at a good price. On one occasion, I think it was General Grant who addressed the audience from a platform. The crowd was so great that it was almost alarming. We were protected by our counter, but those just outside seemed in danger of being crushed. A young man, whom I recognized as a member of the Italian Opera company, jumped over the counter, among our pretty, useless knick-knacks, and landed at my side. When he discovered that I spoke French fluently, his joy knew no bounds and he straightway began making desperate love to me, declaring that American girls were far too charming to marry American business men. I was immensely amused and perhaps — who knows? — a little flattered, not having been over-spoiled by masculine homage. When I try to recall the singer's name, or even his looks, I fail to do so.

And here is a very different picture. One March day came the sudden, terrifying, tragic news of Lincoln's assassination. It was as though each and all of us had lost one near and dear. A whole nation weeping is a tremendous and magnificent sight. I do not know how it was accomplished, but scarcely had the news come to be understood, than Chicago was draped in black: every shop, every house, had its signs of mourning. How so much black material had been instantly found, I cannot tell, but the fact remains.

With this picture of universal sorrow my souvenirs of American life come to an end.

My father, terribly overworked, needed a long rest, and my mother decided that the only way to force the paint brushes from his hand was to go back to Europe for a year or two. This "rest" lasted until 1892, with many a journey to and fro for him alone, except when my mother, with one or two of the younger girls, accompanied him. He was already an old man when he decided that he wanted to return to his native land and to die there. The end came in 1894.

X

A KENTUCKY COLONY

By Carter H. Harrison

If you will look at the map of Chicago, you will find a subdivision marked down as Ashland Second Addition to Chicago. Just what its boundaries are, has escaped my mind, and I used to class myself as a pretty fair real-estate man at that. The old Harrison homestead, which formerly stood at the southwest corner of Ashland Avenue and Jackson Street, however, was within this territory.

In my boyhood days Ashland Avenue was known as Reuben Street. When "Hey! Rube!" came into its greatest vogue as a term of ridicule and reproach, the name of the street, upon petition of its sorely-tried residents, was changed to that of the subdivision.

The name of Ashland was taken from the country home of Kentucky's greatest statesman, Henry Clay. The "Millboy of the Slashes" lived and died at Ashland, the splendid mansion on the outskirts of Lexington, Kentucky, the shade of whose ash trees still mellows the fresh green of its blue-grass lawns.

As may readily be assumed, the subdividers were Kentuckians — clear-eyed, sharp-witted, big-hearted Kentuckians — lovers of man and beast, sons of the farm whose affections naturally ran to trees and flowers, to horses, dogs, and chickens; to the pleasures of a hospitable table, groaning under the weight of good things to eat and drink for the elders; to the joys of the dance for the young people.

In the days of which I write, Reuben Street was a dirt road bordered on either side by a deep ditch to carry away the surface water — no light task in the early spring weather of nearly a half-century ago when, from the scattered houses which fringed the rambling city as far as the Des Plaines River ten miles away, the prairies, flooded knee-deep, became a lake.

South of Union Park to the Burlington tracks at Sixteenth Street — the limits of my boyish territorial ken — there were seven houses in Reuben Street.

At the southeast corner of Madison Street and what is now known as Ogden Avenue, stood the rambling frame structure of the Washingtonian Home. In the earlier days, this had been the Bull's Head Tavern, the hostelry for the first Stock Yards of Chicago. In the late fifties the Stock Yards were moved to Bridgeport, their present location, and the old tavern passed into the hands of the Washingtonian Home. For years this corner was the western terminus of the Madison Street car-line with its seagoing, one-horse rattle-traps, whose drivers had imposed upon them the double duty of serving as money-changer and conductor! There were no street-car men's unions in those days!

About 1874, when the Home became financially able to erect its present structure, the old building was moved away to some site in the northwestern section of the city — just where, I have never been able to learn. But "somewhere in Chicago" the historic structure may still be standing, its erstwhile glory gone, a forgotten relic of early days when farmers and cattle-breeders were wont to come to town on the old plank road to meet stockmen and packers at trade by day, to enjoy by night the bright lights of what was then but little more than a frontier town.

There was as yet no Ogden Avenue to perpetuate the name and memory of Chicago's first mayor. The street was notorious as the Southwestern Plank Road, compared with which the corduroy "tote-roads" of the lumbermen in the pine-woods country would seem veritable boulevards.

There were then seven houses in Reuben Street. One of these was "the chicken-woman's," at the southwest corner of Reuben and Monroe streets. She probably had another name — a good old Irish patronymic on the order of O'Brien, McInerney or Gallagher: I did not know it. She was "the chicken-woman" to all of us. Her home, an eye-sore to the neighborhood, was a tumble-down frame shack, fenced in with a dilapidated barricade originally intended to keep her two cows, her goats, and her geese within an enclosure, but which, long since fallen to pieces, had ceased to serve its purpose.

If I close my eyes to-day, even after all these years, I can see myself, a barefooted boy, crossing the road to give the dogs on the place a wide berth; the hissing of her geese, the quacking of her ducks, and the clatter of her chickens still ring in my ears.

The first of the old homes of the district was built by Henry H. Honoré, who, in 1916, passed away at the age of ninety-two years, one of the most vigorous, most public-spirited, most ambitious, most progressive of the men Kentucky contributed to the up-building and development of Chicago. He built at the southwest corner of Reuben and

Jackson streets. For years the mansion, for such it really was, served as a landmark of the West Side; its breezy air of hospitality, its jutting bay-windows, its spacious pillared front porch, its cupola, and its cheery, smiling grounds are still remembered by old-time Chicagoans.

Judge John G. Rogers, another good Kentuckian, father of the late George Mills Rogers, of Mrs. Samuel P. McConnell, and of Mrs. Joseph M. Rogers, built a home and lived at the corner of Monroe and Honoré streets. Somewhere in the same neighborhood were the firesides of Judge Samuel M. Moore and of Judge Murray F. Tuley. Farther west, at the southwest corner of Madison and Robey streets, lived John E. Owsley. All were Kentuckians and prominent in the early business and political history of the city. The A. C. Badger home at the southwest corner of Reuben Street and Tyler (as Congress Street was then known) had been built by another Kentuckian, Colonel Winchester. A. C. Badger was the father of Mrs. Turlington Harvey, of Mrs. Robert L. Henry, and of the famous beauty of those days, Eva, who became the wife of Charles Angell. At the corner of Sangamon and Van Buren streets lived Judge Morris, the second mayor of Chicago, whose wife played such a prominent part in helping the rebel prisoners at Camp Douglas.

My father, in those early days, lived in the home he himself had built at the southwest corner of Hermitage Avenue and Tyler Street, to which he moved in 1860 from the Boardman House, a fashionable *pension* hotel, in which, by the way, I was born in April of that year, located and still standing at the southwest corner of Clark and Harrison streets.

In 1866 the Honorés moved to Michigan Avenue on the

South Side and were thus the first in the long line of those who established the fashion of peregrinations of west siders to the more modish districts of the North and South sides. Our family thereupon moved to the quarters vacated by the Honoré family which my father had bought, and our old Hermitage Avenue home passed into other hands, finally to be torn down to make room for the buildings of the Presbyterian Hospital.

The homes of the Honoré, Winchester, Owsley, and Harrison families had grounds covering the entire blocks on which they were located. These Kentuckians were farmers' boys; plenty of space and fresh air were necessities to them. On their grounds they kept their horses, cows, and chickens, and here they had their gardens in which all the family vegetables were raised. My father, a farmer to his finger-tips, went further in this path perhaps than any of the others, for he cured all the hams and the bacon needed for his family use.

And I had good cause to remember it. For upon me, at the early age of eight to ten years, devolved the duty of keeping the hickory-wood fire ever alive upon the altar in the smoke-house. Speaking of a smudge-fire in a smoke-house as an altar may smack of the irreverential to some. Let them but remember that the obligation of keeping it going to an old time Kentuckian came close to being a religious ceremony. They will then pardon me.

The late fall and early winter was hog-killing time. Long before daylight it was necessary for me to roll out of bed to start the smudge for the day. On many a morning I had to brush the snow from the wood-pile and kick apart the hickory sticks which during the frosty night had been frozen into a solid mass. With fingers half-congealed, with eyes smarting and running copious tears from the acrid smoke, I learned in the task one lesson which has stood me in good stead during all the years of a busy life: the need of constant care and attention to things if they are going to be done right.

On the day the body of the martyred President Lincoln passed through Chicago to lie here in state, before being laid away in its last resting-place at Springfield, a terrific windstorm, approaching a hurricane in its intensity, lifted the Hermitage Avenue smoke-house of my father from its underpinning, and laid it low, its framework and planking, as well as all its valuable contents, a jumbled mass of debris.

As Chicago advanced in dignity and prosperity, Reuben Street became Ashland Avenue and the old homestead was given a street number — at first 163, later 231 Ashland Avenue. Here our family lived from 1866 to 1904 with the exception of three years, from 1873 to 1876 to be exact, which we spent in Germany.

During these three years the home was occupied by Samuel J. Walker and his family. He was also a Kentuckian, one of the breeziest of all the dashing real-estate operators of the early days in the Windy City, the father of Judge Charles M. Walker, of the present Cook County Circuit Court, and of Dr. S. J. Walker, also of Chicago.

A fine lot of hams and sides of bacon, all sugar-cured in the most approved Kentucky style, as well as a quantity of home-made sausages, were left for the delectation of the Walker family palates.

In the dining-room of this old home on the night of

October 28, 1893, in the closing hours of the World's Fair, at which he had put in a busy day, my father passed away — the victim of an assassin's bullet. Thenceforth the old home had such trying memories of his tragic death, that none of his children cared to live there, even had they been able to afford to keep up the roomy house and spacious grounds in the old accustomed manner.

As a child I used to hear an interesting story connected with the building of the old home. The building was up, the roof almost shingled when, for some reason, the carpenters quit work. Whether it was a forerunner of the modern strike, the result of a disagreement, or just an ordinary laying down of the tools on a job, I do not know. It is enough for the purpose of the story that the men stopped their labors while the roof remained incomplete. A thunderstorm was brewing. Black clouds lay off in the southwest, darkening the skies. It was important that the shingling of the roof be completed before the storm should break. So in good, neighborly, whole-souled Kentucky fashion, Mr. Honoré commandeered the services of his friends, among whom were Colonel Winchester, John G. Rogers, and my father. Off went coats and collars and in a short while the remaining shingles were laid and the roofing completed.

Now comes the nub of the story. While the work was in progress, at the corner of Reuben and Harrison streets, only three blocks away, the sheriff of Cook County was publicly executing a criminal, and Mr. Honoré furnished his guests with an opera-glass that they might take turns in watching proceedings and, incidentally, that he might keep them on the job!

The Honorés' and Winchesters' were two of the seven

Reuben Street homes. At the southwest corner of Adams Street lived S. S. Hayes, the donor to Chicago of Union Park; not a Kentuckian, but having many of the characteristics of that strong race. At the northeast corner of Jackson Street lived Henry Waller, who, with his brothers, James B., Edward, and William, did their share towards keeping up the traditions of the Kentucky builders of Chicago. At the northeast corner of Van Buren Street the house, still standing on the spot, was built in the later sixties; it remained idle for some years, for reasons unknown to me until finally it became the home of Jasper D. Ward, who served two terms in Congress from the old west-side district. Halfway between Van Buren and Tyler streets, on the west side of the street, stood the W. S. Bryan home. This completed the roll-call of Reuben Street houses prior to 1866.

The two blocks east of us from Reuben Street to Loomis Street were vacant prairie. Like all the other land of the neighborhood, what with the rains and melting snows, these blocks were flooded deep all winter long and here we had our skating-rink. In the summer-time they served as cow-pastures for the milch-cows of the neighbors, except on rare occasions when a baseball game was played by the better known nines of the city.

I recall, for instance, how just before July 4, 1868, an imposing grandstand, capable of seating at least two hundred people, was erected in the block between Reuben, Jackson, Van Buren and Laflin streets. On the Fourth, the ball players with their friends, families, and sweethearts drove out in buggies, barouches, rockaways and omnibuses and an exciting game was played between — was it the Excelsiors and the Eurekas? — ending in a score of something like 98 to 87! I was hired at the princely pay of "two bits" to pass the pink lemonade to players and guests between innings, as well as to chase foul balls during the progress of the game.

The frozen, flooded prairies made it possible for the boys and girls to skate miles and miles over ice, wind-swept until it was free of snow and smooth as glass, even to Riverside and the Des Plaines River, ten miles to the west of us — in the latter case, however, only when we were in sufficient numbers to protect ourselves from those we were wont to term the "Micks." These were sturdy, aggressive youngsters, whose homes were along the C. B. & Q. tracks. They were better skaters and better fighters than we. As good skaters, the "Micks" had an artist's admiration and an *amateur's* coveting for the Barney & Berry club-skates on which we more prosperous children of fortune were accustomed to flash about in all the intricacies of the "double roll" and "spreading the eagle."

In the good-humored, daredevil, Celtic faces of some of Chicago's old-time "cops" from time to time I have caught a fleeting hint, an ephemeral suggestion of resemblance to a face I have known in trying circumstances in the long ago. Is it possible that as mayor I have been called upon to command policemen who in our mutual boyhood days had put the fear of God into my heart, before whose fiery attack I had shown my heels in reckless flight?

There was fresh air a-plenty in the Ashland Avenue section in these early days. The cupola on our home was a favorite stamping-ground for the children, because from it great vistas of things unknown, and therefore alluring, opened up in every direction. It was one of my boyish joys to sit there, high above the street, opera-glass to my eyes, and watch the life that went on about me.

In the morning, in a cloud of dust on fair days, in a sea of mud when the weather was "soft," the cow-man took his herd of milch-cows out on Harrison Street to pasture on the rich prairie-grasses somewhere out west, to bring them home again by the same route in the evening. In the herd there would be a hundred or more cows owned either by milkmen, or by the prosperous Irish residents of the territory adjacent to the Jesuit Church in Twelfth Street.

To this church, by the way, there was a well-beaten footpath, striking catty-cornered across the prairie blocks from Reuben and Van Buren streets, for St. Jarlath's Church had not yet been built and the Jesuit Church, a good mile away, was the nearest sanctuary for the Catholic faithful of our neighborhood, as well as of the section to the west of us.

Still farther to the south our childish eyes could watch the trains moving east and west along the Burlington tracks in Sixteenth Street. To the west there were a few houses: our first home at Hermitage Avenue and Congress Street; the Jennings home in Marshfield Avenue; immediately behind us, in Hermitage Avenue near Adams Street, a charming old place belonging to a family whose name I have forgotten; the Hugh Maher place at Ogden Avenue and Adams Street, where stands to-day the Mary Thompson Hospital; the Silver Leaf Grove, a good old-fashioned beer-garden, at Ogden Avenue near Twelfth Street; as well as scattered homes in Monroe Street. The houses were so few and far between, however, that with the glasses, from our old home I have watched croquet games in the Owsley yard at Madison and Robey streets!

Every Sunday morning in the summer season there would be a picnic of some German society either at the Silver Leaf Grove, or in another beer-garden of the same type in Madison Street near Western Avenue. Out on Madison Street the procession would move, with band playing and flags flying; the leaders on horseback, the well-to-do, the women and children in open barouches, buggies or rockaways, *hoi polloi* on foot, trudging vigorously to get up a good thirst. Bayern or Schwaben, Singing Society or Turngemeinde, the procession would move to the distant garden where the day would be spent in a round of singing, laughter, eating, drinking and dancing, with a few speeches interpolated in memory of the Fatherland beyond the seas.

The Kentuckian's hospitality and his love of social life are proverbial, whether he remains in his native State, or whether he moves his *Lares et Penates* abroad in quest of fortune. The Kentuckians who came to Chicago brought with them all the characteristics of their sturdy stock. I was too young for my mind to carry more than the faintest recollections of the social pleasures of the early days.

Indeed, to folk of these days of the Casino and the Saddle and Cycle clubs, the Assemblies, and the Butchers and Bakers balls at the Virginia, and coming-out parties at the Blackstone, the social life 'way west of the river in the sixties would seem hopelessly crude.

The principal dances were given by a social organization known as "The Grasshoppers." The trysting place alternated in the spacious parlors of the old homes. Round-dance and square-dance took turn and turn about until at eleven o'clock the musicians struck up the supper-march, when all the guests lined up in gay and formal array to move with dignified step to the dining-room, where the center-table was weighed down with great dishes of chicken salad, escalloped oysters, sandwiches of various kinds, coffee and chocolate, oranges and Malaga grapes, ice-cream and cakes.

The grapes always carried a powdering left over from the sawdust in which they had been packed for the long journey across the seas from far-away Spain.

English walnuts in those days, be it remembered, came from England in fact as well as in name. A barrel of apples, of hickory nuts, butternuts or walnuts, each in its appropriate season, for us youngsters was a genuine treat. As for oranges and bananas, these fruits were real luxuries. There was no cold-storage transportation. Communication with the semi-tropics, because of its infrequency, was a negligible quantity. Florida fruit-lands had not yet been developed. California was still an arid waste. There was no Imperial Valley to glut the market with early melons. Grape-fruit, casabas and honey-dew melons had not yet been dreamed of.

This reminds me that years ago, in Pasadena, I asked a waitress where the casaba melon came from. "Oh!" she answered, "it's one of Burbank's freaks — a cross between a cantaloupe and a cucumber!"

Toward the end of the sixties William Waller, eldest son of our neighbor, married a Louisiana belle. One Christmas her father sent her a box of Creole oranges. Well do I remember the envy and the heart burnings with which I watched Jim Waller,[1] William's youngest brother, take a big yellow

[1] James Breckenridge Waller, a well-known Chicagoan of to-day.

orange from his pocket during the recess at school, peel it with critical care and eat it slowly down to the last shred. Even the discarded peeling seemed a delicacy to me!

In the beginning the merrymakers were married couples, still too young to have children of an age to sit up to the late hours of the festivities. Gradually the children grew up and became young men and young women, supplanting their parents in the social life of the community.

When the "Grasshopper" dances were held at his home, by the way, Mr. Honoré was wont to place a lamp in the cupola high above the street, that its cheery rays of welcome and promised hospitality might light the way of the guests across the open prairie. The Reuben Street community was a sparsely settled section of the city, but socially quite on a footing with the gay life of the North and South sides. Only in later years did it become the fashion to ignore the great West Side as the social Brooklyn of Chicago!

In all likelihood there were young people who took part in the merry-makings of the group in the early sixties. Who were they? I do not know. Not until the two or three years prior to the great fire of 1871 do names appear in the social life, headed by the west-side colony of Kentuckians, which I am able to recall. Colonel Nelson Thomasson, Edward C. Waller, Henry H. Walker, Adrian and Harry Honoré, Harry Rogers, were some of the young beaux whose names occur to me. The beautiful Bertha Honoré (later Mrs. Potter Palmer), the equally beautiful Eva Badger, who married Charlie Angell, and her elder sister Belle, who became Mrs. T. W. Harvey, Judith Waller (now Mrs. William Johnston), and her elder sisters were among the most attractive of the young women.

What old-timer can ever forget the feverish joys of New Year's Day in the sixties? Few were the houses to hang out a basket as a receptacle for the cards of those who wished to call — an inhospitable way of telling callers that the doors of the mansion for the day were closed to them! Practically every family kept open house. The front doors were constantly opening and closing, as the throng of visitors, young and old, entered into the realms of hospitality beyond, regaled themselves with the good things provided for the inner man, and proceeded on their joyous way to visit other friends until the early hours of morning. How they ever carried the food they ate, the drinks they imbibed, was a mystery to my young mind. Great bowls of egg-nog of the good old kind, made of genuine Bourbon and "with a stick in it" and no mistake, stood on every sideboard. In some homes port and sherry, a rare bottle of champagne, but many a jug of an especial distillation of Kentucky corn-juice, were at hand to add their potency to the egg-nog in rendering the callers *hors de combat*, and incidentally in bringing the custom of New Year's calls into such disrepute that finally public opinion forced its abandonment.

While not strictly in line with the life I am describing, it might not be amiss for me to recall that in 1866 the second annual banquet (or was it the first?) of the Chicago Yale Club was held in the parlor of our old home at Ashland Avenue and Jackson Street. Among the songs which, with my ear at the keyhole, I heard this night for the first time, the rollicking refrain of "*Upidee! Upida!*" stands out the freshest in my memory.

The winter cold of the earlier days must have been more intense, the snowfall greater, than what we now experience.

I have seen the snow-drifts in our side yard so deep, that when a way had been shovelled for the horse and cutter to reach the street, my father's slouch hat could just be seen as he held the reins over his spirited trotter dancing gaily to the music of the jangling bells. It was my duty at this period to help shovel the sidewalks clear of snow of a Saturday morning. The unwilling labor in which I was forced to indulge, while the other boys were skating on the prairie across the street, may have something to do with my recollections as to the depth of the snowfall! As an evidence of the utter unreasonableness of youngsters, while I detested the job of clearing the family walk of snow, in common with my companions, after every heavy fall it was my practice to shoulder a snow-shovel and solicit a like job from house to house, a half-cent a foot, two bits for a fifty-foot lot, being "Union wages!"

My sister, Mrs. Heaton Owsley, recalls that in 1864 a Kentucky cousin visiting at our home was taken sick and died. Trained nurses were then aids unknown. The last sad rites of laying out the dead were not left to the cold, unfriendly hands of the undertaker. My mother not being well, it was necessary to call upon a woman friend to dress the body for the grave. The night was bitterly cold; the snow was too deep in the wind-driven, prairie drifts for a horse to break through without the greatest difficulty. There was no alternative to my father's walking to the Bryan home, five blocks away in Reuben Street, to ask aid of an aunt of Mrs. Bryan, a Miss Rogers of Boston. Together, Miss Rogers in high rubber boots as partial protection against the drifted snow, they set out on the slow and painful return. Before the distance had been half covered, my father's heart was cold with fear lest his companion should lack the strength to complete the journey. All traces of the road had been obliterated by the swirling snows; the drifts were waist-deep; the cold drove to the very marrow. It was with a feeling of intense relief and with thankfulness to a kind and watchful Providence that he finally opened the door of his home after an experience fraught with the gravest dangers.

In Union Park of a summer Saturday afternoon, concerts were frequently given between the hours of five and seven by Voss' band, Voss being the Johnny Hand of early Chicago. Billy Nevins, the "drummer-boy of the Rappahannock," as I recall his war-time nickname, played the drum, his *pièce de résistance* being an imitation of the fury of a battlefield, the roll of his drum for the rattle of the musketry, the bass drum at regular intervals furnishing the boom of the heavy artillery.

My one ambition at this period was to serve my country as a drummer-boy, to lead my regiment until I fell, and while my own young life's blood ebbed slowly out, to hear the victorious shouts of those who had followed me!

While the band played, the fashion of the neighborhood paraded in fine array, some strolling, some driving slowly in wide, open landaus, the populace in the meanwhile looking on in rapt admiration. Union Park was the Bois de Boulogne of the West Side!

There were no more zealous patrons in Chicago of the big doings in an operatic, theatrical, and musical way at Crosby's Opera House than these same west siders.

Ole Bull, Edwin Booth and Charlotte Cushman, Brignoli, Adelina Patti, and Christine Nilsson, were names to conjure with among the adults. For the younger generation, Wood's Museum was the scene of countless, ecstatic delights. What boy of the sixties can ever forget the minstrel shows at which the four Billies — Rice, Arlington, Manning, and Emerson — were the star performers on the bones and tambourine?

Black Crook, with its frank display of feminine beauty, came in these days to Crosby's Opera House, scandalizing the community. The women of the period deplored beyond measure the depravity of a performance which they were consumed with curiosity to view with their own eyes! What excuse could they give for patronizing such reckless indecency? A happy thought suggested itself. I was of too tender an age to suffer injury; the bright colors, the merry music, the kaleidoscopic shifting and changing of the tableaux should prove instructive and educational to me in an artistic sense. However, some form of chaperonage was imperative. Whereupon my mother, accompanied by three ladies of our neighborhood, escorted poor little me to the Saturday matinée! Débutantes of to-day would turn up their noses at *Black Crook* in its mildly-seasoned spiciness and find it deadly dull.

XI

OLD HYDE PARK

BY MRS. B. F. AYER

EARLY in the sixties, a jovial Irishman, Dr. William Bradshaw Egan, a practicing physician, ambitious for such an estate as an Irish gentleman at home might have, bought a large tract of land in the marshy wilderness three miles south of Chicago. It had truly magnificent proportions as it extended from Lake Michigan to what is now Cottage Grove Avenue, and from Forty-Seventh Street to South Chicago. The appellation Cottage Grove, by the way, came from a nameless early settler's cabin in the one little clump of trees which broke the wide, flat expanse of water-logged land stretching from the river to the southern horizon. With proper and paternal pride, Dr. Egan called his newly acquired tract, *Egandale.* He selected, as a site for his house and gardens, the western part of his estate. The ground here was somewhat higher than the surrounding territory and thus gave its owner the semblance of a view. There is nothing so cherished by the dweller in a flat country as an eminence, no matter how insignificant. At that time no other house, or sign of man's occupancy, was visible from Dr. Egan's "hill-top." Following the customs of his native land he called in the services of-a landscape gardener, who laid out his grounds in quite a stately fashion. Early settlers remember the imposing rustic gate and lodge which opened on Forty-Seventh Street, and which was the formal entrance to Egandale. In the neighborhood one could walk for miles in grassy lanes shaded by cedar and wonderful, great oak-trees. Some of these endured for sixty years to tell the tale, when came so-called progress which uprooted them to clear the ground for the building of apartments.

Dr. Egan, being a bachelor, kept open house, where convivial friends met far from the gossip of neighbors. Though he was a genial man, his extensive real-estate transactions sometimes made him anxious and distrait. The story is told that, when a patient once asked of him directions as to how a prescription he had given her was to be taken, he answered, "One-third down, balance in one, two, or three years."

Later Dr. Egan returned to Ireland — possibly on account of the cold winters in Egandale, but more probably because he found too few of the leisure class to enjoy his generous and gay hospitality. When, in the seventies, Egandale was subdivided, the village of Hyde Park, the pioneer suburb to the south of Chicago, was formed.

Among the early settlers of Hyde Park were Charles Mather Smith,[1] Lester Bradner, J. Y. Scammon, Benjamin F. Ayer, and Judge Van H. Higgins, whose homes in the city were either burned or made untenable by the Chicago Fire of 1871. These men bought large tracts of land and established their families in what was then open country. Each land-owner was forced to provide for himself all that is usually cared for by public-utilities corporations. There was no gas, no water, no sewers, except as furnished by the owner; even the street sprinkling was a part of his responsibility (my children learned to drive by driving a watering-cart).

[1] Father of Frederick Mather Smith, Francis Drexel Smith, and Miss Mary Rozet Smith.

Immediately after the great Fire it was not so difficult as might appear to be reconciled to the lack of such conveniences as had formerly been enjoyed by city dwellers. The city was gone and its inhabitants, a large proportion of whom were left homeless, were obliged to find shelter in the crowded and, often, primitive dwellings left on the South, West, and far North sides.

We residents in Hyde Park were better off than most as we had new and commodious homes, well-equipped stables and horses and carriages, which provided means of transportation to the Illinois Central trains, or to the little steam "dummy" railroad. This latter primitive institution connected with the south-side horse-cars which carried the citizens of that day from Thirty-Ninth to Lake Street.

By these routes we were enabled to reach the center of the city for shopping or amusements. We were, however, fairly independent of the social pleasures offered in other parts of Chicago. In our little community there were many opportunities for relaxation.

It has been said, "All the pleasant things of life are either unwholesome, expensive, or wrong — some of them all three." Our life in the era of which I write, looked at in retrospect, seems to me to challenge the truth of this statement. We certainly had lots of wholesome, inexpensive, harmless fun in old Hyde Park with the group of notable personalities that chance had brought together there.

Perhaps those early forms of entertainment would not appeal to the folk of to-day. The mad passion for gaiety and artificial excitement, which at present characterizes pleasure, had not yet absorbed our social life. We had lectures; we had charades; we had no balls but many dances — at least that was what we called them. No one thought himself or herself too old or too proud to dance at these parties. The Virginia reel was a favorite and was generally a long reel. The Presbyterians, while they did not really oppose dancing, would only slip in "just to look on."

Dominoes, checkers, and, later, spelling-bees, were among our quiet, home diversions. Whist was often played — "a bright fire, a clean hearth, and the rigor of the game" prevailed, and the evening frequently closed with music, all joining in singing the soul-stirring strains of "John Brown's Body," or telling what that valiant man, "Captain Jenks, of the Horse Marines," accomplished. As Hyde Park had no gas till 1871, and no daylight saving to light the early evening, like "wise virgins" when going to, or coming from, these entertainments, the inhabitants took their lanterns, well-trimmed and burning, and looked like fire-flies, as they wended their way through the gloom.

People living near the lake, had sail- and rowboats, and a sort of community barge, which was a broad, long, ten-oared boat, carrying ten or fifteen people. We often went on the water in the summer-time. Colonel Mason Loomis used to come down from the city in his yacht, and take us for a sail and a gay supper on board. A yacht club, too, was a feature of early Hyde Park days.

George Root, composer of the loved songs of the Civil War, head of the talented family of Roots, famous in musical circles, lived in Hyde Park. His son, Frederick Root, a leader throughout his life in orchestra organization, was well known as such in Chicago, and his daughter, Mrs. Burnham, was distinguished in literary work.

Flood's Hall, a good-sized room over Dow's drug store,

near the Illinois Central station at Fifty-Third Street, was the center of much innocent gaiety. Our public lectures, concerts, political meetings, and dancing classes were all held in Flood's Hall. The entertainments there were colored by the presence of the Roots, who could sing, act, dance, and organize theatricals better than anyone else. It was there that the Gilbert and Sullivan operas were vividly and brilliantly presented by the Roots and their musical circle. Edward Woodel was an excellent "Dick Deadeye," and Frank Fairman an imposing, stately "Admiral."

Hyde Park was a community of music-lovers. At an early day, when the bob-tailed street-car, drawn by a single horse with a tinkling table-bell strapped about his neck, went no farther than Thirty-Ninth Street, these enthusiasts attended operas, concerts, and theaters: there were no people in the city in closer touch with musical events than Hyde Parkers. The return home at midnight was accomplished by taking a carryall or sleigh at the end of the car line, and driving three miles or more, each member of the party being dropped at his or her door.

In proportion to its population, Hyde Park in those days had more able men in its midst than are often found in any community. A number of the leading lawyers of Chicago, and men of affairs, were attracted by finding country life so accessible to the city, and came to Hyde Park in the early seventies. Among the distinguished residents was Judge Lyman J. Trumbull — a close friend of Mr. Lincoln's from the early days when both lived in southern Illinois, where they often met in court sessions or on circuit. He held many distinguished positions, having been Judge of the Superior Court of Illinois, and was United States Senator from Illinois for eighteen years. An interesting incident is told of his campaign for the Senate. Five men were competing for the appointment, among them Mr. Lincoln. A deadlock was the result, which was broken by Mr. Lincoln, who withdrew and turned his votes to Judge Trumbull, thus insuring his victory. Judge Trumbull seemed to enjoy the quiet life of Hyde Park when he finally retired from his many activities, for he lived there happily until his death.

Norman B. Judd, another of our neighbors, was Illinois State Senator for sixteen years. Originally a Democrat, he became, by conviction, a Republican, and was an enthusiastic supporter of the new party. In the Convention of 1860 he had the distinguished honor of nominating Abraham Lincoln for the Presidency. Afterward, Mr Judd was appointed Minister to Berlin — and was a member of Congress for many years. His home was on Forty-Seventh Street, near Lake Avenue.

After the Fire drove them from Michigan Avenue, Mr. and Mrs. J. Y. Scammon occupied a beautiful tract of land of twenty acres facing south on the Midway; the School of Education, connected with the Chicago University, now occupies a part of this ground. They called their place "Fernwood Villa," and no home in Chicago had greater charm or more of an atmosphere of culture than theirs. Mr. Scammon had known the distinguished people of the world: he was a devoted friend and confidential advisor of Abraham Lincoln and other leading men, while Mrs. Scammon, a sister of Mrs. Mahlon D. Ogden, drew to herself many friends and admirers. Her social gift was remarkable and her fireside was always the center of an attractive group. Anders Zorn, the Swedish portrait-painter, visited at Fernwood

Villa during the World's Fair, and painted the portrait of Mrs. Scammon which now hangs in the Art Institute.

Mr. Scammon was a leading lawyer in Chicago for many years, and as a citizen greatly assisted the up-building of the city. He was always a generous contributor to various societies, and was a founder of the Astronomical Society, the Hahnemann Hospital, and the Academy of Science. The first well-equipped observatory in or near Chicago was provided by his gift of $30,000 to the Chicago University, located at that time at Thirty-Fourth Street and Lake Avenue. When the University of Chicago, a struggling Baptist institution, became a beneficiary of Mr. Rockefeller, and moved to its present location, this telescope, with its fine glass, was afterwards presented to the Northwestern University at Evanston, where it now is.

William K. Ackerman was an early resident in Hyde Park, living in Kenwood. He was always interested in the welfare of the public, and was a pillar in St. Paul's Church, holding every office. As a young man he entered the employ of the Illinois Central Railroad and rose, through different stages, until he became president of the Road. The family moved to the North Side, and, after Mr. Ackerman's death, Mrs. Ackerman went to Rochester to live.

Van H. Higgins, a Judge in the Superior Court of Chicago, — his career was marked by unusual energy and talent, — was a long-time resident of Hyde Park. On his retirement from the Bench, Judge Jamieson, another Hyde Park resident, was elected to fill the vacancy.

Charles Hitchcock was a lawyer of great ability and a gentleman of culture and dignity. He left a fortune that enabled Mrs. Hitchcock to build a dormitory at the University of Chicago, and so perpetuate his name. The Hitchcock home, where Mrs. Hitchcock has been living for more than fifty years, was a country place of unusual charm, and is now an oasis in the midst of a thickly-built neighborhood.

Horatio Waite, a lawyer, and formerly Paymaster of the United States Navy during the Civil War, lived in Hyde Park, and he and his wife always kept open house to friends. Their house might well be called the home of the Shakespeare Club. This Club met informally once a week at the home of some one of the members. Chosen ones read the plays selected, and their declamatory and intelligent interpretations made many a delightful evening.

Two attempts were made to establish private schools in Hyde Park, the first one by Mrs. Waite, wife of Judge Waite, a character in the early days. Mrs. Waite was one of the first women to be interested in what was then called "Woman's Rights"; her very walk expressed determination. The private schools were not successful, as taxpayers preferred the public schools, which is not surprising when one realizes that the High School in Kenwood commanded the services of such men as Davis R. Dewey, now head of the Economics Department of the Massachusetts Institute of Technology. Mr. Dewey was recalled after a time to Boston, and William G. Beale, of Chicago, took his place as head of the High School. As I remember, he pursued his law studies while occupying this position. Even then he gave promise of his aptness for his chosen profession which has since been demonstrated in his very successful career.

Forty-Seventh Street leads from Lake Michigan west, passing through a part of Hyde Park called "The Ridge," between Vincennes Avenue and Grand Boulevard. Mr.

Horatio O. Stone lived in this part of the town for many years, having a spacious home, with elaborate lodges at the gates. Among their neighbors were Judge and Mrs. Henry O. Sheppard. Mr. and Mrs. H. H. Honoré, and Mr. and Mrs. Potter Palmer had houses near-by for the summer season. It was at this country residence of Mr. Honoré that his daughter, Ida, was married to Colonel Frederick Grant, son of General Grant, an event of great social importance, the President and Mrs. Grant having come on from Washington for the wedding.[1]

It is to Paul Cornell, called the "Father of Hyde Park," that Chicago owes its South Park System. He was one of the largest land-owners here, and was deeply interested in the city's betterment. He had visions of great and beautiful play-grounds, and in 1867 he spent much of his winter in Springfield in the interest of the South Parks' Bill, securing its passage after much opposition. The Legislature finally passed an act authorizing the condemnation of certain lands located on each side of the city to be used as boulevards and parks. This was the first step in the City Beautiful. The realization of this scheme, as it is now carried out in Jackson and Washington Parks and the Midway Plaisance, testifies to the foresight, the imagination, the ambition, and the ability, of a few men in Chicago. It has been said of the establishment of the South Park System, that for honest management and judicious expenditure it stands without a parallel in the history of our city. Certainly it has no superior.

Paul Cornell was appointed by the Governor on the first

[1] Other prominent Hyde Park residents, besides those mentioned in the text, were: John B. Calhoun, Homer Hibbard, James A. Root, Charles Gossage, James Morgan, and Norman Perkins.

Board of Park Commissioners,[1] and was its secretary; he was reappointed several times, and served for fourteen years. He further testified to his belief in his part of town by building the Hyde Park Hotel at Fifty-Third Street and the lake.

The World's Columbian Exposition would never have come to Chicago had there not been the beauties of Jackson Park to offer the Commissioners. They saw great possibilities in the wide meadows, the Wooded Island and its surrounding lagoons, and the wonderful background of blue lake and sky. It is not surprising that architects, inspired by this scene, gave us those marvelous buildings.

Many questions have been asked about the origin of the name Midway Plaisance, which was given to a drive-way connecting the two parks—Jackson and Washington—later made famous by the World's Fair. For a long time this roadway was not improved. Its shaded walks and drives made it a resort of equestrians and others enjoying real country. It led through a grove of trees just south of J. Y. Scammon's place. The name Midway came from its situation between the two parks, and Paul Cornell, while a Park Commissioner, brought *Plaisance* home with him from Paris. I cannot find the exact meaning for the word, but it may be roughly defined as "a place of pleasure." The Midway during the World's Fair was surely a place of pleasure and delight.

Six miles south of the City was the Washington Park race-course, with its well-equipped club-house, which had followed the improvements in Washington Park and the

[1] The other members of the Board of Park Commissioners were: J. M. Wilson, President, Paul Cornell, Secretary, Benjamin F. Ayer, Attorney for South Park Board, George W. Gage, and Chauncey Keep Bowen.

boulevards, making the race-course very accessible, and situated in such a way as to attract crowds. The annual June races at the Washington Park Race-track were the first call of summer to the fashionable world, the feminine part of which turned out in becoming gowns, hats and parasols. The grand-stand was like a terrace of flowers. It was an amusing excitement to watch the anxiety in betting circles. On the opening day the line of perfectly appointed landaus, victorias, and tandems on the boulevards brought out a crowd of the less fortunate who waited at the road-side to see what, to us all, seemed a real pageant, and to point out the noted beauties and business-men of Chicago.

The dashing up to the Club-house of Potter Palmer's four-in-hand, and the equally well-equipped coach-and-four of Arthur Caton, was always an event in the afternoon. In these days could such an excitement ever be produced by the passing of a limousine, even if a President were boxed in it?

In that simple era, the church was much more of a social and domestic factor in our daily lives than it now is. Every-one attended at least one service on Sundays, and there were many occasions during the week when members of the various denominations were called by their pastors to some kind of church meeting.

The first church erected in Hyde Park was a small frame building at the north end, built by Charles Cleaver. It was a Congregational organization. Paul Cornell erected a second building "For the Worship of Almighty God," which had no sectarian organization behind it. Union serv-ices occasionally were held there when a wandering min-ister could be obtained. The Presbyterians would meet in the morning, and the Episcopalians in the evening. The utmost harmony prevailed, but, on one occasion, through some misunderstanding, they both attempted to meet at the same morning hour; the spirit of the Church Militant became so aroused that one section of it finally became the Church Triumphant. But it was not long before a new cause of trouble arose; the usual fraternal feeling, not untinged by suspicion, existed in the sects (or was it the sextons?), forcing the situation. Each congregation had its own woodpile in the cellar. The sexton of the Episcopalians seemed to miss something and put up a sign "Episcopalian woodpile. Hands off." There being no special dispensation as to woodpiles, there was no more molesting. Both churches prospered moderately.

Later on, the Episcopal Church left Hyde Park and moved to the more aristocratic Kenwood; it was a pioneer at that end of the town. The Calvinists were left in full possession of the one little church in Hyde Park — enlarging it so that it accommodated the Presbyterians for some years, until they built a more pretentious stone church.

The Episcopalians at first held services in the upper room of the Kenwood schoolhouse. The room was not adapted to church service; the blackboard served as reredos, and the imprint of the last mathematical effort, or some rude sketch made the previous Friday, was generally left on the board. An old melodeon led the singing. It was not long before a frame church with a high steeple was built, which was called St. Paul's. I remember that about this time the treasurer of the Church, W. K. Ackerman, reported that the magnificent sum of $45 had been raised and expended on the services of *several* clergymen.

The simplicity and contentment of the early days in Hyde Park, and the Mid-Victorian flavor of their somewhat ceremonious hospitality, seem to me in retrospect, to be rather fine and distinguished. Men talked well, and comported themselves with dignity. Women were witty and accomplished, as well as good home-makers. We were bound together by the strong tie of the pioneer, and friendship was an evident fact. I like to remember Sunday afternoons at our house, when, in hot weather, friends would gather for a cooling "Tom Collins" on the porch, or, on cold days, for a hot toddy by the library fire. Mr. Dewey, then a brilliant young man, frequently called. Mr. Wirt Dexter, out for a constitutional, on his big, dappled-gray horse, would often ride down from the city, and "drop in." "Long" John Wentworth, driving down to inspect his Wentworth Tract, and other properties, would always stop at our house and review with my husband the palmy days of New Hampshire politics, when Franklin Pierce was President, and he and Daniel Webster were leaders of their party. Both were friends of these gentlemen, and ardent Democrats of that day. Melville W. Fuller, later Chief Justice of the United States, was a frequent visitor, as were many other men who were associated with large affairs of that time.

In the eighties, the city of Chicago began to cast longing and jealous glances at the contented and prosperous village of Hyde Park and sought its annexation to Chicago. For several years the village made a strenuous fight at the polls to retain its independence,- but the time came when all efforts failed, and Hyde Park lost its identity in the embrace of the great city. So passed into the shades of other days the one-time simple, friendly customs and manners suitable to a village, but not possible under the more complex conditions which mark city life.

XII

BEFORE THE FIRE

By Mrs. Frederick Greeley

I am glad that I can remember some of the aspects of the North Side of Chicago before the great fire.

I seem to myself to have passed my childhood and grown up in the midst of gardens; to have had my play in quiet streets, made pleasant and beautiful by arching trees, with soft, unpaved roadways and wooden sidewalks; with houses set back from the highway, and surrounded by flowers and shrubs.

Our own house stood in the center of the east side of the block bounded by Huron, Rush, Erie and Pine streets — the latter now North Michigan Avenue.

The house, square, stucco-finished, and stained or painted a gray-brown, was a two-story structure, with high basement. A broad flight of steps led up to the front door, which opened into a large, square hall, from which a comfortable, winding stair ascended to the second story. On the right of the hall was the drawing-room — an Early Victorian room, with furniture, hangings, and decorations of the period. Long French windows lighted the room; a carpet, gay with garlands of flowers covered the floor. In the middle and at both ends of it were designs of wreaths of roses. To me that carpet seemed the acme of beauty and elegance.

The prevailing color of the library was green. Book-cases lined the walls and extended to the ceiling. Back of the library was a large bedroom, or nursery, with dressing-room and bath-room adjacent. The dining-room and conservatory were in the English basement. We descended to these rooms by inclosed, perfectly dark stairs. Opposite the lower door of this steep and un-lighted staircase was the conservatory, with its fresh greenery, its warm, moist fragrance, and its sunshine. Opening from this shadowy lower hall were mysterious doors leading into various service rooms and pantries.

On the south and east sides of the house were broad piazzas looking into the garden. Directly in front of the high flight of steps which led to the front door, was a fountain, a mossy pool, in the center of which was set an oval-shaped boulder[1] of red granite, which for years had stood within the inclosure of Fort Dearborn. This rock had been cut out and used first by Indians, later by soldiers of the garrison, as a place in which to grind corn. On the face of this massive boulder had been roughly carved, by some embryo sculptor, the features of Waubansee, an Indian chieftain of renown in the neighborhood.

My father, Isaac N. Arnold, had purchased the boulder and had it removed from the Fort and placed in our garden. A hole had been pierced through the rock for a water-pipe which came out through the depression made by the aboriginal corn grinders. From a bronze mouthpiece a slender jet of water sprang into the air, to fall back into the corn receptacle, and from there to trickle down over the features of the old chief into the pool below. Around and above the boulder grew a tree, completely enveloped by festoons of wild grapevine.

[1] This stone is now in the rooms of the Chicago Historical Society.

From the fountain to the Erie Street entrance extended lawns and shrubberies, intersected by paths and walks. A sun-dial "numbered the sunny hours." Tall evergreens made secluded nooks of shade, where children played, and rejoiced in rabbits and other domestic pets; and where birds and wild creatures found sanctuary and shelter.

A croquet-ground occupied the lawn east of the house. On the rear of the property, and facing Huron Street, were grapevines and greenhouses, as well as a substantial barn. Fruit- and flower-gardens filled the land in between these buildings and our house.

On the block south of us was the Newberry place, with its gardens and grape-arbors. West of the Newberry domains and across Rush Street, William B. Ogden's beautiful home occupied another whole block, bounded by Rush, Ontario, Cass and Erie streets. Farther north, old St. James's Church — the Mother Church of the Protestant Episcopal faith in Chicago — cast its protecting shadows over the homes of many of its members.

The two Rumsey households, [1] on the corners of Huron, Cass and Rush streets, were bulwarks of faith and strength. It is pleasant to remember how much of the policy and plans for the welfare of the parish may have emanated from informal conferences and meetings held on the hospitable front steps of the Julian Rumsey mansion.

Opposite George Rumsey's house on Rush Street, was the delightful home of the Henry W. Kings — a Presbyterian stronghold this, but none the less devoted to community interests. Back of Mr. King's residence, and facing

[1] That of Julian Rumsey was on the corner of Huron and Cass streets, while his brother George Rumsey's home was to the east on the corner of Rush and Huron streets.

our place on Huron Street, was a row of two or three houses, made of yellow Milwaukee brick. In the east end house lived Mr. and Mrs. William McCormick.[1] The west end was occupied by two maidens from the south — the Misses Forsyth.

Still farther east, and filling the corner, was the home of Mr. and Mrs. Perry Smith, a brown, wooden house, filled with bric-a-brac, paintings, and statuary.

Across Pine Street, in what seems, as I remember it, the most palatial of all these beautiful homes, Mrs. W. W. K. Nixon dispensed elegant and gracious hospitality. Dancing-school at her house was a social function of the first magnitude. I seem to remember with awe and reverence a dignified butler, and a wonderful form of afternoon tea.

One of the early recollections most clear in my mind, was a day (it must have been about 1865) when Huron Street was filled with an angry, remonstrant crowd of men and women. The Misses Forsyth, whose sympathies were intensely southern, in their zeal to show their allegiance to the Confederate cause, had hung the Confederate flag from their windows. This was probably on some occasion of rejoicing over victory for the northern armies. The poor ladies held their own for some time, vociferating and gesticulating to the people in the streets; but finding that their ill-judged demonstration was creating serious trouble, they finally withdrew the offending ensign, and the crowd dispersed. The little girl peering through the cracks of the "back fence" felt that she, too, knew the meaning of war.

In those days of my childhood one of our favorite amuse-

[1] The parents of the late Hon. Robert Hall McCormick, William McCormick, Mrs. Samuel Jewett, the late Mrs. Perry H. Smith, and the late Mrs. Edward T. Blair.

ments was to go down to the end of Rush Street and watch the drawbridge open to allow shipping to pass through, and many an exciting hour was spent jumping on to the bridge for "a swing," as steamers and schooners were towed in and out of the river.

In those days, too, most of us attended Miss Whiting's School, held in a little white, wooden cottage at the end of Ontario Street, where the sands came up to the high wooden sidewalk. One could jump down at least six feet, landing in the soft, white sand of the shore of Lake Michigan. Returning home towards evening, it was fascinating to stray from the straight and narrow path over to Rush Street, past the rows of cottages on the south side of Ontario Street, and the tall picket fence on the north side of the street, which bounded the Newberry place and through which one gazed, as into a forbidden paradise. Arriving at Rush Street, and perhaps lingering in the cool of the evening, one soon descried the herd of aristocratic cows coming home from the pasture, leisurely pursuing their deliberate way down the street, each one turning into its own barnyard. There was the Henry King cow, the McCormick, the Skinner, Ogden, and Newberry cows, and if one hurried quickly up to Huron Street, the Rumsey cow could be seen sauntering to the west, the Arnold cow to the east — all obedient to habit and direction.

As all who remember the great fire know, the fateful day was Sunday, October 9, 1871. The weather had been unusually warm and dry, with high winds. Dead, crisp leaves lay in drifts along the streets and in the gardens of the North Side.

I had heard my parents speak of the fire of Saturday

night, but had no definite impression of anything impending, until I was awakened in the darkness of Sunday night and told to get up and dress and come out into the garden to help put out fires, which started in the leaves from falling sparks.

The sky was an angry copper-color, while what seemed rushing flames of fire spanned the high arch of the heavens. The family were all astir; probably my father and the gardener had been up all night. At that time there seemed not so much alarm as excitement in fighting an enemy who was sure to be conquered. I remember how gaily we children ran from one to another of our favorite spots in the garden to stamp out the little beginnings of fires. The air grew hotter and hotter, the rain of sparks and burning brands more ominous; then came a voice from the street, someone running and shouting: —

"Mr. Arnold! the water-works are burning, the end is coming!"

With a gasp the fountain gave up its last flirt of water; no drop came through the house faucets — the end, indeed, was near. Then I believe for one moment the valiant heart of my father faltered. In the next instant he was himself again. Alert, resourceful, undaunted by the terrible situation, he at once set himself to meet the immediate and ever-increasing danger, and started efforts to save treasures from the house — family portraits, valued pictures, beloved books; but it was too late. The barn was on fire, a corner of the house began to blaze, and a great burning brand fell with a crash into the conservatory.

My mother and my little sister Alice had already left us to go to my married sister and her husband, because their house seemed less in the path of the fire. The rest of us remained behind, believing our home was safe because of its distance from other dwellings, and being surrounded by green things which would not easily burn. Almost before we realized it, flight became imperative. My father gathered about him the little group, consisting of my elder sister, Katherine, my brother, Arthur, and myself, with the gardener and maids. Quickly we ran into the house to snatch up "one more precious possession"; quickly the horses and the cow were brought from the barn, now beginning to burn. Then, slowly, reluctantly, we turned our faces from the house so dear to us all. My father's plan was to go to the lake shore — a plan which was also a last desperate resort, as north, south, and west of us, escape was impossible. Well does the picture stand forth in my memory — the forlorn little cavalcade making its way from the place through the Pine Street gate, the father, the children, the faithful servants, the patient animals.

As we moved slowly into the street, we heard a jovial, cheerful voice, and, looking up, saw our opposite neighbor, Samuel Johnston, a well-known bachelor and householder, standing on his front doorstep, the door open behind him, the house looking dark and empty, save for the red glare of the flames; in his hands he held a decanter of wine; on the step beside him were wine glasses. Lifting one in his hand and filling it, he offered it to my father, saying: "We must take one more drink together, Mr. Arnold; here's to your very good health!"

I think he joined us on our way to the lake shore. Arriving there we found a motley crowd of people — some neighbors, among them Edward S. Tinkham and his family, who stayed with us until we escaped on the following day. There on the sands we spent the remaining hours of the night, until morning broke and turned the lurid flames into lowering clouds of smoke. I remember sitting on a sofa that had been pushed into the water close to the shore.

The wind blowing from the land made the lake gentle and quiet, and I think we children must have dozed and slept. I have no recollection of hunger, nor of food. Later in the morning, we, with other refugees, were ferried in small boats across "Ogden's slip." From there we made our way to the lighthouse at the mouth of the river, where kind people provided coffee and refreshments.

In the afternoon of that unforgetable day, a tugboat came to our rescue, and we were taken up the river, through the burning bridges, past the ruined and still smoldering warehouses and elevators, to the West Side. Thence, in a dazed condition of mind, we were conveyed in wagons and carriages to the home of our friends, the Alonzo Huntingtons, on the corner of Indiana Avenue and Sixteenth Street, where we stayed two or three weeks until we could collect the family and make plans for the coming winter.

XIII

THE CHICAGO CLUB

BY EDWARD BLAIR

THE position occupied by the Chicago Club is rather unique. Being the pioneer club of the West, and for many years the only club in Chicago, it included all of Chicago's early settlers who had any use for a club, a patronage which in other cities is usually found divided. This is partly accounted for by the youth of the community as well as the Puritan antecedents of its early settlers. They did not come here for their health; few of them had any previous experience of clubs, and if their opinion had been requested the majority probably would have pronounced them an undesirable influence in the community.

The Chicago Club may be said to have been the outgrowth of the old Dearborn Club, a congregation of two- or threescore congenial spirits who, towards the close of the Civil War, began to meet in rooms on State Street opposite the spot on which the Palmer House now stands. They afterward moved into the upper floor of the old Portland Block, on the southeast corner of Washington and Dearborn streets, where a few of their number in a desultory way met to pass the time of day, sample "wet goods" or play "draw." Their membership was so heterogeneous and their attendance so irregular that, before the Dearborn Club was closed by the sheriff in the fall of 1868, their president, W. J. Barney, and several of their prominent members, among them Judge Hugh Dickey, General Stager, John Janes, Henry R. Pierson, Philip Wadsworth, J. K. Fisher, Howard Priestley, Octavius Badger, David Gage, John B. Raymond, Henry W. Farrar, Francis Morgan, and others, had already begun to discuss a new organization.

To this end a meeting was called in January, 1869, in the Sherman House, which was then Chicago's leading hotel, kept by Gage Bros. & Rice. A number of the Club's members boarded there and ate together, as they did at the Grand Pacific after the great fire. About forty attended this meeting, at which U. H. Crosby, of Crosby's Opera House fame, presided. Nothing came of this meeting; but at a succeeding meeting, of which David Gage was chairman, and John Janes, secretary, it was decided to appoint a committee to select a hundred men to form a club to be known as the Chicago Club. The committee consisted of Charles B. Farwell, Philip Wadsworth, John Janes, Henry R. Pierson, David Gage, W. J. Barney, and Octavius Badger. It was said that only about a dozen of the original hundred members of the Chicago Club had ever belonged to a club before, and there was considerable doubt in the minds of the gentlemen approached as to the nature of the organization they were requested to join. Even when this was successfully explained, a further opposition on the part of their wives had frequently to be encountered.

The names of the original hundred members of the Chicago Club, as nearly as can be ascertained, were as follows:

Ayer, B. F.
Ayer, John V.
Badger, Octavius
Barnes, Charles J.
Barney, W. J.
Barter, T. O.
Bishop, H. W.
Boal, Charles T.
Brown, Andrew
Burley, A. H.

Campbell, B. H.
Carrey, Edmond
Cobb, Walter F.
Connell, C. J.
Coolbaugh, W. F.
Corwith, Nathan
Crerar, John
Crosby, U. H.
DeKoven, John
Dexter, Wirt
Dickey, Hugh T.
Drake, John B.
Dunlap, Geo. L.
Fairbank, N. K.
Farrar, H. W.
Farwell, C. B.
Fisher, J. K.
Fiske, D. B.
Fox, Harry
Fuller, S. W.
Gage, David A.
Gage, George W.
Gale, Stephen F.
Gossage, Charles
Hall, Phillip A.
Hopkins, George B.
Howard, W. B.
Isham, E. S.
Jackson, Obediah
Janes, John J.
Johnstone, Samuel
Jones, S. M.
Kattee, Walter
Keith, Samuel L.
Kimball, Granville
Kirkwood, William
Lincoln, Robert T.
Loomis, J. Mason
Lyon, John B.
McCagg, E. B.
McKay, James R.
McLaury, T. G.
Minot, Edward J.
Morgan, Francis
Munger, A. A.
Murray, W. H.
Nickerson, Samuel M.
Palmer, Potter
Parker, J. Mason
Pelton, William T.
Pierson, Henry R.
Priestly, Howard
Pullman, George M.
Rauch, John H.
Raymond, John B.
Rice, John B.
Ross, William M.
Rozet, G. H.
Russel, E. W.
Rutter, J. O.
Scammon, J. Y.
Sibley, S.
Smith, Perry H.
Stager, Anson
Tappan, Charles S.
Tilton, Lucius
Tinkham, Edward I.
Tracy, John F.
Tree, Lambert
Wadsworth, Philip
Walker, Charles H.
Walker, George C.
Walker, William B.
Washburne, Jr., Emory
Wheeler, Charles W.
Wheeler, G. Henry
Wheeler, Hiram
Whitman, George R.
Wilson, Charles L.
Young, George W.
Young, James R.

David and George Gage, Wirt Dexter, General Stager, C. B. Farwell, and George M. Pullman each advanced five hundred dollars, — which was afterward repaid, —

toward the preliminary expenses of the Club. Edward S. Isham prepared the papers of incorporation, and the old Farnham mansion, on Michigan Avenue between Adams and Jackson streets, was rented and furnished for the Club. When it was ready for occupation, a meeting of the hundred members was called for the evening of May 1, 1869. Nearly all of the members attended, but the omens were anything but auspicious. It was a terribly rainy, stormy night, and during the meeting one of the members was seized with a fit and had to be carried out.

Ezra B. McCagg was elected president of the new club. He was one of Chicago's leading attorneys, a partner of J. Y. Scammon, who at that time was among the largest real-estate holders in Chicago and, besides his real-estate and his law business, owned and managed a daily newspaper, a bank, and an insurance company. Mr. McCagg had married the sister of William B. Ogden, Chicago's first mayor and wealthiest citizen, and his house, in which he had collected one of the finest libraries in the country, was one of the social centers of the city. He was a man of polished manners, culture and discrimination; had travelled much abroad and was, altogether, of a type not at all common at that time in Chicago. Philip Wadsworth was deservedly elected vice-president, and Edward Tinkham, secretary and treasurer.

Although the Club nearly doubled its membership in its first year, it was not much frequented except on Saturday nights, when a free lunch was spread to attract attendance. There appeared still to be some doubt in the community as to its character and purposes, and a perusal of the early records indicates that this feeling was not entirely absent from the minds of the members themselves. One of the by-laws declares: "The Club-house shall not be used as an exchange or salesroom of any kind," and at one of the annual meetings it is resolved that "the corporate seal of the Chicago Club be a circle of adhesive paper with the words 'Chicago Club' written thereon." At this same meeting the Club voted its "thanks to Mr. P. C. Maynard for his present of a *Webster's Dictionary*," a gift which evidently filled a long-felt want. Candidates for membership were voted on by the entire Club, with the result that a member whose candidate was blackballed frequently revenged himself by excluding all the others proposed.

The Club-house, being then considered distant from the business center, established a lunch-room on Washington Street west of La Salle Street. This resulted in its being less frequented than ever, except occasionally in the evening, when a few congenial spirits would come for a game of cards. Among these was Granville Kimball, a courtly, old-fashioned gentleman who, like Hannibal Hamlin and Daniel Webster, always wore a "swallow-tail" suit, resembling our present evening-dress. Before coming to Chicago he owned and operated several stage lines in Michigan, among them one from Chicago to Ypsilanti, which was then the western terminal of the Michigan Central Railway. The latter was an old strap railroad, over which three trains ran each day in the same direction, getting back as best they could.

Another dignified, old-school gentleman who frequented the card-room was Colonel Lucius Tilton, resident director of the Illinois Central Railway and one of the oldest and most experienced railway men in the country. The Gage brothers were also frequent attendants of the card-room.

They were from Massachusetts, where one of them, David, had been a railroad man, and the other, George, the proprietor of the old City Hotel of Boston. Among other frequenters of the card-room were Colonel Henry Farrar, also from Boston, and editor of the *Evening Journal*, a great wit and *raconteur;* Dr. Eldredge, after whom Eldredge Court was named, a well-known character among the early settlers, with an explosive temper and an appropriate command of language; Arthur Burley, Sam Johnston, John B. Lyon, H. G. Loomis, Sam Keith, George Hopkins, Charles Tappan, Francis Morgan, who roomed in the Club and was one of its first secretaries, the Fisher brothers, two big, genial Irishmen, who also roomed in the Club and were great card players and general favorites; John B. Raymond, a society beau of those days, like U. H. Crosby; Howard Priestley, a Marylander, who was prominent on the Board of Trade and quite a man about town.

Edmond Carrey, the French Consul, one of the few that have taken much part in the social life of our city, was very popular in the Club. He and Edward J. Minot were respected for their judgment of wines and *cuisine*. Mr. Minot was a member of the old Minot family of Boston and had been a captain in a Massachusetts regiment during the war. At its close he came west and entered the firm of Henry W. King & Company. Mr. Minot was a member of the Somerset and Athenæum clubs of Boston, and was, in every respect, a cultivated gentleman. One of the few others who had enjoyed any experience of club life was Henry R. Pierson of Albany, resident director of the Chicago and Northwestern Railway, who had been president of a club in Brooklyn and was a college man and a natural leader. Among others of the railroad men prominent in the life of the city and the Club in those days, were: T. B. Blackstone, a man with a rugged Henri Quatre face and beard, who built up the Alton road into a great railway system, with an integrity and conservation exceptional in those days; Perry H. Smith and George L. Dunlap of the Northwestern, and John Van Northwick, president of the Burlington, a regular attendant and card player.

Among the prominent lawyers who became early members of the Chicago Club were two of the ablest and oddest geniuses that ever belonged to the Chicago bar, Judge Beckwith and Francis H. Kales, of whom many anecdotes survive. Judge Fuller and Judge Skinner, both fine Christian gentlemen and interesting conversationalists, were only occasional frequenters of the Club. Wirt Dexter, Judge Dickey and Judge Tree were also among our most distinguished members, but although there were several of national reputation like Melville Fuller, afterwards chief justice, Lyman J. Gage, Franklin MacVeagh, Robert T. Lincoln, who all became cabinet ministers, our most distinguished member, without doubt, was General Philip H. Sheridan. When he came to Chicago to take charge of the Department of the Missouri, he was invited to become an honorary member of the Club, without payment of dues, but, with characteristic independence, he declined, saying he preferred to be elected in the regular way and pay his initiation fee like any other member. He was a frequent visitor of the Club, affable to all and as unassuming as the humblest. His appearance was in striking contrast to his manner; a short, thick body and neck, a massive, bullet-shaped head, close-cropped hair, a complexion crimsoned by exposure and high living, and features of a stern, predatory cast, like those of an Indian; a personality eloquent of the ruthless determination which harried and pursued the Confederacy to exhaustion — an energy so fierce as to be even equal to changing defeat into victory. From Sheridan's appearance you would have expected the harsh voice of command and the assurance of one who had never been withstood, but the reality was quite the contrary. In private life his voice was low and his manner deferential. He would chat any length of time with anyone who stopped him. His reminiscences at such times were far more interesting than anything in his memoirs, which are a bare relation of facts, written with the brevity of a military report.

Sheridan, as a man, has been misunderstood, but not in Chicago, which he always considered his home, having spent the best twelve years of his life here. His kindness was so great that he was often imposed upon by people who abused his good nature. He gathered around him the most brilliant staff we have ever had in Chicago. It included General Rucker, whose daughter he married; Generals Baird and Rufus Ingalls, who were great frequenters of the Club, and General Whipple, whose daughter became Mrs. Charles Deering of this city; Colonels Schuyler Crosby, Fred Grant and M. V. Sheridan, too well known to require further mention; the two Forsythes — "Tony," quiet and dignified, the picture of a French colonel, with his prematurely gray hair and imperial; "Sandy," who was sometimes called the bravest man in the army, as he certainly was one of the handsomest, a great diner-out and the very type of a *beau sabreur* with his soldierly figure, manly face and flashing blue eyes. The "staff" never cut such a figure in Chicago society as it did in Sheridan's day. Probably the handsomest dinner seen here up to that time was given in the Chicago Club by Colonel Schuyler Crosby. His guests numbered forty or fifty, and the tables occupied the entire ground floor of the Club.

The last dinner given in the old Club was the week before the great fire, when General Stager asked a number of its members to meet James Gordon Bennett, "Larry" Jerome, "Johnny" Hecksher, and Fairman Rogers, who were returning from a hunting-party General Sheridan had given them in the West. The second day of the great fire a number of the members, among them Generals Corse and Ledlie, George and James Young, J. K. Fisher, and John Janes, who had been burned out during the night and had had no sleep, assembled at the Club and were refreshing themselves with what might be called "a champagne-supper for breakfast," when the house caught afire. Hastily filling their pockets with cigars and taking a demijohn of whisky and a red satin sofa with them, they finished their meal on the, lake shore.

The great fire, coming so soon after the organization of the Club, was nearly fatal to its existence. The Club lost everything, even its records, and its members were for a long time too busy trying to recover from the great calamity and rebuild their homes and places of business, to have any leisure for clubs. The Fire of 1871 was followed so closely by the panic of 1873 that many who had borrowed money to rebuild their property or reëstablish their business were prostrated by this second catastrophe, a succession of misfortunes as fatal to our "peerage" as the Wars of the Roses. Many who were prominent before lost everything and dropped out of sight, while others, who might have retained their places, thought it a good time to sever their connections with Chicago and return east.

The Club maintained a precarious existence, first in the B. F. Hadduck house on Michigan Avenue near Park Row, then in the Gregg house on the northwest corner of Wabash Avenue and Eldredge Court, but these locations were inconvenient and any member who went to the Club at night through the ruins of the burnt district usually walked in the middle of the street and carried a pistol in his pocket. The attendance of the Club became so meager that its officers refused to accept reëlection, and the members began to resign in such large numbers that those left finally voted to disband. In this emergency, N. K. Fairbank, with characteristic public spirit, offered to buy a lot and build a clubhouse where DeJonghe's restaurant now stands, opposite the Monroe Street entrance of the Palmer House. The Club moved into its new building in July, 1876. It was regarded as a marvel of luxury at that time and for sixty days members were allowed to bring in residents to view its splendor, also to have lady guests on Thursday of each week. With a view to increasing the membership and dispelling any suspicions which might still linger in the feminine mind as to the character of the Club, Mr. and Mrs. Fairbank gave an evening reception in the new Club-house, which gave rise to a fierce argument between the older and younger elements of the Club as to whether evening-dress was obligatory on such occasions.

On September 13, 1878, the Club gave a reception to President and Mrs. Hayes, who happened to be passing through Chicago. The reception committee on this occasion consisted of General Sheridan, Franklin MacVeagh, Levi Z. Leiter, Ezra B. McCagg, and George C. Clarke. On November 14, 1879, the Club gave a reception to General and Mrs. Grant on their return from a trip around the world. It was notable for a reunion of the "Blue and the Gray" in the café, which lasted until the small hours of the morning. As Judge Lochrane of Georgia, an ex-Confederate, rose to speak, Henry Norton, amid general applause, threw an American flag over Lochrane's shoulders. Without a moment's preparation, the Judge, who was an eloquent speaker, made an address so mingled with pathos and patriotism, that his audience at one moment was almost weeping, and at the next wildly cheering. This was the last public reception ever given by the Chicago Club, with the exception of the one it tendered its president, Robert T. Lincoln, eleven years later, May 29, 1890, on his appointment as minister to England.

In those days a number of the younger members, who were of sociable habits, lived in the Club and were fuller blooded and more riotous livers than their successors. The genus might now be termed extinct. A crowd of them were in the habit of coming from the Board of Trade in an omnibus, rushing into the hall of the Club-house at noon and finishing their trades while they ordered their lunch. At night their favorite rendezvous was the billiard-room, which was in the basement adjoining the bar. Here they held frequent meetings, appointing a chairman, whose duty was to see that hospitality was equitably distributed, and a sergeant-at-arms, robust enough to be able to remove such members as became obstreperous, or otherwise violated proprieties, to the adjoining coal-cellar, where they remained until they promised repentance and "liquidated" their fines. "Derby Day" at the old Washington Park Club was a great occasion for this crowd. There was a big *table d'hôte* dinner that night, and from the moment the first arrivals, in the stampede for town, began to come in, until the last noisy reveler sought his couch in the early morning's light, there was continuous celebration.

In contrast to this noisy crowd, a group may be mentioned more characteristic of the serious and commercial nature of the Club, a number of men sometimes referred to as composing the "millionaires' table." The men who started it,—Robert T. Lincoln, Edward S. Isham, Henry W. Bishop, and Norman Williams, — were anything but millionaires at that time. These young men, all college-bred, and of distinguished antecedents, came to Chicago about the same time and formed a friendship which was never broken. Henry W. Bishop was for several years president of the Union Club, on the North Side, and later of the Chicago Club, and as such was noted for his urbanity and tact. Norman Williams, who succeeded him as president of the Chicago Club, was such a delightful and amusing companion, so bubbling over with kindness and good-fellowship, that he might have been called the most popular man in Chicago. Edward S. Isham, their companion, soon became known as one of the most brilliant young attorneys in Chicago. His partner, Robert T. Lincoln, although he was the son of Abraham Lincoln and became Secretary of War and Minister to England, was simple and unassuming, and much too straightforward for political life.

The "millionaire" element of the round table consisted of Marshall Field, George M. Pullman, N. K. Fairbank,

John Crerar, and T. B. Blackstone. Marshall Field, a tall, dignified man, with hair and mustache prematurely gray, a fresh complexion, clear-cut features, and keen, blue eyes, would pass in Europe for a nobleman or a diplomat rather than a business man. George M. Pullman also was endowed with a striking personality, an expression of calm confidence and resolution which never changed. N. K. Fairbank, without whom the Club would not be in existence, was for fourteen years reëlected its president. He was a man of distinguished appearance, a born leader and a daring speculator, who won and lost several fortunes in his day, and was prominent in every public and charitable movement of his time. John Crerar was one of the most original characters in the social life of his day, an old bachelor, with strongly-marked traits from his Scotch ancestry. In appearance, he was the typical British capitalist, with florid complexion, white side-whiskers, and merry blue eyes twinkling under bushy white eyebrows. For forty years no social function in Chicago was complete without his cheery presence. While he was alive he headed every subscription list, and when he died he left a large fortune to the city. Heaven send us more such!

Henry W. King seldom missed a noonday meal at the round table. He was president of the Relief and Aid Society, which distributed several millions in charity after the great fire. He was also a pillar of the Fourth Presbyterian Church, and, on account of the social activities of his family and the interest he took in his neighborhood, was sometimes called "the mayor of Rush Street." Among others, who at various times frequented the round table, may be mentioned John de Koven, director of half a dozen railways and banks, a thorough man of the world, generous and companionable; L. Z.

Leiter, the father of Lady Curzon, a short, broad-shouldered man, a shrewd investor with very decided opinions and a voice often raised in their defense; Charles B. Farwell, a brother of John V. Farwell, and one of the founders of the Club, who rounded out a successful business career by becoming a United States Senator; General Anson Stager, the father of Lady Arthur Butler, a nervous little man, who was a general favorite and played an important part in the Civil War, as well as in building up the telegraph system of the country; General A. C. McClurg, a gentleman of the finest character and culture, who acquitted himself with credit in the Civil War; Franklin MacVeagh, a man of fine critical and social abilities, a college-bred business-man and a student of politics, who became Secretary of the Treasury; John M. Clark, another standard-bearer of reform, whose strong face and cheery voice inspired confidence; Edson Keith and Ezra Warner, representative business men, of fine appearance and courteous manners; the two Spragues (A. A. and O. S. A.), Warner's partners, college men and conspicuous in every public and charitable movement; George C. Clarke, whose attractive personality won him many friends; and B. F. Ayer, for many years attorney of the Illinois Central Railway, and one of the original members of the Club. The Monroe Street location in a few years was found to be too much in the business center; the Club-house also had run down and become dark and noisy, so, the year before the Exposition, the Club bought the Art Institute building for the sum of $425,000, and remodeled it. The land alone would sell now for three times what was then paid for it.

The Exposition of 1893, like the great fire of 1871, marked an epoch in the history of Chicago, as well as in American architecture. Nothing of the kind had been attempted before and its beautiful white palaces, connected by colonnades and bridges, were a dream of beauty mirrored in the waters of the lagoons and lake. The swarms of graceful gondolas which carried the crowds from one building to another enhanced this Venetian effect. The exposition closed an era which might be referred to as the "Middle Ages," and marked the adoption of metropolitan standards in the future social and business life of our city. It was as much of an education to the people who produced this splendid spectacle, as it was to the strangers who extolled their public spirit and liberality. As a foreign diplomat expressed it "What we see here was what we might have expected in Paris: and what we saw in Paris was all we expected here." During the eventful summer of 1893, Chicago was the country's center. Artists and journalists rubbed shoulders with titled foreigners, and French, German, and Spanish were heard in thc halls of our new Club, — this, then, would seem a fitting place to close its history, which has since differed little from that of other clubs.

XIV

THROUGH A CHILD'S EYES

By Mrs. Frederick T. West

It is not paucity of years, but the lack of a good memory, which will make the facts here set down so few and far between. Then, too, to my great regret, I did not glean as much from my elders of those thrillingly interesting early days as I now wish I had.

My uncle, Charles Butler,[1] was the first member of our family to come to Chicago. His description of the journey from New York to Chicago in 1833 dwells on the beauties of the Erie Canal as far as Buffalo; then describes the nearly three-days' lake trip from there to Detroit. From the latter place he and a friend proceeded on Indian ponies, by trail, to Fort Dearborn, taking ten days to cover the three hundred miles.

There were only a few hundred inhabitants in the town at this date, and not more than twenty houses. But my uncle writes: "Chicago is a beautiful place; the north and south branches of the Chicago River unite in the center of the town and form a beautiful river,[2] . . ." He stayed at the Green Tree tavern on the point formed by the junction of these two streams, from which he says the view was very lovely. Considering present conditions in this section of the city, it is amusing to read what he writes of its charms in

[1] Charles Butler married Eliza Ogden, eldest sister of Mahlon D. Ogden.

[2] *Life and Letters of Charles Butler.*

those days of long ago. But he not only saw its charms, he saw its possibilities; and, encouraged by my uncle's view of the situation, his friend and travelling companion bought a large tract of land. This included one-half of Kinzie's Addition, which runs from the river to Chicago Avenue, and from the lake to forty feet west of State Street, and the whole of Wolcott's Addition, which runs from Kinzie Street to Chicago Avenue, and from forty feet west of State Street to one-hundred and nine feet west of La Salle Avenue; also Block "1" in the original town, running from Kinzie Street to the river and from forty feet west of State Street to Dearborn Avenue. It must be remembered, however, that in those days the lake came almost to Pine Street, or North Michigan Avenue as it is now called. For this large piece of property the lordly sum of $20,000 was paid. The next year Mr. Butler and some of his friends bought this same tract for $100,000, and the following year, 1835, he persuaded his brother-in-law, William Butler Ogden, to come to Chicago to take charge of it. The property looked very unattractive to the latter on his arrival. It was marshy, muddy, and covered with scrub-oak and underbrush. There was a Government auction coming on. To take advantage of this, streets and lots were laid out in the new purchase, and it was ready for sale in the required time. Although it was only two years since the first transfer, one-third of this property sold for $100,000. In the next year, my father, Mahlon Dickerson Ogden, a young college graduate, just having been admitted to the bar, came to Chicago.

Letters written in 1850 tell of how my aunts used to spend two days a week with each other; how their children were carefully drilled in their French lessons, these same lessons being bestowed by a very charming Swede, Count von Schneidau;[1] how two evenings a week all the members of the family, including the children, and a few of the neighbors, met together and danced, "It amused the children and improved their manners."

A mist of happiness and content seems to envelop my childhood days, through which I can see very little of the outer world. A large and devoted family circle, constantly intermingling, is the background. Doubtless we took meals alone, but I cannot remember ever doing so. There were always several house-guests, who often stayed for weeks at a time, an evidence of the hospitality so universal at that period. These visitors were of all sorts and kinds, and, to my childish eyes, very interesting and delightful, even including a young man of our own name which, he seemed to think, entitled him to stay indefinitely. My surprise was great when one day I overheard my parents discussing how they might persuade him to leave, for they had become convinced that he was really an adventurer. One friend spent an entire winter with us, to be under the doctor's care. Of her stay, I remember nothing, but her going is indelibly impressed upon my mind, for when we went to help her to her carriage, there stood, not only the carriage, but a little ball of a black pony with a red velvet saddle, her gift and my delight for years to come.

I can only remember the interior of three houses, besides our own, before the Fire, and they were those of my aunts, Mrs. Jonathan Young Scammon and Mrs. Ezra Butler McCagg, and of my uncle, William B. Ogden. Mr. Scam-

[1] His daughter was adopted by William B. Ogden and afterwards became Mrs. Eugene N. Jerome, of New York City.

mon's house stood on Michigan Avenue, just above Congress Street, its lovely garden occupying the spot where the Auditorium Hotel and Theater now stand. This was the last house to burn in both of the great fires. It was blown up at the time of the first by General Sheridan, to arrest further southward progress of the flames. When one thinks of the traffic on this corner now, it is amusing to picture our favorite sport when we went down there on summer evenings. It consisted of a run and jump across the street which enabled us to clear successfully the rail fence that conserved the beauties of what is now Grant Park from too great trespassing on the part of the public. This process had a never-ending charm, and how proud we were when, occasionally, we could prevail on the beautiful Miss Louise Clark, who lived next door, to join us!

Mr. Scammon's library is the room which stands out most prominently in my mind. It was big and high and filled with books in every possible corner; books, by the way, mostly bound in brown leather, with a shield derived from Mr. Scammon's Swedenborgian proclivities, in gilt on the back of every one of them. The largest globe I have ever seen stood in one corner of the room, and a large orrery in another. Both interested me intensely and, to this day, I wonder over Mr. Scammon's unfailing kindness and patience in explaining them to me.

It was these same books that were saved when, on the morning of the great fire of October 9, 1871, many teamsters, whom Mr. Scammon happened to be employing at the time, came and backed up their carts alongside of the house proffering their use as vans. Mr. Scammon sent the loaded vans forth into the unknown, anywhere to escape the destruction approaching on every side. In this connection it may be interesting to know that two young men, Robert Lincoln and John Hay, came to Mrs. Scammon that morning to offer what help they could, but when they saw the rather wholesale way in which she was planning to move her belongings, they advised against it, saying it might complicate her insurance arrangements later on. Considering the condition of the insurance companies that fall, it was fortunate that Mrs. Scammon took counsel of the heavens by ascending to the lookout on the top of the house, and, influenced by their angry glow, decided to move everything she could lay her hands on.

I like to think of its being Colonel Loomis who roused the Scammon family, as well as the whole of Michigan Avenue, to their dangers, that morning. I can see him now, mounted on one of his seven black horses, with his army-blanket behind him, riding up and down the street. It was a veritable call to arms, for surely it was a deadly foe they had to fight.

Of the north-side houses, William B. Ogden's is the one I remember least distinctly, though a picture comes to my mind of being there one lovely spring morning and finding my aunt, Fanny Sheldon, sitting on a wide, side piazza with her work, a large cage with her beloved cooing ring-doves and her dogs beside her. The flowering shrubs were in bloom and the square between Rush and Cass, Ontario and Erie streets, was a delightful spot in which to wander. Not the least interesting thing was the smoke-house, where were cured the hams, — a delicious place and most fascinating to us children. The main dwelling was spacious, with large and high rooms which my youthful memories ever picture filled with guests. There were in those days no clubs, fine restaurants, or other general rendezvous for gregarious and cultivated people, so many of the interesting men and women who visited the young city of the West, gathered under William B. Ogden's roof.

Samuel J. Tilden was a great friend of his and a frequent visitor at the Ogden home. How we children dreaded the advent of New York's famous governor! If the older members of the family were not at home, one of us had to give the two gentlemen their tea. How many afternoons I have sat, impatiently waiting for them to finish their tea, — a protracted feast, as you may imagine, as Mr. Tilden was known to take as many as eighteen cups of tea. What wouldn't I give now to remember what they talked about! But nothing remains with me beyond recollections of my longings to get back to my game of "I Spy."

At Mrs. McCagg's house, which stood in a large garden on North Clark between Chestnut and Locust streets, everyone sang or played some musical instrument. It is here I remember William B. Ogden, sitting at the piano, both playing and singing his favorite airs, *Guide Me, O Thou Great Jehovah; Martha; Rise My Soul and Stretch Thy Wings, Thy Better Portion Trace,* being most prominent among them.

My cousin, Louis McCagg, writes: —

"I remember our house in Chicago with much clearness. The two parlors, dining-room, and library, as well as my mother's bedroom, and the nursery, all on the ground floor in the good old generous way. I have vague memories, too, of much company in the house, music, and especially quartette singing by amateurs. Mrs. George B. Carpenter, Mrs.

Stella Dyer Loring (Louis Dyer's sister), Mr. Nillson, and 'Jim' Kelly, are names I recall; also George Bostwick, who had a beautiful baritone voice."

Louis forgets to mention that all the older members of the family, including the eastern cousins who were afterwards Mrs. C. C. Tiffany, of New York, and Mrs. A. C. McClurg of this city, took part in this singing. The letter continues: —

"Showing in what near relation that part of the North Side[1] stood to the country in those days, I remember hearing that a fox had been caught in our place when I was a very little boy; and I distinctly remember discovering a nest of little wild rabbits in the grass near its southern border. The Lake Shore Drive was something very new and very primitive; part of it ran through or alongside a cemetery. Then you came to some land belonging, I think, to the Newberrys, which they would not let one drive across and a detour had to be made. But what a treat it was if you caught sight of Potter Palmer driving four-in-hand, with his old mother, in her Quaker garb, beside him; of Fitzhugh Whitehouse driving tandem, with a negro groom up behind!"

The library referred to by my cousin had a large bay-window at one end, but was chiefly lighted by a skylight from above. It was faced with books from floor to ceiling. Here was my first experience with one of the little travelling ladders by means of which one reached the topmost vol-

[1] The square between Clark Street and La Salle Avenue, Locust and Chestnut streets.

umes. It was a fascinating affair, and we children used to peek around the corner to see if "Uncle McCagg" looked serene enough for us to venture to beg the privilege of mounting its dizzy height. Here, too, hung some carved scallop shells telling, as with the knights of old, of the McCagg pilgrimage to Palestine, Jerusalem, and Mount Sinai, made with my aunt and uncle, Mr. and Mrs. Edwin H. Sheldon, in 1854. How they made me hope and pray that some day I, too, might earn the right to such trophies!

In thinking of the venturesome souls who braved those early days in the West, one is apt to forget that they all came from the East, and that most of them were accustomed to every refinement and all the existing amenities of life in an older part of our country. The difficulties of providing themselves with comforts, to say nothing of luxuries, were, of course, nearly insurmountable, even as late as in 1854. My mother used to tell a tale of the vexatious delays and ultimate disappointment when, in her early married life, she had secured a very lovely Wilton carpet in New York, and how impatiently she waited for the carpet, which was an interminable time in arriving. The boat by which it was shipped, the method by which all freight came in those days, ran into one of the furious lake storms we all know so well, and went to the bottom. The transportation company, however, got it up, and delivered the carpet in apparently perfect condition. It was put down and much enjoyed, until the hot weather came, when an Egyptian plague of flies settled down upon it. Investigation disclosed the fact that the main cargo of the boat by which it had been shipped had been molasses, with which the carpet had become saturated. So, though the company had had it thoroughly cleansed, as they supposed, the flies were not to be deceived. Of course, it had to be entirely destroyed.

My mother was only six years old when she came West. Her father, General William Billings Sheldon, of Delhi, N. Y., suffered from asthma which he thought the change of climate would cure. She remembered, in the very first of her days in the new country, a little girl coming to school with her dress very neatly pinned down the back with thorns from a thorn-apple tree, nature's substitute for pins which were not then as plentiful as now.

To pass on to the great event of my childhood —

The day of October 9, 1871, began for us about one o'clock in the morning, when the watchman roused my father at our home at North Dearborn Street and what is now Walton Place, and told him that there was a fire which was spreading rapidly, suggesting that he might like to go to his office before it was too late. This my father did at once, thus being able to bring home a buggy-full of books and papers. The office vaults, however, did their work well, so a duplicate of the official city atlas, written up to within a week of the day of the Fire, was saved in perfect order.[1] This was the more fortunate as the originals at the City Hall were completely destroyed. My father used to tell me how he was the last person to cross Rush Street bridge before it fell. Later, but still in the early morning, I was amazed to find a strange woman in my mother's bed, and was told she was ill and had been brought for safety from the Sherman House. She was moved on after a time, and we never knew who she was. Then I opened the front door to see what was going on outside. The vestibule was a large one and, on either

[1] From letters written by Edwin H. Sheldon, October 19, 1871.

side of the door, stood a good-sized arm-chair. In these Mr. and Mrs. William M. Scudder were discovered sitting, crying bitterly, and each holding a bird-cage. The sight beyond beggared description. Nothing but flames as far as the eye could reach. The scene was like a vast roaring furnace. Against this background the New England Church, ablaze from steeple to cellar, stood, roof gone, with sparks and jets of fire outlining each rafter.

At this point, my father came in, after having battled in vain with the flames at Mr. McCagg's house, saying, "Does anyone know anything about Grandma McCagg?" as we all called Mr. McCagg's dear old mother. No one knew. It was not a morning to think of much beside the immediate present.

"I must go and find her," said he, and off he rushed into that vortex of flames, on foot, for it was something no horse would have faced. I was frightened then, for it did not seem as if he could come back alive. He found her with her daughter, Miss Carrie McCagg, sitting in the McCagg house quite composedly and unconscious of their imminent danger. A few minutes more and rescue would have been impossible. The old lady was very feeble and, after walking a short way, gave out entirely: it was an ugly few minutes to remember, my father afterwards said. He stood by her side in the street where the air was already suffocatingly hot, she, unable to move, and he, equally unable to carry or leave her. But just at this juncture, Mr. Sullivan, the painter, dashed by in an express wagon. It took but a moment to hail him and help her into the vehicle. So all came safely forth from their terrible danger.

The streets were already very crowded, almost everyone

walking, and almost everyone loaded down with a burden of some kind or other — empty picture-frames, washbowls and pitchers, mirrors, and what-not. Our block was the first enclosed open space they had passed in a long time, so many a Christian divested himself of his pack and threw it over the fence, to be reclaimed or not later on. Such a crop of piano-legs as met our amazed eyes on our return home after our own hurried flight, I imagine, no one ever saw before or since!

And our flight was hurried, for my father, from the first, expressed his conviction that our house would not burn. Of course its position was most advantageous, standing, as it did, in the middle of the square[1] between Lafayette (now Walton) Place and Oak Street, and Dearborn and Clark streets, and in the midst of large elm trees, all of which, by the way, my father had planted himself. Washington Square, with its many trees was directly in front of us, and the block containing only my aunt's house diagonally to the southwest. All this vacant space was a great protection, though it didn't seem sufficient, as the huge firebrands fell about us in fiery showers. The heat from the flames to the east was so intense that it was quite uncomfortable to sit at the side of the breakfast-table nearest the windows. Breakfast was served to any and all who cared to stop for it. And still we had no thought of leaving the house.

Finally, about eleven o'clock, Major Daniel Goodwin came in and insisted that, if my father would not go himself, he should at least send my mother and the children. I don't remember any especial excitement, but there must have

[1] The present site of the Newberry Library

been some, for we made the trip to Lakeview in a lumber-wagon, my mother sitting on a trunk filled with family silver. Our regular carriage-horses were standing harnessed in the barn. Later in the day, they appeared with a relative-in-law, of whom we were none of us very fond, sitting in solitary grandeur on the back seat of the big carriage! By the time the carriage reached the Goodwins, where we had gone for safety, everyone had become convinced that the flames were still pursuing, so once more we started forth, this time across the prairie to Riverside. Here we stayed until the following Thursday.

Many friends and acquaintances were there, too, in the large new hotel, and never shall I forget the looks on their faces, when, one evening, the band began playing *Home, Sweet Home!* Having been one of those cheerfully tone-deaf children, I could not imagine why one of the party made such a dash for the leader, bringing the music to an ignominious ending. In those telephoneless days news travelled slowly, but many tales came to us from the burned district. We heard that our house, like everyone else's, had gone, and that my father and all the men who stayed to fight the fire with him had been burned. So you may imagine with what thankful hearts we listened to William W. K. Nixon when he brought us word that all were safe, and we were to return home the next day.

Such a trip! And such desolation! The scorched, blackened, and leafless trees — and there were many of them, I remember thinking — were one of the most painful evidences of the fiery storm. Never shall I forget jolting over those burned, hollow blocks of "Nicholson" pavement, as we drove up the absolutely deserted streets. Not another soul was in sight. Years afterwards, in going through Holland on my bicycle, I was transported in a trice to this same dismal afternoon, when a portion of the old brick pavement just outside of Haarlem, worn hollow by the tread of many feet, produced exactly the same effect on my little wheel that the fire-tortured wooden blocks had on the old, lumbering carriage.

But there was our home! Our yard was full of piano-legs, and eighteen cows had taken refuge in our garden. These same cows rather appalled us at first, but in the end they proved our salvation, for no one claimed them until spring. We had forty people in our house all that winter. All the servants of the various members of the family slept on mattresses laid in rows on the floor in the large rooms in the basement. Upstairs were my uncle, Edwin H. Sheldon, and his son and daughter; my uncle William B. Ogden, as he came and went; Mr. and Mrs. Volney Turner; General and Mrs. William E. Strong, nurse, and baby; and my uncle, E. B. McCagg, for part of the time. These are some of the many who come to my mind as having spent that winter with us. You may imagine the difficulties of providing for such a family, with every bridge between us and the West or South Side gone!

Our nearest neighbors were four or five miles away. The only method of reaching a shop of any kind was by way of the La Salle Street tunnel, which was pitch black. The horses were really afraid to go through it, so it seemed quite an adventure to undertake it. This, however, did not frighten me, and I was always keen to go; but what did bring terror to my soul was to look out of the windows after lights were out. Every forehanded resident had apparently gotten in his winter supply of coal before the Fire, and as the evil eyes of these many smoldering coal-piles glared at me from under all the debris, I can assure you I scuttled into bed in short order. We were under martial law in the city, and I can remember the men going out with their guns to keep watch every night, for a time. This was the more necessary, as it seemed there was some ill-feeling about our house not having burned. This ill-will became more evident after we had achieved many new neighbors in the hastily run-up barracks, which soon filled Washington Square. Later on, smallpox developed in this settlement, so I imagine my elders were much relieved when one night, towards spring, these buildings, having served their purpose, were set afire and burned to the ground.

A letter from William B. Ogden to his niece, Julia Wheeler, in New York, written from Springfield, Illinois, October 19, 1871, only ten days after the fire, tells so well of the spirit in which everyone met that disaster that I will give some extracts from it: —

"Dear Julia:

"You will have learned from the papers and from a letter I wrote Uncle Charlie much of the particulars of the fire that destroyed so much of Chicago so ruthlessly and so completely. It was an awful, unprecedented catastrophe, wonderful, almost inexplicable, and in a good degree, incomprehensible.

"We have only to see and admit that it is, to accept it without speculation or complaint as an event we can only deal with by trying to repair, so far as we may, its injury.

This I have set myself to doing cheerfully and with confidence, but hardly in the expectation of ever seeing the past literally restored.

"Chicago will be built up again in good time and will continue to expand in business, wealth, and numbers,— perhaps in ten years may contain 500,000 people, — but a great many of the old citizens who have assisted in building it up, and lived to enjoy it thus far in peace and great prosperity and happiness, will never, I fear, be able, at their more advanced period of life, to regain their former positions, but will be obliged to give place to new-comers with money, and leave to others the city they have assisted so much in creating, and the beauty and extent of which creation they have been so proud of, and until now loved and enjoyed so much. It is a sad picture and result to contemplate, and yet must unavoidably be submitted to by many, for aught I can see.

"I feel as if I should be entirely willing, so far as I am personally concerned, to give all I have left, and to live and die a poor man, if by so doing, I could see the city I have loved, enjoyed, and toiled for so long and with such hope and realization and joy, restored to the beautiful and happy position it occupied previous to its recent unparalleled calamity. Indeed, I might well give the remnant of life that is left to me to that end if it would avail anything, but it will not. So far as I am concerned, I have all I need left, and much more than I shall need personally, but with many of my friends and neighbors this is not the case.

"I am here to aid in the passage of a bill by the Legislature restoring to Chicago about three millions of dollars expended by that city in deepening the State Canal, and diverting the waters of Lake Michigan through the Chicago River into it, to the perfect cleansing of the Chicago River and the improvement of the Canal.

"The bill passed a few hours since, and I go home tonight. With the money it provides, we are to rebuild all our bridges and our public buildings where they now stand, are to pay interest on our city debt for years to come, and provide for our fire and police departments.

"This reëstablishes things as they were, overcomes many obstacles, gives confidence to the people to rebuild, and to capitalists to loan the money to do so, and will give heart and courage to all, and I now hope to see active and hopeful and successful efforts in reconstruction everywhere. Were not the winter so near at hand, much would be done before spring. . . .

"Don't understand me as in the least desponding or as pining or unhappy on account of all that has happened here so far as it concerns me personally, for that would be very wide of the fact. On my account not an hour's grief or unhappiness should I suffer, but be just as thankful as ever that my lot and path in life are strewn with so many friends and flowers. But for the loss of the beautiful city I spent the best and almost the majority of the years of my life in assisting to build, and which it gave me such pleasure to labor for, and the growth, expansion, strength and beauty of which it was such a joy to see — I do grieve, — and far more for the greater calamity which has fallen so much more severely on so many of my friends, associates, and co-laborers in that great and interesting work. Never before was a large and very beautiful and fortunate city built by a generation of people so proud, so in love with their work; never a city so lamented and grieved over as Chicago. For this, I do weep with those who have far greater occasion to weep than I."

As I have said before, William B. Ogden came to Chicago in 1835, and when, in 1837, the growing town became a city, he was chosen to be its first mayor. The panic of that year made the payment of indebtedness awkward, to say the least, and a public meeting was called, at which it was proposed to suspend the courts in order to prevent the compulsory payment of debt. By my uncle's influence and personal appeal the scheme was overturned. A little later, he worked with equal vigor and success in preventing Illinois from repudiating her state debt. In this connection, it may be interesting to note that his brother-in-law, Charles Butler, by his own unaided efforts before the legislatures of Michigan and Indiana, likewise prevented both of those commonwealths from following Mississippi's unfortunate lead in this respect.

We have all been brought up on the theory that Chicago grew with lightning rapidity; and this is easy to believe when we realize the spirit of the early days. Because the City Fathers did not work fast enough to satisfy him, William B. Ogden, alone, caused to be laid out and constructed more than one hundred miles of city streets at his own expense.

In 1853, Mr. Ogden felt the need of rest from his many activities and went abroad with his sister, Mrs. Butler, and her husband. They went first to London and, as it shows how Chicago was honored, perhaps a letter from Charles Butler written at this time may be of interest:—

"We went to the Lord Mayor's dinner last evening, which was a most gorgeous banquet, and to us green Americans, a great novelty. The places assigned to us were at the head of the table and directly opposite to the Lord Mayor and his lady and the cabinet ministers, so that we were within a few feet of the speakers. We met the Lord Chancellor, the Earl of Aberdeen, the Earl of Clarendon, Lord John Russell, Lord Palmerston, Sir James Graham, the Marquis of Salisbury, Mr. Buchanan, the Lord Chief Justice of England, the Lord Mayor, and the ex-Lord Mayor. All were seated according to rank, William B. Ogden, as ex-Mayor of Chicago, being placed among the distinguished guests next below the foreign ministers. All the guests appeared in uniform, making a splendid spectacle in the finely lighted Guildhall." [1]

Although rest was a prime necessity, there was another object of Mr. Ogden's trip, namely: the examination and study of the great public works of the older civilizations. Having been president of the Chicago Sewerage Commission, as well as of the Chicago Branch of the State Board of Sewerage Commissioners, he was interested in the canals of Holland and his examination of them first suggested to him the practicability of the free flow of the waters of Lake Michigan through the Chicago and Des Plaines rivers to the Mississippi.

I never hear this trip mentioned without a shudder, when I recall how nearly none of them ever came back. They were waiting in Paris, preparatory to sailing for home in a few days' time. One morning, Aunt Eliza (Mrs. Butler), came downstairs saying she had dreamed that the ship which

Life and Letters of Charles Butler.

they expected to sail on had gone down on the way to America. The next morning she looked a little disturbed and said she had dreamed the same thing over again, and the third morning she begged the gentlemen of the party to wait for another boat, "For," said she, "I not only dreamed the same thing over again, but I saw the children and every one of us drowning in the water." All this was so foreign to her usual calm, matter-of-fact nature, that they yielded to her entreaties, and so escaped the lot of those others who sailed by the ill-fated *Arctic*, which went down on the next westward trip.

When I cross Rush Street bridge, I am reminded that William B. Ogden, who had never seen a swinging bridge, nevertheless, caused the first one in the city to be built. An interesting incident in connection with the early days of this same bridge occurs to me. Another of my uncles, Mr. Sheldon, in crossing it one morning, noted a heavily-veiled woman walking before him. The bridge started to open and for some reason this person was thrown forward, and, but for his quickness in coming to the rescue, would have fallen into the river. Great was his surprise, as he pulled her up, to discover that she was none other than his good friend, Mrs. G. P. A. Healy.

It was at William B. Ogden's suggestion, and on his original plan, that an underground railway for the relief of the already congested traffic of New York was considered. Mr. Ogden's plan was being publicly discussed at the time of his death, and contained the embryo of New York's complex subway system.

These samples are chosen at random from among the many activities of Chicago's first mayor. A dictum on his life and personality published in the *New York Sun*, August 4, 1877, speaks of him as "a great spirit, of a well-regulated activity, of immense energy, of captivating address and winning manners. Mr. Ogden has contributed more than any one man on this continent to the development of the great Northwest."

It is a far cry from rapid transit in congested New York City, to conditions such as those that met my uncle when he first came to Chicago, and yet, I think, it may be of interest to revert to them. At the time he came West in 1835, there were only five thousand people between Chicago and the Pacific Ocean. Charles Butler, writing to his little son, describes the prairie-schooners, the fastest method of progression in those days, and tells the story of the famous Winnebago Chief whom my uncle, in his wanderings on the prairie, had often seen: —

"Prairie-schooners, as they call them, going into the city loaded with wheat or fruit, come from a great distance, some of them more than two hundred miles and are long on the road. They call them prairie-schooners because, with their swelling canvas tops, they look like schooners coming over the prairie. Generally, they have six or eight yoke of oxen to draw the wagon. It is a sight to see fifteen or twenty of these great baggage-wagons coming along together; they look more like a caravan of the East than anything I have ever seen."

There were no roads on the prairies at that time and not a house to be seen, but this is one of the sights we might have chanced upon had our lot been cast in those days that are no more. The letter continues: —

"Big Thunder was a famous Winnebago Chief who lived and died here a few years ago [this was in 1842, in the prairie, west of Chicago], an inveterate enemy of the white man who kept plundering his countrymen and taking their lands from them. He was an Indian of great size and a noble-looking fellow. Just before he died, he directed that after he was dead they should place him in a sitting posture on the top of a beautiful mound in a prairie overlooking a grove, with his blanket around him and his war-club in his hands, and surround him with a paling, so that with his face to the east he could keep the watch. For, he said, there would be a great battle fought on that field between the Indians and the white men. The Indians would come up out of the woods and the white men over the prairie, and he promised that he would keep a lookout. If the white men should win, he would remain forever silent, but if the Indians, then he would give a shout. They buried him just as he said, and there Big Thunder sits, with the paling built about him, with his blanket wrapped around him and his war-club in his hands, looking out upon the wood."[1]

And there, other early settlers report in letters to eastern relatives they found him waiting the great battle. What finally became of his remains is not recorded in the early annals of Chicago. They vanished in the great tide of European civilization which swept from across the Atlantic, westward over this mighty land to the waters of the Pacific.

[1] *Life and Letters of Charles Butler.*

XV

EARLY LAKE FOREST

BY MRS. ROBERT GREAVES MCGANN

A DESCRIPTION of the important men who came to Chicago in the early days includes the familiar names of nearly all who lived in Lake Forest. Brilliant, individual pioneers they were with large vision and with the ability with which to realize their ideals.

My father[1] used to describe how Chicago looked to him when he came. It was then a small town of three thousand inhabitants, but I think even he could hardly appreciate all the changes that had come in one lifetime.

The education we put our children through now may bring a higher average of cultivation and general intelligence, but I wonder whether, in the rush and scurry of our lives, where everyone is trying to be a little and do a little of everything, the individual is not becoming less individual, less rugged, less interesting. Perhaps, because we all travel so much, and are so seldom in one place long enough to identify ourselves with anything, we shirk responsibilities rather than assume them. How different it was when people lived their lives the year around in one place, when one was arrayed, willing or not, for or against every subject, whether an institution or the actions of individuals!

In 1857, a number of men, mostly members of the Second

[1] The Hon. Charles B. Farwell, United States Senator from Illinois, 1887–1891 —*Editor.*

Presbyterian Church, — and I am sure I need not explain that this was an important center in the social life of the Chicago of that day, — decided that they would go up on the North Shore and select a place to live in the country. A special train was chartered and, headed by the Rev. Dr. Robert Patterson, the minister of the Second Church, this large company set forth. Arrived at what is now Lake Forest, they walked on a deer-path down to the lake, and, finding nothing but lake and forest, decided on its name.

Having selected it for its beauty, they were clever enough to have the streets of Lake Forest laid out by Olmsted & Company, the most famous landscape gardeners of that time in America. And, furthermore, they had in their minds that they wished to make, not only beautiful homes to live in, but a university of the first order for the education of their children.

Dr. Charles H. Quinlan, Sylvester Lind, Harvey M. Thompson, Gilbert Rossiter, Judge Mark Skinner, Edward S. Isham, D. R. Holt, Samuel Dexter Ward, and H. G. Shumway were among these early settlers.

Sylvester Lind, a rich Scotch banker, said that he would endow a university if it were named "Lind University," but, soon after, he lost his fortune, and the university project was dropped.

The Academy was the first public building of any consequence that was built in Lake Forest. It stood where the Durand Art Institute now is, only close to the road, having two turnstile gates, one leading up to the school-room door, and the other to that part of the structure where the principal and his family lived, on the other side. The building was an imposing one for its epoch, being very large, high and white, with green blinds, and having two cupolas, one on each side. This is where the boys' school started. Girls went there, too, for a short time, and in it the Presbyterians held their church services for three years.

Mr. and Mrs. Richard Baxter Dickinson managed this school, and a son of theirs was the first minister of the church. Soon the Dickinson daughters started a young ladies' seminary, and had about twenty boarders. The young girls of the very "nicest" families in Chicago went to it. The Dickinsons themselves were unusually attractive and cultivated people, although very prim according to our present standards.

The boys and girls of the schools in those days were kept religiously separated, never allowed to speak to each other in the street and, even in church, they sat on opposite sides of the aisle. The story goes, that young ladies used often to faint in front of the Academy so they would have to be carried in there.

The next group of people who came to Lake Forest included Simeon Williams, William S. Johnston, and Robert I. Fabian, owning the I. P. Rumsey place, Deer-path Inn, and the James Viles places respectively. These three families were related to each other and had numerous and picturesque offspring. They and the H. G. Shumways were very socially inclined, and were responsible for much gaiety and hospitality. W. H. Ferry, president of the Northwestern Railroad, the Carl Bradleys, William S. Warren, Amzi Benedict, D. J. Lake, Edwin J. Larned, the E. S. Barnums, the Hotchkiss family, Edwin S. Skinners, P. W. Pages, William V. Kays, the J. V. Farwells — all these my family found when they came in 1871.

The picture I have in my mind of some of these men, as they came home from their business every night on the five-o'clock train, is typical. Their seats in the parlor-car were always reserved for them, and they sat in the following order: first, my father; then, my uncle, J. V. Farwell; then, D. R. Holt, prosperous on account of his large lumber interest; Simon S. Reid, tall and slight, with a pronounced Scotch accent, dignified, with old-fashioned courtly manners; Ezra Warner, of the old school, handsome and charming; William S. Warren, head of a large insurance company, and one of the most interesting men in Lake Forest; then, Judge Henry Blodgett, an eminent lawyer in Chicago, but who lived at Waukegan. All these men seem to me to be much more distinguished than the types we produce now. A curious combination they made, however, of busy men in the midst of the making of a big city, coming back each day to quiet Lake Forest and their families, and living as simple a life as could be lived in any New England village.

The early days of Lake Forest should be written down by Miss Wilkins, with a first-hand New England pen, and not by one a generation removed. That it should have had that particular flavor is not remarkable, as the heads of every house had so lately come from New England or other eastern states.

The people who thus settled in Lake Forest within a few years of each other, had many interests in common, beginning, of course, with their families of young children, all to be educated.

The life centered around the church, naturally, and everybody went to the services on Sunday, and to most of the other weekly meetings, from Wednesday evening prayer-meeting to the young people's meeting on Sunday night at seven. Each family, from father to the youngest child, took some part, either singing in the choir, teaching in Sunday School, praying or speaking in the prayer-meetings, or reading a verse at the young people's meetings.

The specialties of the various families seem vivid to me still; there was one family, prominent in every way, where the son played the organ violently, working the pedals with his feet and shoulders as well, while the daughter sang soprano, showing her fine row of white, large teeth, and striking triumphantly the top note, never quite on top.

The Ward family amused us all even then, they were so emotional and sentimental; Samuel Dexter Ward sat in the pew on Sunday, surrounded by Mother, Lucy, Ella, Amy, Lilly, and Frankie — the last a girl like the others, so named because they had given up hoping for a boy. Mr. Ward was always to be depended on for the longest extemporaneous prayer, and he moved himself so much that he invariably wept. One Wednesday night he prayed with extra fervor for my cousin Fannie[1] and me, entreating the Lord "that his two young friends who were going to Paris to school, might return safely and uncontaminated." And we giggled out loud! The eldest daughter, Lucy, pale, blond, and ethereal, married a missionary and went at once to China.

The young people's meetings were conducted by a different young man, from eighteen to twenty years old, each Sunday night. He would start by praying, reading the Bible, and then perhaps making wise remarks. He would call on first one and then another to lead in prayer or speak; then, if the spirit was not moving them sufficiently, spaces would

[1] Mrs. Henry Tuttle, daughter of John V. Farwell.

be filled by verses recited from the Bible. On one occasion, Lawrence Williams, nervous and easily embarrassed, was asked to give a text from the Scriptures, so he stood up and loudly said, "While there is life, there is hope."

Then there was old Dr. Nicholas, a retired clergyman, "Father Nicholas," they called him, who used to go to sleep in church, and often he would take out his false teeth and put them in his pocket.

At the right of the pulpit, almost facing the main aisle of the church, in the front pew, sat a man named Stripe, a house-painter, and his large family. He was English, of the pronounced, toothy type, and his wife was fat and ruddy. Of his numerous children, I remember the names of two, Violet Stripe and Ida Centennial Stripe, because she was born in 1876.

At Christmas time, all sorts of ideas were used to amuse the children. Mrs. S. S. Reid (who managed all these affairs) on one occasion decided to have *The Old Woman who Lived in a Shoe.* A mammoth shoe was built where the pulpit usually was, and dozens of children burst out of the top or poked their heads out of holes in the toe.

Other years, a Christmas tree was the center of festivities and the children were expected to come to the church and help trim it. We strung pop-corn and cranberries, and put green and blue candy in tarlatan bags made in the shape of stockings. On Christmas Eve, five of us stood in a row, with arms stretched high over our heads, each holding a large letter, spelling "P-E-A-C-E." Each child recited a verse beginning with her letter. All went well until it came to me, but looking at the church filled with all the familiar faces was too much. I could not remember a word, and sat ignominiously down, thus early forming my own particular view about doing anything in public.

The little white, wooden church, with its tall, thin steeple, stood where the Presbyterian Church is now, and was moved away to make room for the present building. The new church was built out of the original stones of which the famous Second Church had been made before the Fire.

Dancing in that era was looked upon as the last form of wickedness, — Mr. Holt said he would rather see all his children in their coffins than to see them dancing. Mr. Holt also rebuked Mr. Warner for allowing his daughter to be overdressed; he had noticed her one morning on the station platform in a dress made of silk. Incidentally, the dress had been made from an old one of her mother's, but even that did not condone its crime against Puritanism.

Mr. Holt also belonged to the session of the church when they summoned Carrie Benedict, Allie Smith, and my sister Anna[1] to rebuke them for undue levity with Academy boys. These men likewise insisted that a small dancing-class for little children, which had been organized, should be abandoned. *Tempora mutantur et nos mutamur in illis!*

All the boys in the village attended the Academy, until one Saturday when two boys, named Charlie Dole and Edward Pritchet, decided they had had enough school, and, having made careful preparations by soaking the floors with kerosene, they set a match to the building and burned it all up.

The Seminary, Ferry Hall, was started later by Senator Ferry of Michigan, a brother of W. H. Ferry, and has been, from the beginning to this day, a prosperous school.

[1] Mrs. Reginald de Koven, of New York, the well-known writer.

There had never been a college until my mother decided she would like to have one (a coëducational one at that) so that my sister Anna could have a college education without leaving home. She then set forth, first to convince the people in Lake Forest that they wanted one, and then to procure scholars, for there were none.

Miss Annie Williams tells me that in asking her family for their support, she told them how nice it would be for the three young women in the family to have so many young men in town. Miss Williams says she mentioned that she thought they would be rather too young to be interesting, so my mother quickly said, "Oh, but think of the professors!"

For the scholars she went to Chicago, and there in some high-school she found young men and women who were willing to have it done to them, incidentally to be paid for, and brought them to Lake Forest.

The effect of this innovation was almost as a southern feud; those who were in favor of the college and those against it were drawn up in battle array.

The college started in the hotel which long ago was very fashionable, and stood where the tree-shaded village park now is. That building also was set on fire, though accidentally this time, and burned to the ground. When the hotel was first built it was a popular hostelry. The MacGregor Adamses, Kings, Franklin Spencers, Arthur Catons, Augustus Eddys, Charles Townes, Henry Tuttles, Joseph Medills, Wrights, Eugene Pikes, Perry Trumbulls, T. W. Harveys, A. C. Badgers, T. T. Shreves, R. L. Henrys, James H. Taylors, and others, used to spend their summers there. Such bachelors as Scott Keith, Huntington Jackson, Archie Fisher and

Wayne Chatfield also frequented it. There were hops every Saturday night, and much gaiety.

The opening of the schools in autumn was always the occasion for the greatest excitement among the young people. We were occupied with deciding which of the boys looked the most attractive and needed to be selected, or which girl we would choose for a dearest friend.

The concerts in the middle and at the end of the school year were the most important events of all. Then our long-suffering hair, braided in infinitesimal braids for days in advance, was finally liberated. Tied with a bow on the top of the head, it floated in crinkly blond or dark waves down our backs. We were proud when, in the final year of our musical education, we played duets, the master playing on one piano and we on another. We realized fully the importance of having young ladies trained early to play upon the pianoforte.

Before my family built their house in Lake Forest, they used often to go there for the summer, when they occupied a house owned by Mr. Lind, the Scotchman. This stood where the Kent Clow residence now is.

My mother has often told me that there was nothing at that time between that house and the lake, and that she used to walk on a deer-path through the woods to what was called Clark's Ravine — the ravine between the Poole's and McLennan's — owned by the Pages and Kays. The clear, delicious spring on the Pages' side was always a delightful objective point.

The only houses that are just as they were in my earliest recollections, are: J. P. Rumsey's belonging to the Simeon Williamses; the D. R. Holt place and garden; the Burns,' which used to be the David J. Lakes'; and the J. V. Farwell house and grounds. I cannot think of any other place that has not been in some way altered.

The greatest change in the looks of Lake Forest was perhaps made in taking down the fences. My mother, who was president of the Village Improvement Society at that time, was, I am sorry to say, responsible for it. She said she thought it would be nice to have it look more like a park, so the cows which had always roamed in the streets, each with bell attached, were herded in the outskirts of the town, and each owner was obliged to care for his hitherto unkempt roadsides.

Up to that time, white picket-fences were the most popular barrier, but there was an occasional one, like that still standing around the Spragues' old place, or the delightful one around the J. V. Farwells', which had no pickets and, if one ran it fast enough, by placing one foot neatly on the middle bar, and the other on the top, it could be cleared very easily.

The gates showed some taste as well. Some were "Cleveland" gates, to open and shut which one drove the carriage over an iron wicket, before and after entering; a most fascinating contrivance! Sometimes a handle hung up high on the right-hand side, which was pulled down and started the necessary mechanism.

Over the Bradleys' gate was a lovely arch on which was proudly placed in rustic letters, CARLSRUHE. Mr. Bradley's name was Carl.

The village street was a very different sight from what one sees there now on a summer afternoon, when the row of motors extends from end to end of the long block. Then, the railway station, a little wooden building, stood alone on one side of the broad village main-street, and on the other, Taylor's meat-market. (The Arthur Aldis' present house was where he and his family used to live.) The Anderson store, a small frame house, the post office, another grocery, Pratt's, then O'Neill's hardware store, completed Lake Forest's façade.

The only livery carriage was owned by an old colored man named Samuel Dent, an escaped slave. He met all the trains, and I can hear him now, as we sat on the porch, telling the casual visitors whom he drove about the town, all the details of our houses and our persons, when passing our homes. His manners were informal. Sometimes when he was engaged to drive people to or from evening parties, on arrival he would whistle, and if his fares did not come at once, he would drive away. He is buried in the cemetery by the lake, and over his grave is a large tombstone, bought by his many friends.

There were not many social distinctions in this artless community, and if anyone was very poor or very rich there were few evidences of either. The houses were all managed in the same simple manner; we knew the names of all the old family servants in every home, and they were just as much our friends as were the family. The names of the horses and dogs were equally familiar, and the coachman's, too, who invariably milked the cow.

I remember well the sad day when the first family came to "spend the summer," precursors of the present hordes. Also I recall when livery first appeared upon the individual who took the place of our well-beloved "hired man."

What distinctions existed were of a subtle order; the

tradespeople all lived "across the track" and, although their children went to the same schools as we and we were with them every morning, they did not come to skate on our pond in the afternoon, and we did not often go to see them in their homes. I used to ask my mother why she did not have a sewing-machine in the dining-room, and a dish of rosy apples always there on the table to eat, as I used to find in the houses of some of my friends, but I never had a satisfactory answer.

And now when I call up O'Neill's on the telephone and tell them who I am, the answer is, "Yes, this is Jo" or "Will," and I ask how Grace his wife is, who was named after me because her mother did the washing at our house at the time; and when I see them, I tell them how like their father they are growing to be. So there are a few, but very few, reminders of the sweet, old days.

The social life had its main expression in the diversions of the Entre Nous Club. These included serious essays by the older members. William Henry Smith, for instance, was a shining light. There were also musicals, Dickens parties, when perhaps the children were allowed to come, or original plays written by brilliant Effie Neef. One of these was long remembered. She called it, *Gentlemen, We Can Do Without You,* and after the actresses had involved themselves in every sort of complications, she ended it by saying, "You see, Gentlemen, we cannot do without you."

This troupe included Mrs. William Henry Smith, who was the star; Mrs. A. F. Ferry,[1] young and very beautiful; George Holt, Will Fabian, Walter Neef, Effie Neef, and Nellie Warren.

[1] J. V. Farwell's only child by his first wife.

William Henry Smith's[1] house, next door to ours, was a unique place. As manager of the Associated Press, he was in the midst of National politics for many years, and the important man of the hour was sure to be a visitor there. I recall seeing in Lake Forest celebrities like Whitelaw Reid, General Philip Sheridan, William Walter Phelps, President Hayes, Senator Allison, Senator Ingalls, General and Mrs. Logan, and Robert Ingersoll. Whether these men had their interesting talks on my father's piazza or on Mr. Smith's, it is sometimes hard to remember.

When the wonderful reception for President and Mrs. Hayes was planned, Mr. and Mrs. Smith were with the Presidential excursion in the West. Mrs. Smith wrote home that she wished a party arranged. The neighbors did it for her, and she walked in with the other guests, having had no worry on the subject whatever.

Some of the oldest houses were built originally by men who later left Lake Forest, and were no longer associated with it. The old Warner place, for instance, was put up by William Blair, Edward Blair's father. He had at that time two sons and, while the house was under construction, one of these sons died. The Blairs were so unhappy about it that they decided they would not live there, and sold it to S. B. Williams. He it was who cut down the thick woods and made the sloping lawn of which he was extremely proud.

Dr. Charles Quinlan soon after built a large brick house (now the Rumseys'), but found he had spent more on it than he had intended, so this was also sold to S. B. Williams, who moved there and lived in it for many years. The Ezra

[1] Father of Delavan Smith.

Warners then bought the frame house built by William Blair, and came to Lake Forest in 1873.

Deer-path Inn was originally in the middle of the block, and William Johnston, when he bought the property, moved the market which he found there, across the track, making then that dividing line between residences and the trades-people which remained for so many years.

Harvey Thompson's house was the show-place for a very long time. It was directly across the street from the church. He had greenhouses and a large art-gallery, filled with really important pictures, and the ravine was all neatly smoothed and terraced to the bottom. At the ends of walks or vistas were iron benches or marble statues. The only thing that now recalls this early luxury is an occasional iron deer or vase on the lawn. After him, Alexander White owned this show-place, and then, many years later, Joseph Durand, and now the George Fishers.

The Gilbert Rossiter house, only lately moved away, stands out in one's recollection. Here Mr. and Mrs. Norman B. Judd (the latter Mr. Rossiter's sister) used often to be guests. Mr. Judd was very important in Illinois politics, and was sent as Minister to Germany by Lincoln. Mrs. Judd was one of the most cultivated people I have ever known. When she visited my mother a few years ago, she, Mrs. Judd, who was then more than eighty years old, used to read aloud in German every day so that she should not lose her accent; and so human was she in her sympathies, she used to say to my sister and me, "Please do not talk while I am out of the room, because I am afraid I may miss something."

H. G. Shumway, the first mayor of Lake Forest, built the

old house on the property where the Finley Barrells now live, but soon sold it to William S. Warren. Mr. and Mrs. Warren were a most distinguished couple of the old school, dignified and graceful in manners. Mrs. Warren had a very marked literary gift, as I recall it, and wrote essays and papers on all occasions. Her daughter, Nellie Warren,[1] is the one whose name occurs so often in the newspaper accounts of that day. Very beautiful and witty and gifted musically, she was perhaps the most attractive of any of the young women.

The little cottage, next but one to the church, was built by General Webster, then owned by the Neefs, and then the Nathaniel Sawyers, who lived in it many years.

The Neef family had a very distinct character. Mrs. Neef was Mrs. R. W. Patterson's sister, and the family consisted of a son and two daughters. The girls were sent to Paris to school when ten or twelve years old, and I think of them all as the gayest and wittiest people who ever lived in Lake Forest.

The two most important entertainments that I remember hearing about were Miss Clarine Williams' wedding to Mr. M. L. Scudder in 1873, and when William Henry Smith entertained President Hayes.

For the former, a special train brought the guests from Chicago at noon, and they stayed until six. General Sheridan, an intimate friend of the family, arranged to have his military band play all the afternoon. After the ceremony in the house, it really was a lawn fête as well as a wedding.

[1] She married a Frenchman, M. Moreau, and was accidentally burned to death in her Paris home.

The Smith reception for President and Mrs. Hayes was described at length in the *Chicago Tribune* as follows: —

"The reception on Thursday evening at the residence of William Henry Smith at Lake Forest was one of the most complete affairs of the entire Presidential trip. It was the subject of frequent remark that the proportion, not only of well-dressed, but positively handsome ladies was much greater than is usually seen on similar occasions. And then, the reception being a general one to the citizens of Lake Forest, and there being but few guests from abroad, the occasion partook more of the nature of a social party than a state affair. Add to this a fine brass-band, playing at intervals on the lawn, a quartet from the city composed of Messrs. Sabin, Sprague, Barnes, and Powers, elaborate floral decorations and a roomy and handsome mansion entirely at the disposal of the company, but little more can be required.

"Among the floral contributions was a large rosette with a border of white lilies and heliotropes with a center of tuberoses and "Welcome" in small blue everlasting flowers. It was the gift of the employees of the Custom House. Mrs. Henry Durand presented an American flag skillfully wrought in flowers.

"Mrs. Hayes was most becomingly attired in a gray silk skirt with brocaded overdress, relieved in blue and shell trimmings.

"Mrs. William Henry Smith wore a heavy black grosgrain with point-lace trimmings. Miss Abbie Smith blushed in pink brocaded silk, relieved with black velvet, and Mrs. J. N. Jewett wore an ecru silk and velvet mixed."

I am conscious that my recollections of those days must be those of a child, but I have found some articles published in various newspapers that describe them at short range. The following is from a Chicago paper, June, 1878, under Suburban News: —

"*Lake Forest* —

" 'The past week has been one grand whirl of dissipation,' remarked a Lake Forest belle to a companion, 'and it seems really as if this pleasant village were determined to equal Newport.' "

An elaborate description follows of private theatricals at Miss Johnston's; impromptu charade party at Mrs. Smith's, under the supervision of Effie Neef; Tuesday, a concert at the Seminary, and Wednesday evening the graduating exercises; Thursday, a party at Miss Williams', then a reception for Mrs. Sabin in the Academy; the next day, graduating exercises of the Academy and University; then a lawn fête given by Miss Nellie Warren and a "German" by Miss Johnston the same evening.

From a later newspaper account of May, 1880: —

"Lake Forest has put on her Spring beauty, and her woods and ravines are lovely indeed. The weather has been such as to suggest picnics and lawn parties, but though we have had none of these as yet, still, other social events have not been entirely wanting. That they have been few we will admit, in face of the fact that the only entertainment that could be offered a young lady visitor during a stay of a week and a half, was four prayer-meetings, three missionary meetings and two church services. Let no one call Lake Forest gay.

"However, the affair of the season was the elegant party given by Mr. and Mrs. E. S. Warner on the evening of April 15. Their beautiful house, which has recently been entirely rebuilt, was thrown open, and the handsome, well-arranged rooms were the source of much admiration and comment. The supper was furnished by Kinsley and the music by a superior orchestra. Over a hundred invitations were extended and were generally accepted, many being present from Chicago, notably Mr. Walter Neef and bride.[1]

"The company was given as a farewell to Mrs. Neef, who sails for England next month to be present at the wedding of her daughter, Miss Effie Neef, to an English naval officer.

"To this young lady is due in great measure the credit of raising the subscription by means of which our church bell was obtained and put in position; and we understand the bell will be rung long and merrily on her wedding-day, and could its tones be heard in England, they would doubtless convey to her the hearty good-wishes of her many friends here."

From the *Lake Forest Reporter* of August 1, 1872: —

" 'Beautiful for situation on the sides of the North,' was the comprehensive language of the prophet in describing the position of his beloved and holy city. Our readers must pardon us if we find ourselves uttering these words, 'beautiful for situation,' as we walk around about our city of Lake Forest, on the sides of our glorious North.

[1] Miss Annie Douglas, a daughter of John M. Douglas, a prominent Chicago lawyer.

"Elevated more than a hundred feet above water-level, with a bold, clean shore, where no miasma can find a lurking place; crossed in many directions by deep, wooded ravines which wind their way to the lake and perfectly drain the whole territory, while they outline the lots and give direction to the streets; covered with an original forest of oak, hickory, and other deciduous trees, now reduced in many places to cultivated parks, while enough remains to remind us of the country which God made; laid out in generous lots, so that every man's home is ample, fresh and airy, while as a rule the dwellings themselves correspond in style to the place which they occupy; — we know of nothing which our city lacks to deserve the encomium so often bestowed upon it, as 'by far the most beautiful of all the suburbs of Chicago.'"

What I have perhaps not quite expressed, was the real intimacy that existed among all the families in Lake Forest; they were much more like one family than it would be possible to describe. There was only one church, and no one ever spoke of wanting any other.

When Charlie and George Holt went around the world, the letters they wrote were passed about from house to house. When Mr. Warner found that they had an extra crop of raspberries or currants, he would mention it at the station in the morning, and any Lake Forester could go and pick all he or she wanted.

There were no diversities of interest; there was no social climbing, perhaps because, as one old settler says, all the original settlers were confident that Lake Forest was far superior to Highland Park or Evanston, or any of the other towns along the road. It is hard for the original Lake Forester not to be prejudiced even now. Perhaps the opinion was even universal, for Mr. Benedict told us that he asked a friend who lived in Highland Park why he did not move to Lake Forest, and he replied, "Not for me, it is too d—n pious and too d—n aristocratic!"

When a cousin of mine, last summer, heard that the streets were being renamed, she said with intense indignation, "How absurd that new-comers like this should have anything to do with such a thing!" The chairman of the name-changing committee, poor dear, had only lived in Lake Forest twenty-two years!

A later resident told me that she knew that Lake Forest only began to be fashionable at about the time she went there to live, when the Onwentsia Club was started. How little she knew that we who had grown up there felt perfectly sure that the knell of dear, delightful, distinguished, exclusive Lake Forest was at that moment sounded!

XVI

FROM FIRE TO FAIR

By Various People

A flaming wall between one epoch and its successor, a barrier without its equal in any other community, was the great Chicago Fire of October, 1871. A city chiefly built of wood was lost in that holocaust; a city of brick and stone rose from the ashes. A simple-hearted, church-going, provincial people fled before the flames. There was something in the fiery ordeal that tempered the metal of their souls so that they came out of it more ambitious, self-reliant, and optimistic than ever. The Sunday after the Fire, the Reverend Robert Collyer, the celebrated Unitarian preacher, held service in the still smoking ruins of Unity Church on the corner of Dearborn Avenue and Walton Place, when plans for rebuilding the church immediately were formed. I think it was the late William D. Kerfoot who, on the site of his downtown office, the day after the Fire, set up a sign reading: —

"All is lost save wife, children, and credit."

With such a spirit the new Chicago rose swiftly from the smoking debris of the old Chicago. When a catastrophe like the Fire hits so many thousands it ceases to be an unbearable affliction to the individual. It even becomes a matter for jesting and a stimulus to better effort. Help poured in from all over the world. Thomas Hughes, of England, collected a library of 300 volumes for Chicago, to which Queen Victoria contributed many books, and which was the nucleus for our present Public Library, an institution that, to-day, is said to serve a larger public than any other similar enterprise, except the British Museum.

Vast quantities of clothing and food from all over the country were sent here and distributed. As cheerfully as coral insects in the South Seas start anew after a storm, the inhabitants of the ruined city began rebuilding homes and business quarters before the ashes had cooled.

The Fire had put Chicago on the map, and the new metropolis no longer suggested the large, sprawling, over-grown village that had, before October 9, 1871, earned itself the sobriquet, "Garden City." Brick and stone took the place of wood in the rebuilding of homes; nor was this second crop of residences set in big gardens as before.

About this time there crept a hitherto unknown factor in interior furnishings, — a terrible something called "Art." The Centennial Exposition at Philadelphia, in 1876, gave this a fatal impetus. "Eastlake," with its ebonized, flimsy furniture, its fragile gilt chairs, became the fad. A little later William Morris darkened and blighted our homes by inspiring brown and green wall-papers, adorned with geometric figures, and put on in fearsome, longitudinal sections called respectively dadoes, picture-screens, and friezes. Also there were such diseased moments in the search for the new and original when gilt milking-stools and chopping-bowls adorned drawing-rooms; when bunches of dried cat-tails stood in up-ended sewer-tilings in the most elegant houses; when chair-legs were gartered with big ribbon bows; when cheese-cloth was considered chic stuff for drawing-room curtains; when not to have a spinning-wheel by the fireplace was to proclaim yourself a parvenu.

At the same time, however, society was really taking form and shape. Ladies' luncheons, and formal dinner parties (at which the hour was set as late as seven o'clock) became popular forms of entertainment. The "hired girl" became "the maid." She was induced to wear long white aprons, white collars and cuffs, and to permit a frilled cap to be perched upon her head. A few people even had butlers, though I think these were usually drawn from the colored race. I remember, however, that Mrs. W. W. K. Nixon, then living at No. 156 Rush Street, had a white butler, one Edward, who was the pride of the neighborhood.

Immediately after the Fire, the north-side young men of that time started a dancing-class, appropriately called, "The Cinders," which was for ten or fifteen years the chief social event of the north-side young and gay set. Prominent in it were the Messrs. Cyrus Adams, George Rumsey, Milton Leightner, Bryan Lathrop, James Kelly, Clarence Burley, Joseph Adams, Mahlon Ogden Jones, E. B. Sheldon, Walter and Edward Wyman, John T. Noyes, Samuel Wheeler, Robert H. McCormick, Arthur Ryerson, and James Norton. Among the young women who waltzed and polka'd with these gay young beaux were the Misses Rumsey, the Misses Kelly, the Misses Badger, Miss Fay Calhoun, Miss Lillie Winston, Miss Annie Douglas, and Miss Florence Arnold.

The affairs were gotten up and entirely financed by the young men. Coffee, lemonade, cake and sandwiches were the only refreshments at first. Later, sherbet and salad were added. They were held at Martine's Dance Academy on East Chicago Avenue, and were friendly, informal, simple affairs, though there were folks at that time who looked askance at them. The daughter of one of Chicago's oldest, most eminent families was taken to a Cinder dance one evening and, when asked what she thought of it, said: "There seemed a lack of home influence there."

That expression, "a lack of home influence," became a household phrase in a family closely connected with the writer. It's a most useful phrase to describe almost any kind of debauch.

In the twenty years that intervened between Chicago's two great events, the Fire and the Fair, society emerged, or undertook to do so, from the strict puritanic influences of the old conservative leaders here. It acquired some of the manners and customs of the great capitals of the world and learned to look beyond its local borders for inspiration and guidance. The coming of Oscar Wilde in 1882 caused a terrific flutter. Everyone then — educated largely by Gilbert and Sullivan's famous opera, *Patience* — became extremely "esthetic." Many found great bodily refreshment in simply sniffing a rose or a lily. Sunflowers were, for some mysterious reason, the rage, though the high priest of the new cult on one occasion somewhat wilted the popularity of this blossom. At a "ladies' luncheon" where he was the central figure, when he was asked as to what flower a lady should wear, he sighed: —

"She should wear a lily; she may wear a rose; but never, oh never, a sunflower."

A well-known young débutante present, who wore a bunch of sunflowers as a corsage bouquet, hastily smothered and concealed it under her napkin and maneuvered it to the floor at her feet. Such a trouble it had been, too, to procure those sunflowers!

Even before Oscar Wilde cast his unwholesome spell over

this community, another exotic from a more alien people had appeared for a brief while to shock the pious and give a certain fearful joy to the lighter-minded, irked by the orthodox. This was Sarah Bernhardt, at that time fairly reeking with unwholesome notoriety. With bated breath people spoke of her then, of her unfathered child, — the rumor grew to children; — of her many amours; of her propensity to sleep in a coffin; of her tendency to caress a pet skull she carried about with her; above all, of her unparalleled emaciation. There was the favorite quip of the day: "An empty cab drove up and Sarah Bernhardt got out."

She came to Chicago and played some of her great rôles here, and the question every one asked his or her neighbor was: "Are you going to hear her?" One well-known Chicagoan is reported to have said, —

"I do not consider that anyone who would go to see Sarah Bernhardt play would be a fit guest at my dinner-table."

In spite of this, many did go, though little good did it do most of them, as few then could speak or understand French. One wit said he loved to go to a Bernhardt performance just to watch Mrs. —— (a prominent social leader) smile whenever Sarah said, "oui."

Mme. Bernhardt was then an artist as well as an actress, and held an exhibit of her paintings and sculpture at O'Brien's Art Gallery. She sent out hundreds of invitations to the opening reception and, swathed in a black, clinging, utterly un-American gown, stood in the middle of the gallery, ready to receive and converse with any and all. Crowds came, but they circled around the extreme edge of the room, leaving her in the center of a vast solitude. She looked, they said, like a leopardess at bay. The only one who had the courage and good manners to go up to speak to her was Miss Amy Fay, the musician, whose life abroad in France and Germany, — she was a pupil of Liszt, — gave her a great advantage in cosmopolitan *savoir faire* over her fellow-citizens in Chicago.

The two decades we are considering were a transitional period which developed many striking personalities. Every movement toward emancipation is started by leaders, often solitary, unconscious figures, who strike out from the herd and, by so doing, frequently endure criticism, even obloquy. Such a pioneer, free lance, or social rebel, according as you look at the matter, was Mrs. Herbert Ayer, better known later as Harriet Hubbard Ayer. If I cite her here, it is not because she was in any way typical of the Chicago of her time, but because she was so utterly the contrary. In a strait-laced, conventional community she ventured to be and do what she wanted. As I look back on her, she seems like some rare, tropical bird of gorgeous plumage strayed into a simple country hen-yard. Mrs. Ayer loved everything that was gay and pretty, and especially everything that was French. She was the first to fill her house with bric-a-brac, to read French novels and, worse than all, to act French plays. She became a devotee of amateur theatricals and in a north-side club, the Anonymous Club, which flourished in the seventies, she was prime mover in many dramatic entertainments in which the club delighted. Some of these were given in private houses and some in the parlors of Unity Church. Some were great successes, and some were quite the contrary. There was one performance in the basement of Unity Church that was a series of disasters, which began when the curtain, rising, caught the fringe of a table-cloth on a table at the front edge of the stage, and dragged it up, showering the floor, as it rose, with fragile and precious *objets d'art*. Everyone in the course of the play forgot his or her part. The final catastrophe occurred when Mrs. Ayer, the heroine, was supposed to conclude the piece by either fainting or dying on the stage, and, in so doing, dropped too near the front of the platform and had to draw in her feet and knees to avoid the descending curtain. It is reported that Mr. Ayer was found upstairs in the dark, empty church, lying on the cushions of a pew, his handkerchief stuffed in his mouth to keep in the peals of unholy laughter which threatened the peace of the evening.

Mrs. Ayer distressed the high principles of the community by giving Sunday breakfasts — real French *déjeuners à la fourchette* — at which she served *omelettes aux fines herbes*, chicken livers *en brochette*, *café noir*, and alas! *vins Graves*, *Sauternes*, or *Chablis*; and to which she invited well-known stage celebrities, among whom were Edwin Booth, Lawrence Barrett, and John McCulloch — all of which was not done at that time in Chicago, and was therefore anathema.

So it was really but a just fate which overtook the Ayers when Mr. Ayer's firm suffered in a panic; he failed and had to go out of business. He had for some time been estranged from his wife. Mrs. Ayer gave up her luxuries and undertook to support her two daughters and herself by the manufacture and sale of a cream known as the "Récamier" cream, and other cosmetics, some of which to this day are on the market under her name. Later, she retired from the undertaking and became the head of a department in the *New York World* where she made much newspaper fame for herself.

Whether she was rich or in restricted circumstances, she was always generous in sympathy and money to those with whom she came in contact. An evidence of this large-hearted tenderness was her return to her divorced husband, after years of absence, when she heard that he was alone, poor, mind gone, and body sick unto death at the Palmer House in Chicago. She took care of him, paid all the many expenses of his last illness, and held his hand as he died.

She loved life and especially its beautiful, luxurious, amusing side, yet when reverses came to her she faced and conquered them with a gay courage which, in time, I think, disarmed some of the critics who had watched her earlier career with disapprobation.

What would those critics have thought had they looked on at life to-day when some women smoke cigarettes, drink cocktails, play cards for money, tint their cheeks and lips, and yet are not ostracized, or even looked at askance by many? Times and customs change, but not the relative positions of the conservative and the pleasure-loving unorthodox.

One of the gayest, wittiest of the young married couples in Chicago were the Alfred Masons. Mr. Mason was a son of Roswell B. Mason, a fine type of early Chicagoan who was mayor of Chicago from 1869 to 1871. Mrs. Mason, who was a Miss Minnie Murdock, of New Haven, was a clever actress, and also had a desire to achieve fame and fortune as a writer. She wrote a little novel called, *May Maddern.* Its success may be estimated by the *bon mot* of one of her friends who remarked: "*May Maddern* must madden." She, herself, said that she wrote it to furnish her parlor, but that it barely sufficed to furnish her vestibule.

One of the famous houses of the day was the Perry H. Smith mansion on the northwestern corner of Huron and what was then Pine Street, now North Michigan Avenue. It was a large, white marble edifice, with a dark, slate-covered mansard roof, and impressive stone steps leading up to an imposing, pillared front entrance. It was so built that to the childish mind of the day it suggested a big frosted cake with a large slice cut out of it — if that conveys anything to your mind. It was very stately inside, having on either hand suites of drawing-rooms whose spaciousness was enhanced by high ceilings and handsomely carved, black-walnut woodwork. A very smart little theater, with a rising semicircle of seats, was a feature of the house. Another striking adornment was some large mirrors that could be drawn across the tall windows at night and which, as handsome crimson velvet curtains hung on either side, frequently caused much confusion to guests who, thinking that they were walking through a doorway into another room, would bump into themselves. This was apt to cause great joy to onlookers.

At the great "house warming" which Mr. and Mrs. Smith gave to show their new home to their friends, Mr. Smith took some of his guests into the butler's pantry where three faucets bent gracefully over the "sink." One was for hot water, one was for cold water; while the middle one, when turned on, let down sparkling champagne. There was something of the splendor and decadence of ancient Rome in so audacious a device.

The eldest son of the family, Perry H. Smith, Jr., took a dip into politics sometime about 1880. With him in the experience were the late John Noyes and Alfred Mason. It was much rarer then than now for scions of well-to-do and prominent families, to dedicate themselves to their country's welfare. He offered himself as a candidate for some office, I forget what. That he was not successful is attested by the following lines, which for some strange reason lodged in a childish mind that omitted to retain worthier verse:—

Go bury young Perry
Far out in the woods,
  Where politics never are heard;
Where his neat little legs
Can be folded to rest,
  To the song of the wild mountain bird.

And when winter comes,
And the snow and the ice
  Have covered his dear little bed,
His partner, Alf Mason,
Can go out with John
  And visit the place with his sled.

What simple, rather "high-brow" social gatherings entertained the folk of that time! There was the Anonymous Club, already referred to, whose membership included many well-known people of that era, among whom were: Mr. and Mrs. Alfred Mason, Mr. and Mrs. Herbert Ayer, Mr. and Mrs. F. H. Winston, Mr. and Mrs. Joseph Kirkland, Major and Mrs. Henry Huntington, Mr. and Mrs. Edward D. Hosmer, the Misses Mary and Annie Kelly, Mr. James Kelly, Mr. and Mrs. R. Hall McCormick, Mr. and Mrs. Frank Eastman, Mr. and Mrs. Gregory, Mr. William McMillan and Mr. Frank Wheeler.

This organization had no by-laws or committees, though it had presidents. It met at different houses and its programs varied from grave to gay. There were short literary essays "writ and read" by members. There were musical evenings. One was of a classic character when a band of members played on all sorts of childish instruments, penny whistles, little trumpets, and drums, combs, and their ilk. There were humorous performances of well-known poems. On one occasion, Lord Ullen's daughter escaped her irate father by embarking with her lover in a wash-tub, only to be engulfed in the raging billows of a green travelling-rug, while from the side-scenes someone intoned the lines of the ballad in hollow voice.

On another occasion, at a meeting of the Club at the residence of Mr. F. H. Winston, an erudite lady member read a long paper on some none too interesting subject. The host was found pacing restlessly up and down the hall outside the drawing-room.

"What do you think of the paper?" he was asked.

"Fine, fine!" he said, "so spun out, you know."

What would people of to-day think of such a way of spending an evening?

Those were days, moreover, when men's clubs really were in their prime. The Union Club on the North Side had its first home in the Mahlon D. Ogden house, the old, gray, wooden structure which, in its encircling grove of trees, was the only building for miles around to weather the Fire. The members used to give summer garden-parties in the pleasant grounds.

Later they built a handsome, brownstone club-house across the square, on the corner of Dearborn Avenue and Delaware

Place. Here the pace grew swifter for many of the members. It became the fashion for a certain set to gather in a card-room and play cards and drink — well, I don't know what the favorite tipple of the day was, it was before the cocktail flourished. These carousals went on nightly and lasted long, much to the distress of the wives waiting alone at home. At length one determined woman, a well-known and charming young Russian, set out to get her husband. She pushed by the protesting door-man, went upstairs, opened the door of the card-room and said: —

"Bob, you come right home with me!" He did.

There is nothing more gratifying to orthodox and pious critics than the inevitable disintegration of any group of unwisely jovial mortals. The very nature of their communion makes such companionship short-lived. So the gay days of the Union Club passed into limbo. The succeeding habitués were bachelors or widowers, some of whom eventually married, leaving too small a number to maintain the club. The building is now a most excellent home for working-girls and run by the Salvation Army.

In the same way the Calumet Club, on the South Side, passed through its various phases of birth, youth, full growth, and decline.

The old Exposition building on the lake front, — of the vintage and style of London's Crystal Palace, — was a well-known landmark and will be remembered by many a Chicagoan as being the temple of various civic festivals in the two decades between the Fire and the Fair. Every autumn it was the setting of a general exposition of the agricultural and industrial products of this part of the country, which drew thousands of visitors from the surrounding districts to the city. Machinery, manufactured goods, and farm produce all jostled each other in a cheerful, utterly tasteless fashion, entirely characteristic of the cheerful, utterly tasteless age in which they flourished. But off in one corner of the building there was a noteworthy adjunct to this annual affair. This was an exhibition of paintings, occupying three or four rooms, which, under the direction of Miss May Hallowell, became a real event in Chicago's fast-budding life of culture. It was the direct ancestor of our present Art Institute. It is one more proof of the adage that "art is long and time is fleeting," for, while the pavilions built of ears of golden corn, the roaring, champing machinery, the collections of household implements, and the ugly, sturdy, old structure itself, have all vanished from the lake front, pictures—lineal descendants of those early exhibits — are still domiciled there in a fine marble palace. Thus does civilization work its way out from darkness and materialism to light and the life of the spirit!

The Exposition building housed many pleasant undertakings. For several winters there was a good-sized skating rink in one end of it, whose great, black glare of ice was a favorite rendezvous for skaters and onlookers.

During many summer seasons Theodore Thomas gave the first of his famous orchestral concerts there and held several Wagnerian festivals under the iron girders of this primitive birthplace of music and art. He introduced his public gently to music, as, behind the rows of seats that immediately fronted the stage, there were set many tables, backed by evergreen trees in-boxes. Here good Milwaukee brews were served the thirsty music-lover.

What has become of the thick clouds of "sisco flies," as

they were then called, which used to be blown to us from across the lake, to darken the air, hang in festoons from the street-lamps, collect in slimy, fish-smelling drifts underfoot, and last, but by no means least, settle all over the Thomas Orchestra men? The bald cellist of that day had to make a cap of his red bandanna handkerchief to protect his head. The performer on the wide-mouthed cornet frequently was obliged to shake an accumulation of flies from his instrument. The long-bearded drummer could be seen combing them out of his whiskers. These restless, frail, poor-spirited insects were a pest that seems to have been abashed and abolished by our more complex civilization, which likewise did away with the old Exposition building, New Year's Day calling, square-dances, big bustles, the hired man, the family soup-tureen, and various other once familiar institutions.

There flourished here in the two penultimate decades of the nineteenth century a group of men of rare wit and mellow wisdom such as seldom grows and flourishes in so young and, in many ways, crude a community. They did not seek either fame or fortune, so little is left of them today but their fast-fading names. But neither before nor since has their like or their equal been known here. Major Henry Huntington (commonly called "the Major"), Dr. Clinton Locke (who said of himself that his sense of humor stood between him and a bishopric), Edward G. Mason, Professor David Swing, James Norton, and Joseph Kirkland formed the nucleus of a group whose forum was the Chicago Literary Club. Their brilliant papers, their trenchant, pithy wit — now satirical, now more genial in humor — have never been equalled since. Alas, that no record was kept of their clever banquets, their literary meetings, their sparkling sallies and quips! They lived before Chicago's intensely prosperous and material era — an era which developed rapidly after the World's Fair.

There was, on the South Side in the latter part of the last century, a group of men and women who, in a certain worldly sense of the word, added more to the lustre of Chicago's social life than any other single set of well-to-do, cultivated, pleasure-loving people we have had. The Arthur Catons, Augustus Eddys, John M. Clarks, Frank Gortons, George M. Pullmans, Wirt Dexters, Franklin MacVeaghs, J. M. Walkers, W. W. Kimballs, N. K. Fairbanks, Henry Dibblees, Hugh T. Birchs, Norman Williamses, and Marshall Fields, were all prominent in this set. The South Side Dancing Class, which later developed into the fashionable balls of Chicago, was started by Mrs. Dexter and Mrs. Pullman, whose husbands wanted to learn to dance. The class was organized with a teacher and met in the evenings at the different houses, the men wearing business suits and the women high-necked dresses. The evenings ended with light "refreshments" — coffee and sandwiches, or lemonade and cake, according to the season.

There was much hospitality of a simple kind in that epoch and also good music. Mrs. Clark, Mrs. Birch, Mrs. Gorton, and Miss May Allport used to give piano recitals, playing double duets.

It wasn't the custom to fly from Chicago's hot season in those days — it was before our smoke era — and most houses in that neighborhood (Prairie, Calumet and Michigan avenues from Sixteenth Street south) used to have wide verandas, on which gay companies gathered in the warm summer evenings. There was much driving out to the Washington Park Club for the races and lively dinners afterwards. To-day, that once cheerful, sociable neighborhood is, either entirely obliterated by the march of progress — so called — or quite other tenants occupy the big, friendly houses, whose former owners are scattered, some to the North Side, some to other cities, and still others to that country from whose bourne no traveller returns. To go back there is to tread alone a banquet-hall deserted.

There is no other city whose inhabitants have such a habit of emulating the chambered nautilus and building them more stately mansions. Chicagoans even go beyond the nautilus and forsake entirely the locality to which they have given character and prestige. At present the trend of residents, — those who can pick and choose, — is, as it has been for many years — northward. This is partly due to the encroachments of business on the West and South sides, and even on the lower part of the North Side; but the main force behind this movement is the desire to live on or near the beautiful lake shore, a shore unobstructed by railways or shipping.

XVII

THE YESTERDAY OF THE HORSE

BY HOBART C. CHATFIELD-TAYLOR

SHOULD a discerning historian write the story of Chicago in years to come, I feel confident that he will select the age just preceding the World's Fair, as the most engrossing period of our history; and since the horse was its distinguishing feature, he will, I venture to say, dub it the "Hippic Age."

Though the glories of the World's Columbian Exposition were conceived at that time by the genius of John Wellborn Root, and a taste for music was instilled in our reluctant hearts by Theodore Thomas, it is not our artistic achievement so much as our metropolitanization which distinguishes that period from all others in our history. Shedding our small-town ways, we became, by leaps and bounds, a city of cosmopolitan mien, — a metamorphosis largely due, I believe, to the appearance of the horse as a social factor.

Trotting horses with flowing manes and tails having been seen in our shady streets, and the "fast young men" who drove them to sulkies and side-bar buggies having shocked our more sanctimonious citizens long before "Charlie" Schwartz first "tooled" his drag down Michigan Avenue, it is perhaps more historically exact to attribute the elegance of this age to the horse's tail — or rather to his lack of one — than to that animal himself; since not until his tail had been docked did he become a civilizing influence.

Perhaps the credit for the startling changes which took place in Chicago in those days before the World's Fair should be given to the man behind the tail, it being the English coachman, after all, who refined our uncouth manners. Indeed, no sooner did he sit clean-shaven and erect upon the box, where formerly a mustachioed Scandinavian, or colored man, had slouched, than the owner within the carriage began to realize that a genteel era had dawned which made the mending of his provincial ways a duty both to his family, himself, and his community.

To merit the approval of one's English coachman became an obsession in those days, for, oh, what a deal of scorn lay in the curl of that supercilious fellow's lip, if one chanced to call a "trap" by the uncouth name of "rig," or to speak of a pair of horses as "a team!" Indeed, one had need to unlearn all that had been taught by the "hired man" of one's youth, it being no longer permissible to seize a rein in each hand and shout "git ap!" to the horses, or to drive them with the whip stuck democratically in the socket. Furthermore, it became unseemly to jerk one's reins so that a sudden slap of their slack on the backs of one's nags might induce the said nags to increase their speed; while to sit comfortably, with legs apart and feet against the dashboard, was to outrage the proprieties.

Many a recalcitrant millionaire, it is true, refused to mend his primeval ways, even while courting Dame Fashion with a mail-phaeton or a stanhope of the latest build. The tails of such a one's horses were still undocked and the reins with which he drove them were held at arm's length, but whenever he chirped to them to hasten their steps, some passing coachman, in boots and breeches, was sure to murmur *sotto voce* to the carriage groom beside him: "I say, Bill, 'e must 'ave a cage of canaries under 'is seat."

Ah, how superior we younger men, who had learned to keep our knees together and our feet well under us, felt to those lubberly millionaires, as, with reins held correctly in the left hand and whip poised deftly in the right, we sped toward the park! Indeed, we knowing ones saw at a glance the defects of every turnout on the road, and read its owner's character. Clanking chains, for instance, in lieu of modest pole-straps, or a harness mounted as ornately as that of a royal coach, bespoke the parvenu; while an unshaven coachman in ill-fitting coat and unbrushed hat, told beyond the shadow of a doubt that his master was a careworn man, made pale and stoop-shouldered by the weight of business.

From the old-time codger in a buggy, with a linen duster on his back and fly-net on that of his horse, to the flashy young man of the hour, with a brazen coryphée from Rice's *Evangeline* troupe beside him on the seat of his Whitechapel cart, all classes of society paraded on the Avenue in those days. Milady drove in a C-spring victoria, her pretty daughter fared forth in a phaeton, attended by a groom in boots and breeches, or if she was particularly horsey, in a tilbury, or even a tandem cart. Meanwhile, the wife of the butcher, or the baker, clucked to a long-tailed horse in the shafts of a canopy-topped surrey, all sorts of women, as well as of men, being on the Avenue, in those halcyon days.

But the time to view the passing show was Derby Day when all Chicago was on parade and lines of moving vehicles of every description known to the coach-builders' craft stretched from the Hotel Richelieu to Washington Park.

To those of the present generation a sight as splendid as that which met the eye on this day of days is quite unknown. Alas, the white macadam of Michigan Avenue has been oiled a dingy brown, and the chugging motor-car, which has supplanted the horse-drawn vehicle, bears the same relation in beauty to a well-appointed drag that an ocean tramp-steamer does to a clipper ship with a "bone in her teeth."

A drag, it may be said for the benefit of the uninitiated, is a private coach, or "tally-ho," as it was perversely called, because the first public coach put on the road in this country by Colonel Delancy Kane, was named the "Tally-ho." It might as readily have been the "Tantivy," in which case all members of the genus coach — which includes the road-coach, the drag, and the brake — would have been known throughout the length and breadth of the land as "Tantivies." Indeed, in those days mankind might have been classified as those who called coaches "tally-hos," and those who didn't, those who did being Philistines in the hippic world.

While the majority of the Chicagoans who sped toward Washington Park on Derby Day belonged to this class without a saving grace, to your true horseman's way of thinking, even they went forth in holiday spirit to see the great American Derby won or lost by the horse on which their dollars had been staked, Chicago being then an unreformed city, where the personal right to dissipate was still uncurbed.

But I am wandering afield, the Washington Park Club and its sophisticated display of horseflesh and humanity, rather than public morals, being the topic I have in mind.

To stand on the broad veranda of the Club-house on the first day of the annual season of horse-racing, and watch the arrival of the members, was to witness a display, such as the Chicago of to-day cannot rival, there being now no opportunity for society to foregather in such style as the Washington Park Club afforded a quarter of a century ago.

Looking backward to that period, I find it difficult, I confess, to recall the faces and names of all who were prominent in the hippic age, the glories of which I am endeavoring to recount. But a few come distinctly to mind, particularly among the coaching men. Of these, the pioneer, as I have already noted, was Charlie Schwartz, whose Brewster drag and team of bays created a veritable sensation when it appeared in Michigan Avenue for the first time.

For a season or two, Charlie Schwartz had the road to himself; then Valentine Dickey appeared to rival him with a coach equipped in western fashion with whiffle-trees, and soon Hall McCormick was driving a team of roans to a London-built drag. Then Potter Palmer, not to be outdone, turned out both a coach and a French char-à-banc, with marvellous leopard skins spread over the seats of both vehicles, which created a sensation, I acknowledge, but did not win the approval of the stickler for good form.

The fifth coach to appear in Michigan Avenue was my own yellow-wheeled Kimball drag, drawn by a team of golden chestnuts; and I confess that I took particular pride in the fact that both coach and harness were made in Chicago. At a later day, Arthur Caton took to the road with a Brewster drag and a team of bays; but Charlie Schwartz had already ceased to "sit his bench," as they used to say in the old coaching days of England; therefore five was the greatest number of coaches to be driven in Chicago at any one time. General Torrence, to be sure, drove a drag during the World's Fair days, but somehow the rest of us never quite accepted him as one of the coaching set, and my recollection is that before he appeared in Michigan Avenue both Charlie Schwartz and Valentine Dickey had taken their last drive.

Among the drivers of tandems, Frank Whitehouse[1] was easily foremost. Being a skilled whip, his leader was never known to turn and face him. The same cannot be said, I fear, of Ben Lamb, or Norman Fay, or even Jamie Walker, tandem driving being an art in which only those excel who have "hands," as well as an intimate acquaintance with the use of the whip-thong.

Among those who drove to the Derby in less spectacular vehicles than drags and tandem carts, the names of but few stand forth in my memory; yet in those days everyone who was anyone was on the road in some sort of trap or other. I recall, however, Columbus R. Cummings and William B. Howard as men whose turnouts were spick and span, and likewise striking. And I remember Marshall Field in a highly respectable stanhope-phaeton with long-tailed horses; but I confess that my memory of the great parade on Derby Day is rather a panoramic picture, than a "close up" of any individual.

Toward the distant city, stretches a long line of smart vehicles, the mountings of their harnesses glistening in the June sunlight. At the gate of the Club grounds, a stone's

[1] The late Francis Meredith Whitehouse, of Chicago and New York, a son of Bishop Whitehouse.

throw away, there was a turn in the road and from it to the Club-house steps was a rise of ground, up which the horses of the drags were wont to rush at a gallop. "Springing 'em" is the horsey way of describing this spirited dash. When a team had been brought up all standing, and a nimble groom had sprung to the leaders' heads, the more portly coachman placed a folding ladder against the coach. While pretty women in modish finery, and men in top-hats, with field-glasses slung across their shoulders, descended from their proud seats to the ground, a flutter of excitement spread along the Club-house veranda, a coaching party being the cynosure, in those days, of all fashionable eyes.

The occupants of the box-seat were, of course, the observed of all observers, it being a seat akin to a throne. Even the less favored ones on the "gammon" or "backgammon," as in coaching parlance the other seats were called, felt themselves as superior to those who viewed them from the ground, as ladies-in-waiting undoubtedly must feel towards all others of their sex at a Queen's drawing-room, an invitation to drive to the Derby on a drag being the acme of social achievement.

To figure this distinction mathematically, there were but five coaches in a city of a million people. Moreover, even if the number of persons upon the seats exceeded the limit of coaching correctness to that of the seating capacity of the vehicles themselves, only fifty people all told could drive to the races in the finest of style, and only five women, or one to each 200,000 mortals in the city, could occupy box-seats.

But, if there were but five bona fide coaches in the town, there were several four-horse brakes, and at least a score of tandem carts to add their share of sportive zest to the Derby Day parade. I am bound to confess, however, that the girls who went to the races in the ticklish vehicles last mentioned were courageous to a degree, in those days, when social aspirants were in the habit of hastily taking up tandem driving, just to be in the swim. Moreover, if I am to chronicle the entire truth, I must add that more than one of our proud drivers of a four-in-hand was ignorant of the art of "pointing" his leaders when turning a corner, as well as of that of "folding" a whip-thong neatly, after performing the difficult feat of flicking a leader, many a Chicagoan who owned highsteppers being a parvenu in horsemanship.

Once more, however, I am wandering afield, the art of driving being a topic apart from Chicago's hippic age, for while there were but five coaches and a score of tandem carts in our Derby Day parade, there were dog-carts, tilburys, gigs, and stanhopes, galore, and a goodly sprinkling of smart victorias, with pretty rosettes on the head-stalls of their sleek-coated horses, and pretty women within them conscious that the eyes of friend and enemy alike were upon their newest gowns. Even the husbands beside them were, if they happened to be wearing white spats for the first time in their lives, pitifully conscious too, I fear, of the scornful glances of their business associates, the Derby being an occasion of ordeal rather than of joy for many a citizen of our budding metropolis.

Nevertheless, it was a notable event in the life of the city, and the Club-house lawn with its display of well-dressed women and men was a sight to vie in elegance with the Ascot enclosure and the lawn at Goodwood in their palmiest days. In recalling its glories, I cannot refrain from lamenting, Puritan though I am by nature and inheritance, that the "Sport of Kings" has been banished from our midst. I lament in other ways, too, the passing of the horse — the cutter racing in winter, for instance, over the glistening snows of the boulevards, and the horse-shows in the old Exposition building on the lake front, where the winning of a blue ribbon used to fill one's cup of happiness to overflowing. Unlike their successors in the Coliseum, these horse-shows of which I speak were truly amateur affairs, where the contestants were all citizens of the town, and their entries, the horses and traps of every-day use.

To show a four-in-hand or tandem in that tan-bark ring, while the band played, and the crowd shouted, and the pretty women in the boxes clapped their little gloved hands, was as thrilling an experience, I believe, as one can have in this world, short of war in the front-line trenches. The competition was keen and sportsmanlike, and to maneuver a four-in-hand in the midst of that clamor without breaking one's own neck, or that of some guileless spectator, required considerable skill, particularly if you were called upon to cut figure-eights, or drive unscathed between a series of posts, with a leeway of only a few inches between your hub and the obstacles. But the most pleasing memory which comes to me from those glorious days of the horse is that of driving a coach through the parks and boulevards at night.

The clicking of the hoofs upon the hard macadam, the rhythmical creaking of the harness, the merry rattle of the lead-bars are delectable sounds, I recall, as I sit before an autumn fire dreaming of those days long gone. I seem to see my old team of chestnuts before me, and feel the weight of their reins upon my forearm. Sniffing their stable from afar, they spring into their collars with a will, while the coach-lamps shed their glimmering rays upon the white roadway ahead. Pricking up their trim little ears, the leaders shy at a shadow; a wheel-horse starts to break, and as I speak a soothing word, the familiar notes of *Who'll Buy a Broom?* sound sweet and clear upon the night air.

Awakened from my reverie by the snorting of an automobile muffler, opened in defiance of the law, I lament the degenerate age in which I am forced to end my days. No machine, alas, howsoever speedy or noisy it may be, can ever take the place the horse used to hold in my affection during Chicago's palmiest days.

For though the sound of the horn is dead,
  And the guards are turned to clay,
There are those who remember "the yard of tin"
  And the coach of the olden day.

XVIII

THE WORLD'S FAIR

By Mrs. William J. Calhoun

A radiance hangs over the summer of the World's Fair and makes it, to all that part of Chicago that holds it in the memory, a thing apart. The vanished city that rose out of the mists of the marshes by the shore of the blue lake had in it a quality that never will come again. Only those who have wandered through the Court of Honor, from the flashing waters of the MacMonnies fountain to the Peristyle and the great lake, and have seen the white buildings and their gay pennants reflected in still lagoons can believe in a beauty so poignant that it was almost pain. Only those who have floated in gondolas at dusk around the Wooded Island and have come out upon the splendid Court, gay with its thousands of lights doubled in flickering water, the rising sprays of the fountains rainbow-colored, can know the infinite leisure that makes for dreams in the memory. And perhaps too, only those who rode down the Midway in a wheeled chair, guided by a bright young student from some western university, can recognize the enchantment that hung over the life of that street and the villages from far-away worlds that lined it. The tragedy of gayety as of beauty lies in its evanescence and in the powerlessness of words to present it to the imagination.

But to Chicago, the World's Fair was something more than a fascinating festival, a city of dreams. It represented a struggle, a mighty effort, a notable victory. Beyond giving her the opportunity and official backing, the nation did very little to aid the vast undertaking. It was the will of the city working against heavy odds that brought success. It was the sacrifice and devotion of the men who had built the West, laborer and capitalist, that made the White City out of a dream.

The Board of Directors[1] was composed of big men, men who had arrived and had done their part to make the city arrive. The first president of the Board was Lyman J. Gage, the second William T. Baker, and the third and last, who bore the brunt of the battle, Harlow N. Higinbotham. From its first meeting to its last, it was animated by no mean spirit. It saw things large, with imagination, vision and idealism.

[1] At the first meeting of stockholders, April 10, 1890, the following directors were elected: —

Owen F. Aldis	Cyrus H. McCormick
Samuel W. Allerton	Andrew McNally
William T. Baker	Joseph Medill
Thomas B. Bryan	Adolph Nathan
Edward B. Butler	Robert Nelson
William H. Colvin	John J. P. Odell
Mark L. Crawford	Potter Palmer
DeWitt C. Cregier	J. C. Peasley
George R. Davis	Ferdinand W. Peck
James W. Ellsworth	Erskine M. Phelps
John V. Farwell, Jr.	Eugene S. Pike
Stuyvesant Fish	Martin A. Ryerson
Edward T. Jeffrey	Anthony F. Seeberger
Lyman J. Gage	Charles H. Schwab
Harlow N. Higinbotham	William E. Strong
Elbridge G. Keith	Charles H. Wacker
Rollin A. Keyes	Robert A. Waller
Herman H. Kohlsaat	John R. Walsh
Marshall M. Kirkman	Charles C. Wheeler
Edward F. Lawrence	Frederick S. Winston
Thies J. Lefens	Charles T. Yerkes

Otto Young

The qualities that had made the success of big business in the West made the success of the Fair and proved once again that captains of industry are potential artists and poets, that the scope of imagination in the one is as powerful as in the other. With a fine spirit of sacrifice, the directors put aside their immediate concerns and their personal interests to give of their time and energy whole-heartedly to a great cause. Opposition only stimulated them, difficulties became their stepping-stones to achievement.

The triumphal note was sounded at the very beginning when the architects and landscape architects whom they had appointed to design the Fair, — Burnham and Root on the one hand, and Olmsted and Company on the other, — after making the ground-plan which proved to be its firm foundation, asked permission to select, without competition, the greatest designers of the country and invite them to plan and construct the buildings.[1] The directors responded instantly to the superb generosity of this appeal, and from that moment the noble spirit of the Fair was assured. In a measure it disarmed the hostility of the East, to whom no good could come out of Nazareth, and it opened the path-

[1] The plans submitted by these architects were adopted by the Board of Directors on November 21, 1890. A Construction Department was then formed with Daniel H. Burnham as Chief of Construction, John W. Root as architect, Abram Gottlieb as engineer, and Olmsted & Company as landscape architects. At the first session of the Board of Architects selected by these men, in January, 1891, the buildings were assigned as follows: —

Administration, Richard M. Hunt
Agriculture, McKim, Mead & White
Machinery, Peabody & Stearns
Manufactures, George B. Post
Electricity, Van Brunt & Howe
Horticulture, Jenney & Mundie
Fisheries, Henry Ives Cobb
Venetian Village, Burling & Whitehouse (abandoned later)
Mines, Solon S. Beman
Transportation, Adler & Sullivan

At a later date, the *Art Building* was assigned to Charles B. Atwood.

way for an enterprise that was not sectional but national, not for a day but for all time. The architects thus honored assembled in Chicago in January, 1891, and inspected the cold and dreary waste which they were to transform into fairyland. But if the aspect of the marshes of Jackson Park was discouraging, there was enough vitality and imagination in the great ground-plan to inspire their highest efforts. They were skeptics when they arrived in Chicago, but they left firm in the faith which animated the men they were consulting. Even the sudden death of the consulting architect, John W. Root, who had put all his ardent vitality into the labor of preparation, could not then discourage them, and the work went on without him along the lines and in the spirit that he and his partner had marked out. Innumerable difficulties faced the builders and the gallant body of directors as time went on, but they met them like an army with banners and conquered all along the front, until the mirage they had seen over the waters of the lake became the White City.

With this mighty effort, the city reached its maturity and made its début among the cities of the world. The same energy and the same faith went into it that rebuilt Chicago after the Fire, and the idealism that always dominates in America when she faces a great opportunity or a great peril. Contemporary records bear eloquent testimony to the magnitude of the task and give glimpses of manners and customs now changed or outgrown. The long contest on the subject of Sunday closing, which dragged its slow way through the courts, seems as archaic as the persecution of witches in Salem. In this, as in other things, the Chicago directors proved themselves in advance of the times, while the national commission was overhung with prejudice. The directors finally won the privilege of opening the grounds on Sunday, but the exhibits which were under the control of the Government remained firmly closed to inspection.

Banquets and breakfasts were numerous during the exposition season, and official entertainments were not without their amusing side. They began long before the Fair was opened, and this preliminary hospitality culminated in the dedication of the buildings on October 21, 1892, four hundred years to a day, by the revised calendar, after the little caravels of Columbus sighted the new world. The change from October 12th was made out of courtesy to New York and its naval celebration, and it was then discovered that the difference from the old reckoning made the 21st the true anniversary.

The ceremony, preceded by a military parade which was largely an escort to the Vice-President of the United States, Levi P. Morton, took place in the huge unfinished building for Manufactures and Liberal Arts. More than 100,000 people were massed on the floor and in the galleries. At the far end, the chorus of 5,500 singers led by William L. Tomlins, and the orchestra conducted by Theodore Thomas, made a fluttering picture when their waving handkerchiefs flew up like birds. The ceremony was imposing. It began with the Columbian March composed by J. K. Paine; continued with a prayer; an address by Director-General George R. Davis; a speech of welcome by Mayor Hempstead Washburne; selections from the "Columbian Ode," written by Harriet Monroe, some of them read by Sarah C. Le Moyne, others set to music by George W. Chadwick and sung by the great chorus. Then the Director of Works, Daniel H. Burnham, tendered the buildings to the President of the Board of Directors, Harlow N. Higinbotham, and presented to him the master artists of construction. He in turn, after Mrs. Potter Palmer had spoken for the Board of Lady Managers, offered them to the President of the World's Columbian Commission, who presented them to the Vice-President of the United States, for whom was reserved the honor of dedicating them to "the world's progress in arts, in science, in agriculture, and in manufacture — to humanity." Orations by Henry Watterson and Chauncey M. Depew were inaudible to the vast audience, for whom only the music and the national salute fired at the end were eloquent. But they added their part to the dignity of an occasion which required oratory, even though it was unheard.

With hospitable foresight, the Directors, considering it inappropriate to permit the sale of food on the grounds to their invited guests, had provided a light luncheon in the galleries of the Manufactures Building, and over 70,000 persons were successfully served, a colossal feat of western hospitality.

Even before this occasion the city had given many evidences of her generous instincts. When she was struggling to wrest the location of the Fair from ardent competitors, she invited the Congressional committee and the families of its members to inspect her claims, all the expenses of the journey to be paid by the city. The invitation was accepted and the families came, down to the last infant. At Mrs. Palmer's reception for them, a large crop of noisy babies, who could not be left at home, was deposited upon her Egyptian bed. The hospitality of the exposition could not have been what it was without Mrs. Palmer's grace and Mr. Higinbotham's urbanity. As President of the Board of Lady Managers, a title which caused a shiver when Congress imposed it upon a reluctant democracy, Mrs. Palmer played her part with distinguished ability. In December, 1892, she threw open her house for the Columbian Bazaar of All Nations, organized by the Friday Club to raise money for the Children's Building at the Fair. Mrs. James B. Waller was the chairman of the committee which developed this bazaar, and to her graceful ignoring of obstacles, her knowledge of women and what they could do, her gentle persistence, and her ready hospitality to new ideas, was due its success. It was a forward-looking bazaar, in which the Friday Club and all its friends triumphantly arrived. Very lovely were the booths it created in Mrs. Palmer's art-gallery and salons, and the women who had worked for weeks to burst into flower for a few gay nights. That they were efficient as well as ornamental was proved when it became known that the bazaar had raised the then unprecedented sum of $35,000 for the fund for the Children's Building. It was all a part of the great outstanding enthusiasm which animated the people of Chicago and made them for the time as one.

"They have had a vision," wrote Walter Besant when he tried later to describe the indescribable and called it, "the greatest and most poetical dream that we have ever seen." "The people dream epics," he added, but they dreamed them gaily, high-heartedly, to the accompaniment of music and laughter. It was a magical summer and all its gaieties partook of the glamor of that White City whose pennants and lights were always dancing in the waters of the lagoons.

On the opening day, May 1, 1893, it was not considered necessary to repeat the formality of the ceremonies of the previous October. A great crowd assembled in the open and, when President Cleveland touched the button which started the machinery, the veils fell from the statue of the Republic, flags, banners, and gonfalons were broken out, and the waters of the great fountains rose sparkling in the sudden sunshine. In the thrill of the moment, the multitude forgot that the buildings were unfinished and the roads of the Court of Honor still a sea of mud. After this dubious beginning the weather was kind all through the Fair, though it had been cruel and had delayed construction during the preceding winter and spring.

The Duke of Veragua, the only living descendant of Columbus, was present at the opening as the guest of the nation, and numerous banquets and receptions overpowered a figure not made for glory nor accustomed to it. He liked being the guest of the nation better than occupying his debt-ridden haciendas, so well indeed that he lingered on many weeks, "feeling," according to the *Chicago Times* "that it would not be dignified in a guest of the United States Government to be in a hurry about taking his departure."

There were other guests of the nation, also, whom Chicago was called upon to entertain. The most important of them was the Infanta Eulalia, representing the King of Spain. The city was rather overpowered at the prospect of receiving her, and like the cities in the East, a bit too obsequious in its preparations. The fact that she was "Royalty," as the press of the time put it with a big "R," was blinding to a modest democracy, until she proved herself something less than royalty in courtesy and grace. With a certain respect for its traditions, the city selected rooms at the Palmer House for the princess.

"Massive and antique is the furniture in the Palmer apartments to be used by the Spanish princess and her suite," says the *Chicago Tribune* of June 6, 1893. "Twenty years ago Potter Palmer fitted up these rooms, and the same old-fashioned but imposing-looking beds and chairs and lounges and tables will serve the royal guest. Everything is huge and the apartments do not in the least approach the idea of what would be found in an up-to-date hotel. From the heavy and rich fabrics of the curtains and carpets to the mosaic work in the woodwork of the beds, it is all of the olden time, but it does not show its age. Eulalia's bedroom is the most imposing of the suite. It adjoins the Egyptian parlor and is carpeted with a handsome Nile-green Axminster. The curtains and coverings of chairs and lounges are of a bronze-green velvet. The bed is a massive affair of mahogany, with a canopy from which are suspended curtains of heavy gold cloth. The coverlet is of the same rich fabric, with hand-worked designs. The head- and foot-boards are inlaid with pearl and colored woods and the pillows are soft as down. On a mantlepiece stands an ormolu clock with gold decorations, that has a chime attached. The mantel is draped with Spanish colors. Pictures adorn the walls, and in a corner is a silver water-service, while vases, all antique, are placed in available niches. The lounges and chairs hold soft cushions and are placed in inviting positions in all parts of the room."

But alas, even the pillows soft as down and the silver water-service did not create in the princess the suavity which could accept things as they were offered. Hobart Chatfield-Taylor, the consul for Spain at Chicago, did his best for her and gave her refreshing incognito visits to the lovely Fair, but even with that assistance she could not play her part in the ceremony. One of the chief functions in the program was a reception at Mrs. Palmer's house, but, unfortunately, before it took place the infanta learned that her host was to be the owner of the hotel where she was lodged. An innkeeper she thought him, and therefore unworthy to entertain a princess. She was constrained at last to put in an appearance, but she arrived an hour late and she departed outrageously early, making no response meanwhile to the greetings of the guests as they were presented. She sat upon the dais, which, with too much courtesy perhaps, had been prepared for her, in sullen, unsmiling, unbending silence, while her beautiful hostess, standing at her side and offering martyred Chicago society at her altar, tried in vain to thaw the icy atmosphere. Mrs. Palmer did those things well and in the minds of her guests that night, it was she who was the princess.

Many other formal functions were given during the Fair, breakfasts in the beautiful Music Hall, receptions in the Administration Building, and the Woman's Building, banquets in the New York Building, the White Horse Inn and Old Vienna. The mayor of the city, Carter H. Harrison, did the official honors with southern graciousness and northern energy. A picturesque figure, either on horseback wearing his old slouch hat, or after dinner in the vivid grace of his old-fashioned oratorical periods, he imposed his handsome personality on many a pompous ceremonial. It was a grief through all the streets of the city, high and low, when he was shot at his post on October 28 by a fanatic, and the close of the Fair was shadowed by his death.

In all the official hospitality, the president of the Board of Directors, Mr. Higinbotham, did the honors with distinguished ability, a gracious personality, sympathetic understanding, with that simplicity and modesty which are always a part of dignity. And Mr. Burnham, as Director of Works, was another citizen of no mean city who played his hospitable part well. In him was the imagination of a poet — rich, spacious, far-reaching, seeing things in terms of the future, grasping possibilities and making them real, magnetic, persuasive and compelling.

All the world came that summer to Chicago, and all the world was well entertained. At the beginning, things moved slowly and the attendance was too small. But gradually the country awoke to its opportunity, and, as a contemporary newspaper reports Mrs. Paran Stevens to have said, many of "the very nicest people in New York paid Chicago the great compliment" of coming to see the Fair. On the Fourth of July, the admissions reached 330,542, and from that time success was assured. On Chicago Day, dramatically fixed for the 9th of October, the anniversary of the great fire of 1871, a wave of pride and joy swept over the city which sent 761,942 people through the gates. These figures alone explain the Fair, testifying to the enthusiasm and single-minded devotion which made it possible. Even more than the fact that Chicago itself had raised more than $10,000,000 to meet the Government's grudging $7,500,000, they show that the energy and idealism that animated capital and labor in the great work of construction were an impelling force in every heart. It was another evidence that the support of an appreciative public always lies back of a notable achievement in the arts.

But to those who lived in Chicago through that magical summer, each little by-way was touched with enchantment. The Midway was a never-ending source of gayety. It brought all nations to our doors, it gave us the world for our plaything. After a morning riding a donkey through the Streets of Cairo, watching the wedding procession, and buying trinkets of Far-away Moses, one could lunch in the lovely square at Old Vienna, while the band discoursed excellent music, and stroll afterwards down the Midway, with its costumes of all nations and its amusing fakirs, to the Bedouin Camp or Blarney Castle or the theater of the South Sea Islanders, where the Samoans danced their blithe, barbaric rounds. There were many other corners to take one away from the prosaic modern world, — the Dahomey Village, quite untrammeled by civilized conventions; the Ferris Wheel,[1] which was the prosaic precursor of the aeroplane; the Hindoo jugglers; the Congress of Beauties; the startling verities of the *danse du ventre* in Cairo Street; the strange postures and gorgeous color of the scenes in the Chinese theater. Most enchanting of all, perhaps, of the glorified side-shows on the Midway, was the Java Village, with its houses and industries straight from the South Seas, and its exquisite, tiny women, dainty as porcelain, strange as oriental gods. In their own theater a new kind of charm

[1] The Ferris Wheel was afterward transported in sections to Paris for the exposition of 1900. It still stands in the Champ de Mars near the Eiffel Tower, and after the armistice was signed in 1918, many American wounded soldiers looked down on Paris from the windows of its moving cars.

was revealed, a beauty that was partly grotesque, a grace that was stiff with decorative gesture. And beyond the confines of the Midway, there were bits from the old world and the new that were strange to our vision, — the Ceylon Building and the Swedish, the lovely caravels of Columbus and the little Viking ship, the Spanish Convent, La Rabida, where Columbus slept the night before he set sail, the Indian camp with its totem-poles, the moving sidewalk on the pier leading out from the Peristyle over the great lake, and the lovely Japanese houses on the Wooded Island.

Enchantment hung over those evenings at the Fair. A dinner on the roof of the New York Building, overlooking the lights of fairyland reflected in its waters, could be followed by a gondola ride through still lagoons, hints of song and laughter vaguely breaking the silence, and that again by a glimpse of the high barbarities of Java on her dainty stage. Or one could dine at the Café de Marine looking out upon sunset waters, or at Old Vienna,[1] with a dip into the Midway afterwards, or at the White Horse Inn, where the prices alone would have staggered Mr. Pickwick.

Tea at the Japanese tea-house near the Fisheries Building, was another diversion which interrupted the serious business of examining the exhibits or spending an hour or two with the pictures in the beautiful Art Building.

But the special quality of that enchanted summer was that the business of life was its diversion. Here were all the countries of the world at our doors — for a moment, for the

[1] On one occasion there was a fire in Old Vienna while the tables were crowded with diners. It was quickly extinguished, but after it was over and calm re-established, the Turkish fire-brigade trotted in, dressed in the gay uniforms which they had waited to put on. The band rose to the occasion and struck up the *Turkish Patrol*.

space of a breath. It was for us to see and understand and enjoy. To float over the lagoons, piloted by Antonio, the Apache, in a birch-bark canoe, to dream away an evening near Columbia on her throne in the midst of rainbow-colored waters, to sleep in the log cabin on the Wooded Island and see the Court of Honor under the light of the moon alone, to watch through the Peristyle the sun rise over the lake — all this was to drink in refreshment for a lifetime.

Gaiety and humor were mixed in with it all, and even the most serious functions were sometimes touched with laughter. We were a bit self-conscious at times in our new cosmopolitan clothes, and too susceptible to criticism. But we had grown to maturity in a night and won our place among the cities of the world.

Perhaps we took ourselves most seriously in the World's Congress Auxiliary, a series of conferences held on the lake front in the building which is now the Art Institute. Organized to discuss the problems of the world by an idealist who was something of a fanatic, C. C. Bonney, it was considered a visionary and impossible project. But it, too, made good and brought many men of light and learning to Chicago. If they gained more than they taught, we were all the richer for their impressions. We listened to them and applauded them and then, our duty done, took our gay way out to the radiant Fair, where they rapturously followed. But though these congresses had many moments of humor and many of success, they had also in the Parliament of Religions a notable triumph. It achieved the impossible by uniting on a single platform representatives of all nations and all creeds. In variety of costumes and physiognomy it could not have been more picturesque, and its emotional and intellectual appeal was powerful. The Hindoo monks made a sensation which lasted and grew into a cult. For a long time the image of Swami Vivekananda in his orange-colored robes uttering his impassioned periods was a thing to conjure with. And if the Parliament of Religions did not succeed in uniting the people of the world in one belief, it, at least, broadened our outlook and gave us new standards of judgment.

In every way, that summer was the beginning to the city of a larger life. It ended the period of adolescence with an achievement so vast as to be exhausting, so brilliant that it surpassed any possible new endeavor. It was inevitable that a time of inertia should follow, but a city acquires mysteriously its character, like an individual, and keeps it in spite of variations and weaknesses. If the building of a permanent Chicago has gone on haltingly, if it has not risen to the standard set by its own energy in 1893, it is certain that the qualities which made that success are still here and will achieve many another. Every agitation that makes for progress rises to the surface here, every disaster has its turn on our stage, every difficulty and struggle, every failure and high endeavor play their parts here in the making of men. And behind and beyond it all lie the force that redeemed the wilderness, the vision that created the Court of Honor, the faith that makes all things possible.

THE END

INDEX

INDEX

CPSIA information can be obtained at www.ICGtesting.com
Printed in the USA
BVOW051637070413

317508BV00007BA/67/P